ON MY WAY HOME

An Autobiography Of A
Priest In Today's World

Rev. Jay J. Samonie

Ralph & Patti,

May you experience

true Peace & Happiness

that comes from God.

Fr. Jay Samonie

On My Way Home

Copyright © 1998
Rev. Jay J. Samonie

ISBN: 1-57502-788-7

Art Work on Cover Design: from a painting
by Rev. Jay J. Samonie
"Seeking The Eternal City"

Printed in the USA by Morris Publishing
3212 East Highway 30 • Kearney, NE 68847 • 1-800-650-7888

This book is dedicated to:

my parents, Jacob and Mary Samonie,

and my sisters Marie Hellow and Jenny Latiff

who have been called to Heaven

by the Creator of all life.

Contents

Acknowledgments

In loving gratitude to my family for their continued support through the years and for their encouragement in producing my first book: (Those called to the next life are placed in parentheses)

My brother Anthony (Mary Ann), my sisters, Lillian Simony (Joseph), Philip and Rose Semain, Elizabeth Nader (Simon), Craig and Jackie Cebulskie, Anthony Latiff (Jennie), and (Bill and Marie Hellow).

I am also grateful to the following:

Most Rev. Thomas J. Gumbleton, Rev. Edward L. Sheuerman, and several other priests who offered meaningful and constructive advice in the publication of my experiences.

Sally Owen who helped me to organize and edit the material contained in the book.

Joan Lemieux, Mike Assemany, Mary Marchio, Beatrice Marx, and Joan Cullinan for their time spent in reading and reviewing the manuscript.

Members of the Prayer Group whose discussions and prayers contributed strongly in motivating me to write the story of my life.

Preface

All life begins with one Source. That same Source or Creator is the beginning and the end of all things. The Alpha and the Omega. Each of us spends a certain amount of time on this planet and then we return to our Source. In a very real sense we are all *on our way Home*.

Everyone's story is like a flower that unfolds in its proper time. I believe that for me the time is now! I would like to share my story with you on my way back Home.

Allow me to begin by saying that I have over one hundred and thirty-three nieces and nephews. They know very little if anything about my personal life. I decided in the beginning to relate my life story for them. Later I decided to include my friends and other relatives, especially when I discovered that my experiences were considered rare. I had previously thought that everyone had such experiences. I was truly surprised to learn the opposite!

I am a Roman Catholic Priest. I was ordained in 1956 but the experiences I have had through the years have greatly altered my view of the priesthood, my perception of God and the meaning of truth. I have witnessed visions, healings, and had several out-of-body experiences. The most unforgettable of all my experiences was being awakened for 40 consecutive nights at 4:00 am. Each night consisted of a different mystical experience and a most enlightening instruction. Several months later, when direct communication was achieved, I was especially excited when given answers to questions I had been wrestling with for many years. I wanted to know: Where was God when my parents both died suddenly just before I took my vows to be a priest? Is communication with God or his helpers/angels real or imagined? Is there any proof? Is God the violent punisher that many believe Him to be? Why was 4:00 am such a special time to be awakened and enlightened? In fact, I had hundreds of questions that needed to be addressed and explained. They were...and I am still overwhelmed with gratitude.

What I learned always encouraged me to remain in the priesthood. Even the practice of Yoga which prepared me for a quantum leap in meditation, and the experiences that took me into the world of Metaphysics, affirmed my work as a priest.

At the early age of seven, I had an experience which was far beyond my understanding. For over an hour I witnessed a vision over Mt. Elliott Cemetery in Detroit, Michigan (close to the Monastery where the saintly Fr. Solanus Casey lived). I was not alone. Two of my sisters and my brother were present and saw exactly the same thing. As a result of the vision, etched in my memory all through my life, was the certainty that there truly existed invisible, mystical realities about which we know little or nothing. *But they were nevertheless real!*

In my early teens I was present at three extraordinary healings that could never be explained by present day medicine or science. The conflict between what I was experiencing and what I believed was slowly becoming an issue within me.

Less than a year before I was ordained a priest, I had a past-life experience. Not just seeing. Not just remembering. Much more than that! Directly in front of the Sun Pyramid of Teotihuacan outside Mexico City, I suddenly went into trance and actually was re-living the life of a Mayan architect at the time the pyramids were built. The whole detailed story is covered in the book.

Like many adults living today, the world I knew as a child no longer exists. Not just from the viewpoint of scientific progress - television, space age, computers, etc - but also experiencing a glimpse from time to time of the world beyond this one, and the ongoing activity of God in my life. The "veil" that separates us from the world of spirit is very thin. The interaction between both worlds has always been accepted as an important part of Sacred Scripture, but today it is emphasized greatly through a variety of books and television documentaries that affirm the existence of angels sent by God to help us or the direct action of God in our lives.

I no longer expect the concept of Heaven as I believed in my youth out there waiting for me; rather, it has taken on a totally different perspective in the light of Jesus teachings re-visited: He said in Luke 17:21: "The coming of the Kingdom does not admit of observation and there will be no one to say, "Look here! Look there! For you must know, the Kingdom of God is *within you."* (Some versions say: *among you.*) Regardless, the meaning is clear enough! He did not say it will take place at a future event. God's Kingdom is *here* and *now.*

It is a most interesting time to be on this planet. We have most certainly entered the *Age of Spirit* as Teilhard de Chardin, the famous Jesuit Anthropologist, has pointed out. Stories of Divine Assistance are coming from all walks of life with the same theme: spiritual help, unconditional love, forgiveness and another chance to change one's life.

You are welcome to walk with me as I recall the strange path my life took and how my experiences affected my understanding of Reality. The incredible mystical, cosmic, and spiritual experiences have given me a totally new perspective, one that is life-giving, productive and fulfilling. The one single hope I cherish is that the story of how God awakened my spirit and changed the course of my life will assist you on your way Home, where together, we shall be blessed with the Joy and Peace of God.

Rev. Jay J. Samonie
February, 1998

PROLOGUE

The following is an example of an exciting moment - truly a turning point - in my priestly ministry! Here is a brief account of what happened:

It was early evening on November 17, 1970. I struggled with the cold wind and crossed the street to the dimly lit church. As I approached the entrance, I realized that I had taken on more work than I could possibly handle. That left me no time for myself. From early morning till late evening my life was not my own. Almost angrily I pushed the door open and immediately began to pace back and forth rapidly, nervously. I found myself talking out loud, complaining that I had given up just about everything. I even began shouting, "What more do you want from me?"

Exhausted, I stopped. Something was happening...a very bright light was blocking my view of the altar! At first, I thought it was someone's headlights bouncing off some object in the church, but then, as I watched, it began to take the shape of a *sphere of light*. Brilliant and almost blinding, an object I would have quickly turned away from. But, as a matter of fact, I was actually *attracted* to it! *Invited* to it! My mind was brought to complete silence!

Then came an even greater surprise! Suddenly, a dazzling *Being* emerged inside this light making the sphere a mere shadow of itself.

This Being of Light appeared to be the embodiment of all the Knowledge, Wisdom, Holiness, and Power that I could ever imagine. I realized I was standing in the presence of the *One* whom I had been serving all my life. There was no doubt about it! Filled with a sense of unworthiness, I fell to my knees and wept. After the initial shock, I managed to slowly raise my eyes to see if the Being of Light was still there. *His eyes were looking directly at mine and all fear dissipated instantly.* He continued to smile as he motioned for me to stand. For the first time in my life, I understood the meaning of *unconditional love.* No words were spoken but the message of Divine Love was loud and clear. For me it was a peak moment of enlightenment and acceptance.

The vibrations that filled the church were so warm and comforting I wished in my heart that I could stay there forever. This tiny matchbox-shaped church suddenly took on the radiance and beauty of a Cathedral. Regardless of the usual feelings I had toward myself with traces of guilt and fear and sometimes resentment toward my situation, I now felt innocent, free, guiltless, and - yes! - even holy. Then slowly, the church returned to an unwelcomed darkness. It was as before...but I wasn't! I felt like I was *transformed,* and my *hopeless* schedule now seemed workable, changeable, acceptable. After that wonderful visit, I returned to the Parish House, jubilant and spiritually energized.

I thought of Peter, James and John on the mountain top with Jesus when they saw him *transfigured* and compared his face to the sun in all its brightness. As they were descending the mountain, they knew in their hearts that witnessing the blinding appearance of Jesus' true nature was needed to fortify them for the challenging events they were about to face. I seemed to have that feeling inside of me as well. I was living in the fringe inner city of Detroit at the time and life seemed to present one stressful situation after another. But with my spirit strengthened, I was ready to face the days ahead because I knew I was not alone. Ever!

ON MY WAY HOME

1. My Earliest Memories

Blood was gushing from my face and I started to pass out. I was being carried by my aunt Sultana (we had to call my mother's closest friends "aunt") to Deaconess Hospital on Jefferson Avenue, near Belle Isle in Detroit, Michigan. By now, with my head tilted back as when one sleeps, both eye sockets were covered with blood and I couldn't see. I was afraid I had lost my sight. I cried. I was a little over three years old.

The cause of what happened was purely accidental. I was in the wrong place at the wrong time. My brother Tony and my sister Rose were arguing; then they started throwing things at each other as children do. I was standing behind one of the two posts that held up the back porch some ten feet away from my sister Rose. Tony threw a piece of slate at her, but she was protected by standing behind the screen door. I was safe where I was but just when I thought it was safe to peek out from behind the post my brother had just sent a piece of slate sailing toward the screen door. However, the slate being flat and thin moved unpredictably in the air and curved toward me instead. Before I could react, I was hit literally between the eyes!

When the doctor cleared the blood away, I was told to open my eyes. I could see perfectly! The family - me too - sighed in relief. The stitches hurt. But I had my sight! And I carry a scar at the top of my nose to this day!

I was actually born in that same house. I have told people when they ask me where I was born: "In Detroit, just behind Deaconess Hospital!" It throws them off for a moment because it sounds as if I was actually born in an alley behind the hospital. Then the light dawns on them that our home was there.

Not long after I had "the nose job", the family moved from

Larned about a mile away to Mt. Elliott and Waterloo, located across the street from Mt. Elliott Cemetery, still on the lower east side of Detroit.

Again, one of my earliest recollections goes back to an incident that happened when I was four years old. Monsignor Farah, one of my many cousins, was visiting our home along with some friends. We lived upstairs above my parents' grocery store. During the conversation - I am not sure what brought it on - he came over to me and was on one knee in order to reach down to my level and asked: "Do you want to become a priest like me someday?"

I said, "I don't know!"

He continued, " Well, here, let me try my Roman collar on you." He took his collar off right there and put it around my neck. He repeated, "Now, would you like to be a priest?"

I replied, "No!"

He asked again, "Why not?"

"Because the collar is too big!", I insisted.

He quickly responded, "Well, you won't be wearing this one. When you get bigger, we'll get you one that does fit. Now, would you like to become a priest?"

I answered again, "No, I can't!" He started to run out of patience.

"All right! Why can't you?"

"Because I don't know what to say to the people in church!" I said quite timidly.

"You have to spend many years in a special school before you would have to talk to people in church. You will know a lot of things to talk about then. It will be easy. So, tell me, do you wish to become a priest some day?"

I thought of the time when I saw an older priest in church who wore beautiful red garments and a staff of shiny metal and a tall hat, and I gave my final response - to the laughter of everyone present: "I want to be a *bushel*!!" When the laughter died down, I was immediately taught what the word "bishop" meant.

Obviously, I knew a little about religion even at a very young age. The fact is that we went to church every single Sunday. It was unthinkable to miss! So I knew a little about priests, church and such things. But I only once heard the word bishop. That day I added the word to my vocabulary.

2. The Samonie Heritage

My parents were very religious. In fact, my father, Jacob Laba Samonie, Sr., was in a Monastery in Lebanon for 10 years. He was naturally on his way to become a monk for life. However, that was not to be. His uncle, the Superior General of the Franciscan Order, came to him one day and told him that he would have to leave the Monastery. This came as quite a shock! But not as much of a shock as to the reason why. His uncle relayed to him the importance of having a male heir in the Assemani (Samonie) family. My father was being scheduled to get married to someone he did not even know. In accordance with a custom in the Middle East - and still prevalent in some areas - marriages were arranged by the parents of both parties. My father was betrothed to Mary Fadool in order to raise sons to carry on the family name.

As amazing as this sounds there was never a divorce in the entire town of Hasroun. It was not due to one hundred percent perfectly happy marriages, by any means. As a matter of fact, it was *very difficult* to get divorced. You did not marry a single person...you married a whole family. One family marries into another family. Then, there was the influence of the church which did not permit divorce and re-marriage. Added to that was the scandal of being divorced. You would be shunned by everyone and a disgrace to the family. There really was no choice!

Interestingly enough, my mother was born on the ocean coming into American waters off Long Island, New York. She was declared a natural citizen of the United States. She lived here for her first six years until her family returned to Lebanon. She had a great desire to become a nun; rather, she was given in

4

marriage at the young age of sixteen. She once told me that one of my great aunts was being considered for canonization, a long process in which a person outstanding in holiness is placed in the Calendar of Saints. I never knew her name or any details about her life. I simply took it for granted that it was true, and my mother, a very down-to-earth person, was not the type to make up a story. I believed her.

With childlike obedience and complete trust, my parents married according to their parents' arrangement. In an effort to have sons they had a lot of children. They began by having two miscarriages. The first child to live was my oldest sister, Marie. Then came Jennie and Lillian, followed by Maroun. The family was very excited to finally have a son. But Maroun was not around for long. A childhood disease took his life. They kept trying to have a son that would live. Two more girls followed in succession: Rose and Elizabeth (nicknamed Billie). Still no son! The ninth child was a *son* named Tony. He *lived*! They were ecstatic, of course. In order to have a little "insurance", they tried again. I came along, followed by my youngest sister, Jacqueline. I ended up as the tenth child out of eleven, with eight of us reaching adulthood.

I recall my sister Marie (who went to heaven in 1980) telling me about dad's short stay in Nigeria, Africa. He owned a store and had a fairly good business. That did not last. He acquired a bad case of malaria and had to leave the country. Apparently he was there in the first place because his brother and a partner owned a diamond and a mica mine. The mines were a lucrative enterprise. Unfortunately, my uncle never came back from his last visit to the mines. My father's family believed there was a violent underhanded act that took the life of my uncle but the family had no actual proof. There was never even an investigation of trying

5

to locate the body.

Time was moving on. Marie, the oldest, was born in Lebanon. The rest arrived here in the United States. My parents first went to Grand Rapids, Michigan. My dad got a job in one of the furniture companies. It was not necessary to speak English well as long as you could do the job. The same thing happened when they moved to Detroit, Michigan. Dad worked at Cadillac Motors for 25 years. I still have the pocket watch they gave him as an award for 25 years of faithful service to the company. How a family survived on $15 a week, I have no idea...and a large family at that! There were small raises all the time, but I believe it was my mother's ability to produce good meals with a few dollars that helped make it possible.

After leaving Cadillac Motors, my father carried on an unwritten tradition among Lebanese merchants: he opened up a grocery store. It was a good thing, considering all the mouths to feed. Those were wonderful years. We were truly a close family. We lived in the apartment above the store and we all worked in the store. I remember as a child taking cans out of boxes and putting them on shelves or putting empty bottles in their proper cases. We ate meals together. We prayed together. We talked to each other.

While being in the store so often and so long as a child, I took full advantage of my favorite foods...tomatoes and strawberries! Every opportunity I had I would pick up the most beautiful tomato and devour it with pleasure. Also, when in season, I picked each strawberry carefully. This was my reward for my "hard work" in the store. I didn't get paid in money but choice food was good enough. This continued throughout my life. Years later, even after the store was sold, I still ate much more than my share of tomatoes and strawberries. Then it happened! I suddenly broke out with the ugliest sores somewhere on my face whenever I ate my two favorite foods. Nature had struck back! I must have radically changed the acid balance in my system to the extent that at about age 20, I could no longer eat tomatoes or strawberries without a reaction. Sometimes the open sore would appear right on the tip of my nose or on my lips or near them. What a sad story! But the lesson was clear: too much of anything is not good!

When I reached about forty five years old, I discovered that if I removed the seeds in the tomatoes, I had no reaction. On the other hand, with the strawberries, there was no way to remove all the seeds without losing the strawberry itself. So strawberries are still off limits!

3. Life Before Television

We listened to the radio on Sundays. Fr. Coughlin spoke about politics, unions, banks and other current topics, with a few racial slurs thrown in. It was the racist remarks that was his undoing. Cardinal Mooney had to let him go. Fr. Coughlin was such a powerful speaker and spoke without fear about his convictions. Whether I agreed with him or not I admired him greatly. Unfortunately, he stepped on too many toes of people in powerful places and we heard from him no more.

When I was quite young we listened to another exciting speaker on the radio: Msgr. Fulton Sheen. He gave truly dynamic and inspiring talks. As a young boy, I enjoyed hearing his many examples that he used to make a point. There was always a clear message to his talks. Both he and Fr. Coughlin influenced me a lot to someday want to speak out publicly and tell people my views on current issues. Perhaps in those early years of my life a seed was being planted within me. At the time I really was not thinking that strongly about being a priest. But it was a recurring thought that emerged every so often. I can still hear the voice of Msgr. Sheen (Later Bishop Sheen) in my memory. Of course, the favorite programs for me, as a child, were The Lone Ranger, Superman, Flash Gordon, The Inner Sanctum, The Green Hornet and several others.

When I say that we prayed together, it was not by force. My parents never said: "All right, everybody on your knees! We are going to pray!" No, what they did was much more powerful. They simply gave us the example. Both parents knelt down every evening to say the Rosary along with the radio station at 7:15 pm. They never said anything; but watching them was like being drawn by magnetism. We automatically fell to our knees. Besides, it was something beautiful we were doing together.

The atmosphere in the home was quite religious. There were holy pictures and statues of saints in every room. It became part of life to talk about God, the church, good morals and proper behavior. My mother, being a very strong woman, even *argued* with her favorite saints. If we came home from school and saw the statue of St. Joseph or St. Anthony turned around facing the wall, we knew right away it was going to be rough day for everyone. The statue and my mother's disposition remained on the negative side until that saint granted her prayer! Thank God she got her prayers answered quite soon. As strong a woman as she was, she had a childlike faith. Some of it rubbed off on all of us. My siblings can testify to that.

We also shared a lot of laughs. I don't think I ever got through a meal without laughing about something someone said or did. We were not saints by any means. We argued, fought, and played tricks on one another. We were ordinary kids!

I thought my mother was the best cook in the world. I know that is quite typical of children to say that. However, I loved everything she made. Our usual meal consisted of Lebanese food. The only thing I did not like then and still do not like to this day are mushrooms. When I was a child they somehow reminded me of something that was distasteful or ugly. I still brush them aside as if they were a poison. My favorite food was and still is the universally accepted principal dish in the Middle East: Kibbee! I would prefer it before the most perfectly prepared steak! Strangely enough, although I am wild about all Lebanese dishes, I also love spaghetti, which is also near the top of my list of most desirable foods. When it comes to pasta, I probably speak for most kids everywhere.

As a young child, I did not understand anything at all about matters concerning birth. I had no idea how a baby came into this world. When I was about six years, old my mother was pregnant for the last time with my youngest sister Jackie. Since my mother had so many children before both of us, she simply remained on the heavy side. Naturally, I did not presume that she was carrying my sister because there was no actual difference in my mother's appearance...*with* or *without* pregnancy. No one told me anything about such things as how babies were born or where they came from or how they got here. All I knew was that people go to the hospital when they are about to have a baby and they come back with one.

In my young mind, it was all very simple: mom and dad go to the hospital. They see a lot of babies. They pick one out that looks good enough to take home. They bring it home and make it part of the family. It has to be so! Look at all the kids mom and dad got! They must have been well known at the hospital. Maybe got first choice!

The first death that affected me deeply was my grandmother's. My mother's mother, Catherine Fadool, was about seventy-nine when she passed on. I had no idea what it was all about. In those days it was fashionable, at least among our people, to put the deceased in the home for a wake service before burial. My grandmother looked like she was sleeping. My mind was filled with confusion and wonder when I saw my oldest sister Marie yelling at grandma to wake up. She even grabbed the body and lifted her up almost out of the casket. I didn't know if that was part of what grown-ups called a "wake service" during which someone tries to wake up the dead person or perhaps it was something personal in which Marie couldn't bear to have grandma die. I discovered we are all going to die some day. That was a real shocker! I was sure glad when my mother explained to me that we are going to live even after our bodies die...not only that, but we are all going to be together again in heaven with God.

For many years I had a strong dislike for motorcycles. I never wanted to ride one and I didn't even like them on the road. Then one day, one of my sisters mentioned that I was hit by a motorcycle when I was in the first grade. Then everything came back to me. I remembered every detail of what happened. I was crossing Mt. Elliott street. I looked both ways. No cars. I began to cross the street when suddenly a motorcycle came from behind me. He did not stop and was moving pretty fast around the corner. Before I could react and move out of the way, the handle bar - at a perfect level with my neck - struck me hard just under my skull from behind.

I actually remember being airborne. People who witnessed it said I was thrown about twenty feet. I must have passed out upon hitting the pavement. Neither the family nor the doctors knew if and when I would awaken.I'm not sure how long I had lain there. I opened my eyes to see my parents and others surrounding the table. I had no idea how I got in the hospital and I certainly don't remember anyone taking my clothes off and putting a simple hospital gown on me. From the way I was treated, it was obvious that they were very happy to see me alive and awake. And no bones broken! As a matter of fact, there were no other apparent injuries. Lawsuits were not popular at that time. I recovered completely without a lawsuit! When I got back to school after missing a few days I was as good as new. But the thought was still with me, that as a child I had my first brush with death.

I learned two things from that incident and from others as I was growing up: life is very fragile and we only die when we are supposed to regardless of the circumstances.

Since we lived in the city I was not familiar at all with life on a farm. We were invited to a farm one day. It belonged to one of our relatives. It was fun getting that close to animals. I was asked if I wanted to milk a cow. I could see first hand where milk comes from. I agreed to try it. The first time I sat down to begin milking, the tail of the cow swished across my face. It was like getting slapped. I said, " I don't think this cow wants to get milked; do you have any other ones?" They smiled! Then they convinced me that I misunderstood what was happening. The cow was probably just brushing flies off her back and legs. So I tried again! This time I was really excited: I actually succeeded in getting a half a pail from the cow. For me it was a real accomplishment! I not only discovered where milk came from, but with a "hands on" experience I got some! My memory of that experience is still vivid. After some sixty years! I also haven't forgotten the huge difference between the air on the farm and the air in the city. The smell of manure on the farm was very strong.

Probably the scariest moment in my childhood was coming home from a movie with my brother after seeing a Frankenstein movie. It was starting to get dark. Every time we passed an alley, I imagined a monster waiting there for us to do us harm. I wanted to run all the way home. But I remembered there were several alleys along the way...and monsters love to chase little boys. My brother kept re-assuring me that we were safe. That helped a lot.

In the summer of '36, my mother and I were going to Grand Rapids to visit my aunt Minnie, one of my mother's sisters, and her husband, uncle Alex. I especially looked forward to spending much of the summer with their two boys about my age. We always had a lot of fun together. The beach at Grand Haven was not far from there and going to the beach was definitely a part of the visit.

We were all packed and ready to take the train to Grand Rapids. At the last minute my mother said we were not going. I asked why. She never answered my question. She simply said we were not going and that was final. I pouted, got very upset and was deeply disappointed. For a young boy to travel that far in those days was like going to another country. When my mother said "No" to something, she rarely changed her mind. Our whole family can testify to that! Little did I know what would follow. The next day we heard on the radio that the very train we were going to take to Grand Rapids, Michigan was derailed. Many were injured. It seems that some boys as a prank had put some stones or boulders on the tracks to see if the train would crush them. The locomotive went off the track and the passengers cars went with it. We were spared. My mother then said to me: "*That is why we didn't go!*" That day I marveled at my mother's ability to know what was going to happen. What I called "spooky", I found out later was called premonition.

4. A Vision Shared By Four Children

The next memorable event in my life is absolutely true, as is everything else. What I am about to relate was truly a blessing beyond words. I shall forever consider myself blessed for having such an experience. I will not exaggerate a single detail. This is exactly as it happened.

It was 1937. I was seven years old.

It was a Holyday according to the church calendar. We called it the Feast of the Ascension of Jesus into heaven. That meant no school! The four of us - my sisters, Rose and Elizabeth, called Billie, my brother Tony and myself - were all upstairs in the apartment above the store owned by my parents. On this particular morning both parents were busy working in the grocery store. I don't recall what each of us was doing. We were certainly not watching television as many kids do today; mainly, because TV was not invented yet. At least it was not yet on the market. I believe my sister Rose was watching over our baby sister, Jackie.

My sister Billie suddenly cried out: "Look what's going on at the cemetery!!" She made it sound exciting! We all dashed to the window. And we all saw the same thing. We were having a vision! We looked across the street in the area of Mt. Elliott Cemetery. We could hardly believe our eyes! We were watching thousands, perhaps millions of oval-shaped objects going up to the sky and millions of others going down into the earth. (It was impossible to count them all!) This was not a split-second occurrence! The vision lasted for almost an hour. That's what we estimated when it was all over. It was late morning, a beautiful bright day. I remember looking on the sidewalk. I saw no one.

And there were no cars in sight! We did not have to convince each other as to what we saw. We simply pointed out different things and we all knew immediately what it was in the vision. The oval-shaped globes of light were very clear. There were two things I remember about them: there was a light emanating from within and they were in soft pastel colors.

Among the various objects of light were full body images as well. Some were in standing position descending or ascending; others were prostrate as if sleeping. We were constantly expressing the usual exclamations, like: "Wow!" "Oh my God!" "Holy Toledo!" and many others, appropriate to the moment.

For at least ten minutes, I began staring at a particular cross. It began descending from as high as I could possibly see. It was coming straight down in the area closest to us, just inside the cemetery fence. It came down very slowly. Perhaps it took about ten minutes before it reached the ground. It was about three or four feet in height; only a few inches of it went into the ground. The rest remained above standing upright. I could now see it very clearly. There were thorns encircling the vertical bar and cross bar of the cross. I was so fascinated by that cross that I left the window and started to go downstairs. My sister Rose yelled, "Where are you going?"

"To get that cross," I said. "I think it belongs to me."

"You can't touch those things! They are holy and you will get punished if you try to grab that cross!" She insisted.

She scared me sufficiently. I returned to the window overlooking the cemetery. Then we noticed three huge images: in the center of the vision behind the objects ascending and descending, was a most beautiful lady dressed in blue and white. She took up a third of the entire sky. On her left was a man with a beard. He was holding a child in the palm of his hand. He also

15

took up a third of the sky. On her right was a massive cross without a body on it, filling the rest of the sky. The lady in the center seemed to be in charge of all that was going on.

The whole scene was spectacular! I was only a child but I knew that we were experiencing something very rare. Even as a child I was very observant. From my earliest days in grade school, I found myself drawing pictures in pencil of my teachers, classmates or some object in the classroom. No wonder I suddenly began to do oil painting as an adult. I can visualize the scene at the cemetery today as if it was happening all over again. It was so vivid and remarkable that my memory will never forget even the details of the vision.

For many years I was hoping that I would come to an understanding of what we saw as children. Since what happened was actually a mystical experience not given to many people, there would have to be a important message, either for us or for the world. But that was not to be. In fact, there really was no follow-up to what we saw. When this incredibly marvelous scene suddenly vanished after nearly an hour, we all felt free to go downstairs and tell our parents all about it. We were really excited and we all wanted to talk at once.

I will always be grateful to my parents for listening to us and not calling us very imaginative children who made things up. We explained everything we had seen to them. We asked if any customers said anything about what was taking place at the cemetery - just across the street. My father taking out his pocket watch remarked in amazement, "By golly, I don't remember a single customer coming in the store for the last hour. That has never happened before." My mother, religious woman as she was, responded with great insight, "Well, it is Ascension Thursday, the day on which Jesus ascended into heaven. Maybe that's why it happened today." We were delighted. We were not challenged, rejected or laughed at by our own parents. What a wonderful affirmation!

However, whenever we told our peers at school about it, we were met with doubt or laughter at best. Even our relatives weren't supportive. So we did what was the most natural thing in the world to do...we kept our mouths shut. I didn't talk about it for years. Naturally, in the back of my mind I knew there was a reason why the vision took place. Its meaning would have to come in the future.

Not long after the mysterious vision, we moved across the street from the store and bought another store, better situated and with greater possibilities. My parents did the same thing on a larger scale: they not only bought the store but also an apartment complex which took up almost half the block. As before, we lived directly above the store. We even had back stairs that connected our apartment to the store. I enjoyed being together with the family in the store and then eating together. There was no question about the importance of family values in my life. I also loved to visit with my grandfather. We would talk a lot; I loved him dearly. There was something, however, about him I could never understand. Grandpa (we called him "jiddu", which is "grandpa" in Arabic) and I would get a couple of chairs and sit in the store near the entrance. It was a rather open area. We used a barrel upside down for a table. On it we played checkers. It was fun playing with my ninety year old "jiddu". There was only one problem! My grandfather could not stand to lose at checkers, especially to be beaten by a nine year old. This is the absolute truth: whenever he was losing, he would say in Arabic "Who is that coming in the store?" I would turn around and say that is Mr. So and so. Getting back to the game, I would immediately notice the whole checker board had changed! Somehow, grandpa now had the advantage. The first time this happened I was confused; I thought maybe I was imagining the whole thing. But time after time it was the same thing: If I happen to be winning, all of a sudden I would hear, "Did you drop something on the floor?" or Was your dad calling you?" "I think your mother wanted to see you for a moment?". There was always the same result. I always got back to the game only to lose. So I simply said to myself that I had a grandfather who could not handle losing! I was only a child but I went along with the program. I never challenged the ceremony of "*The changing of the checkerboard.*" I loved him anyway. I loved spending the time with him regardless of the outcome. In fact, down deep I felt good about making him happy. To this day, I have only happy memories of my grandfather.

Maybe that's where I learned to say so often as an adult: "It doesn't matter whether you win or lose. Enjoy the game! Have fun!" I have said those very words many times to teams just before a game at the parishes where I was assigned. I meant it! Whether those youngsters won or lost, the whole school was very proud of them for having done their best. That's all that one could ask.

I had a very good memory in those days but sometimes I let some important things slip my mind. How quickly I forgot the wonderful blessings God continually gave us. Having been born to such a dedicated, loving and religious family and gifted with a mystical experience, I was surprised at my behavior at times. My brother Tony and I were alone one day in the apartment above the store; we dared to go into our parents bedroom. This was off limits, verboten! But our sense of curiosity got the best of us. We looked at different family pictures hanging on the walls. We couldn't' help noticing the big mirror and dresser women use to make themselves look pretty, and various items we had never seen before.

Then I saw a statue of St. Anthony I had never seen before. I noticed that on the top of St. Anthony's head was a circle of hair that to me appeared very humorous. So I started to make fun of the funny-looking haircut on the statue. In the middle of one of my silly remarks, the head of the statue suddenly fell to the floor. My brother and I looked at each other breathless for a moment since we were nowhere near the statue. We were about five feet away. I said in defense, "It must have been an old statue ready to fall apart anyway."

I picked up the head of the statue, and, looking at it closely, changed my mind completely. The statue was obviously new. Also, there was a strong wire that ran from the head down through the body of the statue, thereby securing it against any possibility of the head coming off. I was shocked! I turned to my brother, "Oh boy, I think I'm in trouble. There is no way this head could have come off without hitting it with a hammer or a baseball bat. It's wired in!!!" Tony scared me when he said God might punish me for making fun of one of his saints. I believed him but I thought, "I'll probably get clobbered more by my mother when she finds out."

We came up with a plan. We would glue the head back on. No one would notice the difference. My plan also fell apart like the statue! The very next day my mother called us both together and led us into her bedroom. "All right, who did it?" I couldn't figure out how she noticed such a perfect glue job. Well, we found out that the statue of St. Anthony was indeed newly bought. There wasn't a single scratch on it. I guess some of the small chips of white showed under the paint where the head and body were separated. My mother's keen eye picked it up right away.

I was ready to get punished. First by mother and then by God! I came up with my only defense: "I did not touch it, but I did cause it and I'm sorry!"

I got a good strong lecture. There was no punishment. Only shame for making fun of something others hold sacred. I promised never to make fun of saints again. I asked if God will punish me. She said "No...you have learned your lesson."

Years later I found out that the circle of hair on the statue is called a "Tonsure". Seminarians receive it when they become members of the clergy. Two years before I became ordained to the priesthood, I too was tonsured. Instead of the hair shaped into a circle, they cut five pieces of hair in the form of a cross. It indicates the commitment to be a disciple and a minister of Christ

I certainly did learn a lesson! In my work I have met persons of practically every denomination. I have made it a point to respect each person's belief and practice of their faith, regardless of how strange it may appear.

5. In The Grocery Store
During the War Years

I was eleven years old when Pearl Harbor was invaded and forced the United States into World War II. Everyday I read about our troops, their gains and their losses. It was difficult to believe how many lives were lost daily. It was far beyond my understanding why people would kill other people. What was there to gain? How could anyone *win* if you *lose* thousands of young men? It made no sense to me as a young person. It still doesn't make sense.

The times were difficult for many people. Sugar and gas were rationed; they had to use stamps then, much like using food stamps today. We lived in a neighborhood that was well integrated, but my father never showed any signs of prejudice or racism. He treated everyone with kindness...we thought perhaps too much! He would also allow people to buy food on credit. There were many pages in the credit book, especially during the war years. And after! Dad never really pressed people to pay. If they said times were hard and they will pay when they can, he accepted their word. Dad always told me "a person is only as good as his word!" So he trusted anyone who promised to pay back. Everybody liked him, regardless of their skin color. They used to call him "Mr. Jake" (Dad's first name was Jacob). My mother was called "Mrs. Jake" I always smiled when they gave her that name. Both names were meant to be a term of endearment.

While World War II was under way, a minor war broke out in Detroit in 1942. I am not certain of all the details, but as I remember, a race riot started with a fight between a white sailor and a black civilian. I believe it took place around Belle Isle and was well publicized by the newspapers. The riot was not confined to any particular part of the city. It seemed to be everywhere. Black and white people threw caution to the wind. There must have been much anger and violent feelings held back until that time. There was violence all around us. From people actually being thrown off the bridge to local areas invaded by one color or the other.

At one point, my parents had us taken to my sister Marie's home in Ferndale. It doesn't seem far away today, but at that time it was considered out of the danger zone. There was talk of hundreds of blacks who previously lived peacefully with us in the integrated section on Mt. Elliott and Vernor that were now on a warpath of destruction. As a matter of fact, the very next day a large contingent of blacks were coming down Waterloo Street heading straight for my parents' grocery store. Witnesses later described in detail what took place. There was every intent of breaking the windows and helping themselves to a lot of food. There was also a big supply of knives in the butcher section of the store. They couldn't wait to get their hands on a supply of things they could not buy. Regardless of the race riot, right now the store was a bonus, a prize package.

Just as the enraged crowd reached the store after turning over cars parked on the street, they were now ready to take their spoils. Then a very brave black man well known in the neighborhood spoke up. It was James Canard, one of my dad's regular customers. Not only did he love my parents, but his son Jim once told me he looked up to my folks as his second parents. His father threw his hands up to get attention and shouted in a very loud voice, " Now, listen here, You are not going to touch this store. It belongs to Mr. Jake. He's a good man; he gives us

22

all credit...he likes us folks. He talks to us as friends!" Then he pointed to several people in the crowd how they too were well-treated by Mr. Jake and Mrs. Jake. "You can do what you want to the other places around here, but you leave this place alone!" Others then stood with him and helped prevent any harm to the grocery store.

Needless to say, our whole family was amazed at the courage of Mr. Canard and the others, demonstrating true bravery in a very delicate situation. We were able to return home shortly after.

It was quite true that my dad allowed credit to many customers. When he sold the store and we had moved, one of my sisters found the notebook with the names of each customer and the amount of money they owed. It literally was in the thousands of dollars. My father never lost any sleep over it. In fact, he didn't even try to recover the money. He felt sorry for them and let it go. As a young boy, I had first-hand example of my father's generosity and extraordinary response to financial loss.

I was told by my mother that during the depression of 1929 she and my dad had to give up their life-savings. While working at General Motors dad had accumulated a good number of stocks open to employees. One of my relatives had loaned my dad some money and demanded payment immediately. Our cousin didn't really need the money at the time. He was still secure during the depression. But he kept after my father to pay up. All of it. That would mean selling all his stocks at the worst possible time when they were at their lowest value. Well, he sold them and paid this very close relative in full. Years later, my uncle Don who had a good understanding of stocks and their value, told us that those same stocks would have been worth several million dollars about the time when my father sold his store. Of course they would have been worth much, much more today. Again, my father was nothing like those despondent businessmen who actually jumped out of windows during the crash in the Stock Market. Nor did he speak in violent terms about it.

The store was only about two blocks from St. Bonaventure Monastery. The monks would buy their foods wholesale to keep their Soup Kitchen supplied sufficiently. Donations made it possible to feed hundreds of hungry people every day. Sometimes they would happen to run out of certain perishable foods, such as milk, fruit or vegetables. On such occasions, it was usually Fr. Solanus Casey who would walk down the street to buy those items from my parents. Fr. Solanus was known as a very holy man who healed many people. He will be declared a Saint some day.

When I was about five years old, I remember seeing Fr. Solanus come in. I didn't know anything about him at the time but I do remember him taking a large bag of groceries to the counter. He paid for them. But before he could leave, my dad asked him to wait for just a moment. Then dad brought another bag filled with fruits and vegetables and gave it to him. He thanked my dad kindly and walked out. I said, "Dad, he didn't pay for that second bag!" My dad looked at me with a little smile on his face and a hand on my shoulder, and said, "Someday you will understand why I gave that extra bag of groceries to him!" Sometime later, I did come to understand and to realize once again that my father was a truly generous man.

Money was definitely not top priority with my father. He would make any sacrifice for his family...his only concern was being a good provider. And that he was. While working at Cadillac Motors which was on the west side of Detroit, my father walked every day to and from work to save on expenses. I am talking about a distance of five miles a couple of hours before

24

daylight. And that is just one way. In the cold of winter it is almost unimaginable. I am speaking of 25 years working at the same place denying himself a street car or a bus to save some small change every day.

6. School Days

I distinctly remember my first day at School. I was registered into the first grade by my sister Lillian. She told the Sister in charge that my name was Junior. I immediately shouted to the top of my voice: "My name is Jacob Joseph Samonie!" My sister stood corrected, and they both smiled approvingly. I had been called Junior up to that time and, at home, with family and relatives, I was still called Junior right up to the time I was called Father as an ordained clergyman. In a sense, I never really had a name until after ordination. I then chose the name Jay.

School was a lot of fun for me. God gave me a good mind to work with; I never had difficulty with my studies and my average mark was an "A" in every subject. And somehow spelling came easy to me. When I was in the fourth grade we had our annual spelling bee. I beat all the fourth graders. So the teachers decided to put me in the fifth grade spelling bee. I beat the fifth graders. They then put me up against the sixth graders. I beat the six grade class. The whole school became aware of what was going on. So, some of the seventh and eighth grade boys went to the principal, Sr. Lucina, and told her they would beat me up on the playground if she allowed me to compete in their spelling bees. I was told they used pretty strong language. What I heard was: "You put that little brat in the seventh or eighth grade spelling bee and we'll fix him good on the playground!!!" Needless to say, I was spared a black eye or whatever.

I have to admit when I was up against the last sixth grader in the spelling bee, I had to make a big decision. She was the girl of my dreams and - wouldn't you know - we were the last two standing! It was either "her or me." She just happened to be, in my opinion, the prettiest girl in the school. She never knew I was a secret admirer of hers. Why should she be interested in a fourth grade kid? But I decided to deliberately misspell the next word and let her win. It would be my gift to her. Besides, what was I doing in the sixth grade when I belonged in the fourth grade? I waited. It was her turn to take a word. I honestly don't remember what the word was, but she spelled it incorrectly. She was out. So I decided that I might as well spell the word correctly. I did...and won. It broke my heart. But she took it like a good sport.

In 1944, at the age of 14, I went to the seminary to study for the priesthood. It was not a simple road to get there. Rather, it was a strange and extraordinary path that led me to the seminary. First of all, I did not get support from home that one would expect; at least not in the beginning.

Let me explain. When I was in my teens, my parents decided to follow another custom from "the old country". Back in Hasroun, Lebanon, this was the way it was done: Since God gave them more than one son (after ten tries), they were supposed to give one son back to God by encouraging the eldest son to go the seminary or a monastery to become a priest. This was the mark of a truly devout and Christian family. I, in turn, would get married (they had already picked out a cousin for me) and raise sons to keep that *famous family name* going! However, we were living in the United States of America, not Lebanon. My brother, understandably, was not happy with the idea. But the Pastor of Our Lady of Sorrows Parish also encouraged Tony to take the entrance test to the seminary. He was at first hopeful but in the final analysis it wasn't his calling. He did not actually attend the seminary that Fall but rather enrolled at St. Rose High School.

I was in the sixth grade at the time. I thought maybe I was cut

27

out for the priesthood. With my brother free to marry, I no longer had to get married and raise sons! So I told my mother of my intentions. She said, "Son, I think that is a good idea, but they would never accept you in the seminary to become a priest!"

I sadly inquired, "why?"

"Because you're a '*shutshought*'!!!" (*Shought* rhymes with thought) This is an Arabic word that means "a real slob or sloppy kid". That was true. I was never conscious of my appearance, whether I looked good or bad, properly dressed or wearing very old or torn clothes, shoes untied, hair in my eyes, and pockets full of nails, bottle caps, agates or whatever I could find on a given day that seemed interesting. She was absolutely right! But that was when I was younger. Along about the fourth grade on, I began to discover "girls". My mother hadn't noticed that I started to dress better, look better and had one eye on the opposite sex. The change was probably not even obvious to *me!* And so my life direction began to take shape. I then gave up the idea of becoming a priest.

I continued to be a good student at Our Lady of Sorrows School on Meldrum and Benson not far from home. My classmates chose me president of the class when I was in the eighth grade. Sr. Mary Lucina, my teacher in the eighth grade, was also the principal of the school. There was no middle school at that time. You went right into high school after graduating from the eighth grade. Three other boys in my class were planning to go to Sacred Heart Seminary in Detroit. Sr. Lucina was after me all during the eighth grade. "I feel that God is calling you to the priesthood," or "Think about it." I kept telling her I am not going to the Seminary. Then I made what I thought was a final decision. I signed up to go to St. Joseph High School for boys taught by Christian Brothers. It was located behind St.

Joseph Church on Jay Street in the downtown area. The school was close. It had a great teaching staff. I could be well prepared to enter one of the universities and choose a profession. I paid a portion of the tuition. My future was all set...so I thought.

The principal, with a one-track mind, would not give up on me. She continued to pursue me to the extent that I finally agreed to take the entrance test with the other boys planning to go to Sacred Heart High School. I made it very clear to her that I will not be going to Sacred Heart but rather to St. Joseph High School. I took the test just before graduation and passed. We were told that there were several hundred applicants. In 1944, it was considered an honor and a privilege to go to the Seminary. I believe about 125 of us passed and received a letter welcoming us to enter the seminary officially in September. At that time, they took boys into the ninth grade. To become a priest the normal process was four years of high school and four years of college at the minor seminary, Sacred Heart. The last four years of Theology was at St. John's Major Seminary in Plymouth, Michigan. From the time you entered, you had twelve years to make the final decision. One could leave anytime.

Some entered Sacred Heart after finishing high school; others came in after college or with degrees from a university. It didn't matter. As long as a young man could pass the written and oral entrance tests they were welcome. I told the good Sister that I kept my side of the bargain. I then felt very free to pursue my future as I had planned. During this whole process, I never mentioned anything to my family. My parents, brother and sisters only knew about St. Joe's. They had no idea what was going on between myself and Sr. Lucina who kept reminding me that God was calling me to the priesthood. I guess I had no idea either.

29

7. A Calling To The Seminary...
Loud And Clear

The events that occurred that summer and the years that followed challenge my own memory. Yet, this is precisely how it took place. I am making no attempt whatsoever to exaggerate or to improvise.

During the summer, my buddies and I would play baseball almost every day in a field on Vernor Highway and Meldrum about two blocks from home. I was usually in the habit of pounding the fist of my throwing arm into the glove to strengthen the pocket as I walked. Out of nowhere, a clear and distinct *voice* spoke to me as I walked along. Yes, the voice was actually addressing me. There was no one physically present on the sidewalk. There were no bushes or trees to hide behind. Could this be actually happening to me? So I listened.

"Why don't you try going to the Seminary for one year," it said.

I hesitated, then answered very slowly, not knowing if this was some kind of prank or sick joke somebody was playing on me. "Why should I? Besides, I have already signed up for St. Joe's and paid part of the tuition." I could not believe I was speaking to a *voice* coming out of thin air!

"You could easily get your money back. But if you do not try the Seminary for at least one year you will never know whether God was calling you to the priesthood. You could regret never having tried". Naturally, I thought about it. It's not like every day you hear a *voice* counseling you. There had to be a reason. So I said I would try for one year. When I got to the field and saw my friends, I told them I was going to Sacred Heart

Seminary in the Fall. I did not share with them the mysterious advice I had just received. I was really afraid to tell anyone about conversing with someone I couldn't see.

As predicted, I got my money back from St. Joe's. I told Sr. Lucina about my decision. She was delighted. I discussed it with the Associate Pastor of the parish, Fr. Ferdinand De Cneudt whom I admired a lot. He gave full approval. My family was happy for me...a little surprised, but happy.

In spite of the general moral support we received from our families, we were all too aware that we were still a long way off from ordination to the priesthood. They told us in our first year at Sacred Heart Seminary that only about fifteen percent of our class would probably be ordained twelve years later. That percentage did not include the students who would come in after high school or after college. I had no idea whether I was to become a statistic.

Since we lived in Detroit, I naturally chose to be a day student. I would be present for classes and then return home. I was welcomed to stick around after classes and study in the library or play sports or visit with friends, if I wished. I chose none of those! My greatest difficulty was just getting to school and returning home. I had to take four buses just to get to class. We had no car and my father did not drive. My brother was in the Coast Guard and World War II was still going on.

We lived so close to the downtown area that the Vernor bus was always crowded by the time it got to Mt. Elliott. The bus just did not stop when it was full and nobody was getting off. They were all going downtown. Downtown Detroit was a very busy place in those days. The businesses were all flourishing and people went there without fear. The streets were crowded with shoppers and the offices were full of workers. Many times two

31

hours would go by; I'm still standing there at the bus stop. It wasn't so bad in the pleasant weather, but winter was unbearable. I literally experienced freezing to the extent that at some point I thought my fingers were going to fall off from frostbite.

My mother would look at me walking in the door. She knew immediately what happened and would make me some hot tea or hot cocoa. I would hold the cup in both hands to bring back warmth and feeling. It was important that I study what I missed in class that day. I never fell behind in my studies or in my marks on report card day. My marks were not all "A"s. I had a few "B"s, which was not all bad. I spent much of an average school day on the bus. That first year was really tough. My absence from class did not go unnoticed! Within the last week of school in June, I was called in by the Rector or head of the Seminary, Msgr. Donnelly. I wondered what I did wrong. After all, I had no demerits. He asked how I was doing then came to the point rather quickly. "Are you a sickly person?" he asked. "Why no," I replied.

"Then why did you miss almost a whole month of school this year?" He was anxious to know. I told him about my problem of taking four buses. He sympathized with me but spoke in very clear terms. "I'm afraid you will have to board here next year or leave the seminary. You cannot continue to be absent that many days regardless of your grades." I was stunned. I had never been away from home. Even when I went to Camp Ozanam for the summer, I was always accompanied by my brother or my classmates. But to leave home for a whole year ...that was hard to agree to. I told the Rector I would think about it; I had the whole summer in front of me.

You probably guessed it. By this time, I almost expected it. My friend the *voice* spoke to me of the many advantages of living at the Seminary. No more hours of bus rides each day! No more freezing fingers! No more disgusting winter standing at a bus stop! The list is long. I was told by the *voice* that I would make a lot of good life-long friends at Sacred Heart. And there would be time to play baseball, basketball, handball, tennis, and cards. There would actually be a study time where no one would bother you. Just think! Ample time to read. I could come home once a month for an afternoon, a week or so at Christmas and Easter, and all summer. It began to sound quite attractive. I told my parents about my plan to board. They were not overjoyed, but they were supportive since they would see me periodically during the year. Also, they could and did visit me once a month on Visiting Sunday for families.

Two good reasons why the seminarians in general liked it when I got visitors: first, my sisters and some nieces always accompanied my parents. Girls were always a welcomed sight at a boys school, Seminary or not. Secondly, my parents always brought delicious Lebanese pastries, infinitely tastier than Seminary desserts. The boys feasted on behalf of my family and the families of other students.

Boarding at school was certainly much more practical. It saved time. As predicted, life-long friends were established. I played every sport I could, including those I failed to mention: ping pong, pool, and football. I excelled in handball, pool, ping pong and not bad in baseball (I pitched hardball). I even went swimming once a week down the street at an indoor pool opened to us seminarians. There I learned to dive, do flips off the diving board, do the one and a half pike and a host of dives that I wouldn't dare attempt today. I passed the test to become a lifeguard, should I so wish. In the evenings, we played cards. I learned to play pinochle, bridge, euchre and rummy. There was time for everything. Don't get me wrong! Studies came first of course. The curriculum was similar to any high school except for the emphasis on Latin, Religion, Greek and a Modern Language. Math, Biology, Social Studies, Literature, English, Ancient History, Medieval History, American History, Physics, Algebra, etc. were basic to receive a High School Diploma.

When I was in the 10th grade, boarding for the first time, I attended Religion class and had an unforgettable experience. The professor, Fr. Joe Szymaszek asked the class a rhetorical question one day. "Has anyone ever seen a human soul"? He asked, definitely not expecting an answer. But being naive and terribly honest, I did raise my hand. In my innocent mind I was willing to answer his question. Fr. Joe schmo (as he was called since nobody but the Polish students could pronounce his last name correctly anyway!) looked at me surprised and had a smirk on his face like a cat about to play with a canary before devouring it.

"So class...we are going to find out at last what a human soul looks like! He was watering at the mouth. I started out simply: "I believe the best time to see them is on Ascension Thursday." I remembered so vividly the vision I shared with my sisters and my brother at the cemetery. I interpreted the bright objects as souls. This was not the response I got in class that day. Only laughter and giggling filled the air. I knew the professor and my classmates were making fun of what I said, but it didn't matter. At this point I felt impelled to tell my story. So I continued. "They're about this big!" I made a motion with my hands indicating they were oval-shaped and about a foot and a half in length. More laughter.

"What else can you tell us about souls?

"They appeared in different colors, soft pastel colors with a beautiful source of light coming from within." They were now roaring, "splitting a gut" as we used to say. They were finally

34

rolling in the aisles when I pointed out that the cemetery was the best place to see them. This occasion represented my first attempt to share this wonderful experience with persons who were preparing for the priesthood. I had hoped they too had mystical experiences and we could talk about theirs as well as mine. I presumed the Seminary was the perfect place where young men were trained in prayer and meditation, and where they had personal and mystical encounters with the Lord. I thought by chance someone else might chime in about encounters with God or one of the Saints. Never happened! This whole episode in my life was a total bummer! Surprisingly none of my classmates teased me about it after class. However, I did notice at supper, Fr. Joe was the center of attention among the priests/professors on a separate long table about 30 feet away from us. They were all laughing about something. I prayed it wasn't about me.

The next day I was walking in one of the many corridors at the seminary. Coming straight toward me was the Rector, Msgr. Henry Donnelly.

I said the expected, "Good Morning!"

"And they're about this big!", He gestured and laughed. I thought to myself: "I'm finished, expelled, caput!" But, as with my classmates...the topic never came up again.

I felt the need to retain my sanity concerning the vision. So I decided to write to my brother stationed in Greenland, to my sister Rose in California and to my sister Elizabeth in Detroit, asking if they remembered the mystical vision and explaining to them the embarrassing situation I encountered in my Religion class. I also wanted their honest opinion. Did I make it up? Was my imagination overly active? Was I a dreamer as a kid? Was I accustomed to tell wild stories?

I was very excited to hear from all three of them. Each one of them in separate letters strongly affirmed that we did indeed have the vision. It was a real experience! We all saw it! Don't let anyone ever talk you out of it. No, you did not make it up. What you said was the truth! They were all surprised that in a seminary, of all places, it was not investigated as an authentic message from God or Our Blessed Lady. It was all but forgotten. None of us was ever officially interviewed. It was never documented. We were actually afraid to talk about it publicly. I suppose if there were someone, perhaps a priest who reported it to the bishop and called us in to talk about it without fear, something may have come of it.

On the other hand unlike other visitations from the spirit world, what we saw only occurred once. There was never an ongoing communication with a Heavenly Guest. The whole incident remained only in our innocent minds. It became just a memory. But that memory has reminded me all through my life that there really is a spiritual world. There really is a hereafter. And other extraordinary events in my life supported belief in God and other invisible realities far beyond my understanding.

8. Miracles Do Happen

I witnessed three miraculous healings in my teen years. These were, in a sense, affirmations that God is active in the world, and I was blessed to see the work of His hands. Ever since I was a baby, my mother took me and my other young siblings down to the National Shrine of Our Lady of Consolation in Carey, Ohio about 60 miles south of Toledo. The statue of Mary holding the child Jesus has been accompanied by healings ever since it was enshrined in 1875.

In 1945, it was getting close to August 15, the day on which Catholic Christians celebrated the Assumption of the Mother of Jesus into heaven. It was also the same day when pilgrims from all over the U.S. made their way to Carey. In this small insignificant town, tens of thousands of people would gather for the celebration of the Eucharist and for the outdoor procession, ending with a special Benediction (and possible healings).

I said to my mother a few days before leaving on the fourteenth of August that I was going to see a miracle on August 15. She explained that miracles can happen but no one actually sees them. I repeated my conviction that I was going to see one.

"Why are you so sure?" She insisted.

I did not have a good answer, but I could only say, "I heard a *voice* tell me so!"

"Well, we'll see," she added faintly.

At that time it was more practical to stay overnight, making it a two-day trip. Otherwise, finding a parking spot the next morning would be very difficult. Also, it was not possible for the hotels to accommodate such a huge crowd from out of town. People slept almost everywhere imaginable: in their chairs, on the grass, in their cars, in the park nearby, in church and in whatever niche available. We chose to sleep on the pews in the Basilica. That's what the principal church was called.

The next day we attended religious services conducted by the Black Friars (Franciscans) who were in charge of the Shrine and dedicated their Ministry to the widespread devotion to Our Lady of Consolation. They were called Black Friars simply because they wore black garments instead of the usual brown ones.

Soon it was time for the Grand Procession to begin. People were moving into positions to line up for the procession. I, in turn, was looking for someone who desperately needed a healing. There was a lot to pick from. I saw people slowly walking with crutches or a cane, others on stretchers, and still others in wheelchairs. I spotted a young man about my age in a wheelchair. I looked at his feet. There weren't any. And no shoes! Only twisted, gnarled bone from his knees down. He needed a miracle badly! I thought to myself: He's the one!

I asked my mother if I could push him in the procession to the Shrine Park Altar while the thousands of people prayed and sang hymns along the way. My mother saw no problem with that. Of course, I had to ask the mother and her son if they accepted my suggestion. They welcomed the idea with a smile. Our two mothers who till that day did not know each other walked behind me and my newly found friend. We both had the same idea. He wanted to have normal legs and feet...and that was my prayer too!

The procession was about to begin. The distance both ways was about a mile. Everyone was praying devoutly; I was too, but I couldn't keep my eyes off the feet - if you can possibly call them feet - while I prayed along with them.

We finally returned to the front of the Basilica. There were so many people that the Benediction (which is a Blessing with the Eucharist) took place outside on the front steps. There were at least ten steps so that visibility was not a problem. It was impressive to see the thousands of pilgrims on their knees, some kneeling on grass and others on the rough pavement of the road or sidewalk. I did not hear anyone complain. They were happy just to be there!

Then began the sacred moment. The priest raised the Blessed Sacrament above his head and made the sign of the cross with it. All eyes were focused on the makeshift altar, more specifically on the Sacrament which we believed was a powerful gift of Christ's Presence. Then it happened! I saw movement in the young man's legs. I am not sure whether he was paralyzed from his waist down, but he apparently was unaware of it himself. He was still staring up at the altar. The next scene was so powerful with the legs sort of gyrating, turning, twisting or perhaps unraveling, that suddenly before my eyes I was looking at two perfectly shaped legs and feet. That did it! I couldn't hold back any longer. I yelled to the top of my voice, "It's a miracle!!!" I kept repeating it. My mother tried to quiet me for fear of embarrassment. All eyes were turning to this young voice that kept yelling 'miracle'. Benediction was now over and I could hear a ripple of people repeating the word miracle. The mother of this young man asked me if he was able to stand up. I again spoke very loudly, "Stand up? He can walk!" Both of us grabbed an arm and lifted him up. He stood on his own then slowly took a few steps. He was ecstatic with joy. So were we! The boy and his mother thanked me. I said, "Oh, please, thank the Lord. He's the one that did the healing." What I was most excited about was the insight given to me beforehand that I would witness a miracle.

That event stayed with me a long time. Unfortunately, we

never documented the healing although it was witnessed by thousands of people. Today, that would be the first order of the day. I do not remember his name and I do not know what became of him. It really didn't matter. I was only an instrument of Someone much greater than I.

During another visit to the Shrine of Our Lady of Consolation, my mother, my sister Billie and I prayed that Billie would be healed. She was unable to eat and keep the food down. Her entire digestive system shut down to the extent that she could not even keep water down. Naturally, after a short period of time she was starving to death. Dr. Dwaihy, our family doctor, and a specialist examined her thoroughly without success. They were totally baffled as to what was the cause of her condition and what could possibly be the remedy. She had made many attempts to eat only to have the same experience...throwing up. The worst foods, of course, were greasy ones. However, her condition had the same effect even with the most nutritious foods.

The only positive note about the whole thing was that she had developed this rare condition close to August 15, the day we go to Carey, Ohio. It was about the only thing we could do. When the time came for the Grand Procession the three of us walked and prayed side by side. Nothing so grandiose occurred such as the boy in the wheelchair receiving brand new legs and feet. But we prayed with great confidence because miracles were not exactly foreign to us. And Billie was present when we shared the vision over the cemetery.

Upon finishing the procession and Benediction, Billie demanded to get something to eat. She had a great yearning to have a hamburger. My mother quickly reminded her that she couldn't keep anything down much less a greasy piece of meat. Billie insisted on trying to eat again. She said that during the

40

procession she felt some activity within her from her throat to her stomach. It could be interpreted as hunger pains, exhaustion, thirst or something like that. But not diarrhea, since nothing entered her body for so long. Each of us was excited in our hearts hoping, just hoping it was more than just a feeling. We were expecting a miracle. As Billie put the greasy hamburger to her lips, my mother and I held our breath for a moment to await the outcome. Yes! The food stayed down. She ate without any discomfort. She was cured! The three of us hugged each other with tears flowing freely. Then we gave thanks to Our Lady of Consolation who once again brought consolation to those who sincerely asked for help.

Needless to say, the doctors who examined her after we returned home had no idea what she had nor how it went away! Nor were they ready to proclaim the change in her condition a miracle. They simply could not understand how it could have healed itself. And they are slow to admit the cause was Divine in origin.

The third healing I witnessed was, wouldn't you know, back at the Shrine of Our lady of Consolation. Our small delegation from the Detroit area made the trip once again. We left on the 14th of August and arrived around noon. This time we had planned to meet relatives coming in from Richmond, Virginia. They had lived next door to us at one time. The Yesbecks were related on my father's side, but Mrs. Amena Yesbeck was my mother's best friend. It was one of her daughters that they presumed I would marry some day. That, of course, never happened. Tillie and I were the same age, grew up together and were good friends...but nothing more. She eventually married Mr. Oley.

Her sister, Sadie, was part of the plan to meet in Carey. We set up a time and place. Sadie brought her daughter Mary Magdalene, hoping she would be cured of a severe eye condition. She was badly cross-eyed. The glasses she wore were helpful but in no way corrected her sight. The glasses helped a lot, but when you looked at her, it was obvious that she was still impaired with some double vision. With the glasses off she absolutely could not function. It was truly sad to see a child that physically challenged. We all had a nice visit and ate of the food we brought with us. Mother always packed a good meal for travel. That evening we were in the Basilica in front of the altar dedicated to Our Lady of Consolation. We decided to stay right there and spend the night. We prayed together and recited certain devotions. It didn't bother anybody since each family group had their own prayers going in many different languages. We were in the middle of a league of nations.

It was a long day. I imagine I went to sleep in the middle of a prayer. My cousin Sadie and I sat next to each other. Her daughter slept on her lap. Since the girl's body was just a little too long for one lap, Sadie placed her daughter's head on my lap as well. With one hand gently covering her forehead and eyes and the other hand holding a rosary, I prayed myself to sleep. I didn't know whether it was possible for a person to sleep in a sitting position all night. Yes, it is possible! I didn't move at all. When we awakened at daylight we were all in the same relative position. As if by habit, Sadie immediately gave Mary Magdalene the corrective glasses to wear. She tried them on and said the glasses hurt her eyes. We all looked at each other. Either her eyes got better or they got worse. We were anxiously waiting to find out. Her eyes were no longer hugging her nose. Instead, both eyes were perfectly aligned as they should be. She was healed during the night. We had hoped for a cure during the procession later that same day. We did pray with deep faith but it was now a prayer of thanksgiving. With her pupils in the center of her eyes my little cousin's face was a beautiful sight to see and her response of gratitude was overwhelming.

9. Working My Way Through

I was once again reminded of God's continuing action in the world. Miraculous events started to appear natural as there were less and less surprises. God seemed to be very near and very interested in what was happening to me. So when I was encouraged by the *voice* to finish high school at Sacred Heart Seminary since I had put in two years already, I did. The *voice* left the door open. I could go to the University of Detroit taught by Jesuits after high school. There I could pursue a career of my choice. The options were given as before but, as usual, it never happened that way!

First of all, I became more and more involved in the extracurricular activities. My interest in remaining in the Seminary increased each year. Tuition was $300 per year, very reasonable for a Boarding School. It was possible because the Archdiocese of Detroit subsidized the Seminary. Still, in those days, it was a good sum of money. When the occasion arose, I applied to work in the front office on the switchboard. It was great. I could get out of study hall and get paid for it at the same time. It wasn't much: a dollar per hour. It added up. I was able to pay my own tuition and have spending money besides. There were other advantages. I was able to meet all the professors more personally. They would come in to get their mail, stop by to see if there were any phone messages, and sometimes just come in to chat. I even got to read the newspapers without having to share a copy in the library.

Part of the job on the switchboard was taking care of 27 professors each having a separate line. When you see old black and white movies, they sometimes show the girls plugging each call to an outside line. The result: a crisscrossing of many connections. It could keep you quite busy at times. And you had to remain alert. The connection you mess up could be your math teacher.

There was another way of making some money in the seminary. Ron Prebenda (of happy memory) and I use to be called "Corner boys". Since a seminarian was not permitted to leave the seminary grounds except once a month for one hour and once a month for an afternoon, the boys often ran out of certain items like cigarettes, gum, cigars, toothpaste, shaving cream, powder, toothbrushes, soap, pop, etc. Ron and I received a percentage of the sale. We did not make a lot of money but after a full school year, it helped a lot. It was also fun just walking outside the seminary property into what we called "the world". Just breathing the air outside the seminary was a freeing experience.

As I was away from home most of the year, I began to develop a strong sense of independence. It was almost necessary since each seminarian was on his own. Fellow seminarians are your friends but they are also your competitors in class, on the field, or on the basketball, tennis and handball courts. Classmates are a continual challenge. One becomes sharpened as does a soldier in boot camp or simply by living a military life. The key to happy living in the Seminary was to comply with the rules and regulations, become more and more disciplined in body, mind and spirit, and to maintain at least a fairly good academic average through diligence and study.

At Sacred Heart Seminary there was a statue of the Mother of Jesus in front of but to the side of the main doors of our chapel. It was a habit with some of us to pause in front of that beautiful statue after night prayers on our way to the dormitory. Every night I said a prayer to my dearest Mother Mary. I often entrusted my seminary life into her hands. I presumed that if God put the child Jesus into Mary's care and she did so well, maybe she would take care of me also. And I had not forgotten that she seemed to be in charge of the vision I had earlier in my life. I had come to know Jesus' Mother as "Our Lady of Guadalupe" before I was ordained a priest.

Part of our curriculum was a choice of a modern language. I chose French. For whatever reason, French came easy to me. In fact, all languages seemed easy. I had no difficulty whatsoever with Latin, Greek, or Hebrew which were part of the curriculum at appropriate times as a preparation for priesthood. Latin, of course, was the language most used in classes. During the last six years in the seminary the majority of classes were in Latin. And so were the tests. At that time five years of Greek were also required. I had no trouble at all with Greek. In both these languages the rules are fixed and pronunciation is consistent which makes them easier to learn than English; that is , if English is not your mother tongue.

Even though French has a strange pronunciation for a certain combination of vowels and consonants, the pronunciation is still consistent and predictable. Learning French was practical for me. The following summer after learning the basics and being able to carry on a very simple conversation in French I went up to Quebec in Canada. Everything was in French; I got by very well. Only one incident came off badly. I went into this restaurant with a fellow seminarian and ordered my meal in French. The waiter turned toward me and said in a sneering voice and with a French accent, "Monsieur, if you can not speak French right, then don't speak it!!!"

I retorted, "Monsieur, if you cannot speak English right don't speak it!" Then I took the dish, threw it across the table in his direction and walked out. That was the only bad memory I had of that trip. It was another opportunity to learn patience with others.

During my second year of French, I wrote a letter to my great uncle, Bishop Louis of Tripoli, the last of the line of Bishops in

46

the illustrious Assemani Family. He could speak and write in eleven different languages. Instead of writing in English, I wrote in French. It was a two page letter, introducing myself as his grand nephew and that I was preparing for the priesthood. I wanted to make sure it was clear enough in French for him to understand, so I had our French teacher Fr. Hennes check it over for mistakes. He liked it as it was.

My great uncle was 90 years old at the time. I was delightfully surprised to see that his handwriting was a beautiful script and his French was perfect. Included in the envelope was a letter to my dad in Arabic. Dad was happy to hear from his uncle and to know that my uncle and I had corresponded with each other. I wrote to my uncle about two years before he died. They said he had already picked out a casket and made arrangements for his funeral long before it took place. He told his staff he was ready and unafraid. He had lived a full life and welcomed the day when he would enter eternity.

Most young men eagerly look forward to their twenty-first birthday. There is usually a party centering around the first time he could drink legally in a bar. I know families who make a big celebration out of it. Well, in my case it was different. When I reached the mature age of twenty one, I was greeted with a pilonidal cyst. The first symptoms are pain and the inability to sit down without discomfort. I thought I had a boil where the seat of the pants go. Dr. Boutrous at that time was our family doctor and also a well-known surgeon. He examined the area for just a few moments and he knew immediately what the problem was. He explained to me that it was congenital, that somehow a foreign object, usually a hair, got within my system as a young fetus and settled at the bottom of the spine. As time went on, the body built a protection around it so that no harm would come to the body. Of course, that eventually became a full-grown, pus-filled cyst causing havoc to the body.

47

Instead of putting me out completely during the operation, they gave me a spinal block. That meant I was conscious during the whole thing. They gave me a needle with something to relax me. One of the nurses was supposed to keep an eye on me to see how I was holding up during the surgery. I was making conversation with her. Then, at one point, I looked into her eyes, and muttered, "You have beautiful green eyes! I have never seen green eyes like yours before. And you're very pretty...." Just then, the doctor yelled, "Shut him up.!" I remember the nurse giving me another injection. I lost consciousness very quickly. When I awakened after the surgery, I was teased by the doctor and a few nurses about being a seminarian and flirting with one of the nurses during surgery. The doctor laughed and explained that the medication affects people in different ways; sometimes it makes them feel light-headed, like being drunk...and terribly honest.

That isn't all! It was just the beginning of what could have been the ultimate embarrassment for any twenty-one year old male let alone a seminarian living in a boarding school. Dr. Boutrous did not use stitches after the surgery. He said the pilonidal cyst is commonly known to return if simply stitched afterwards. He told me of a woman who had the same operation thirteen times. That's correct! Thirteen times! Every time they sewed her up there was a build-up of liquid causing another surgery to relieve the condition. So my doctor left the incision open to heal on its own from the inside. Meantime there was always liquid or pus to deal with; there were sitz baths to be taken every day. This went for a month at home and another six weeks at school.

The most embarrassing part was that the good doctor recommended kotex to absorb the draining that went on continually. When I returned to the seminary, I had to trust a friend completely, because I could not place and tape the kotex in the right position by myself. I chose Dick Lauinger as my trusted friend. He was true to his word. If he had just once broken his word, I would not have been able to get by one day without laughter and many insulting nicknames that describe a man wearing one of the female sex's "unmentionables"...in a male boarding school yet. It seemed to take forever to heal, but once it did, the cyst never returned. Nature took care of it the long way, and, apparently, the best way.

10. The Next Major Step...With Help

I had to make another important decision in 1952. That was the year I had to decide whether to leave the seminary and go home or, as a college graduate of Sacred Heart Seminary, go on to St. John's Provincial Seminary in Plymouth, Michigan. St. John's Seminary was the Major seminary and it was called "Provincial" because seminarians from all over the State of Michigan were also permitted to take their last four years of study at St. John's before being ordained to the priesthood.

The *voice* was active again inviting me as before to take the step. The voice complimented me on how well I was doing. It would be the right move for me. St. John's Major Seminary was the last stopping place on that twelve year journey toward the priesthood. The voice encouraged me by stressing other advantages over life in the Minor Seminary: the food would be better, the air was fresher outside the city, there were new classmates to meet from other dioceses, there was a golf course right on seminary property, and just think, I would actually be studying Moral and Dogmatic Theology, Sacred Scripture, Canon Law, Homiletics, and Liturgy in the Major Seminary. All of that was true. The staff of professors belonged to the Religious Order of Sulpicians. The Sulpicians dedicated their priestly Ministry to the preparation of major seminarians for the diocesan priesthood. That was their main work.

We had more space to call our own; each seminarian had a private room and bath. And St. John's Golf Course was owned by the seminary and available to us every day during recreation (and the right season.) The outdoors, by comparison with city air, was indeed very refreshing. Once again, the voice had not let me down. In fact, life in the Major Seminary was exciting. It was an honor to attend such a place. Sacred Heart, the Minor Seminary, taught courses that are typical of any college, including a good foundation in philosophy. We earned a Bachelor's Degree in Philosophy. We minored in English. The Major Seminary, on the other hand, offered what was equivalent to a Master's Degree of Divinity. I say "equivalent" because in the 1950's the Major Seminary was not accredited yet for a Master or a Doctoral Degree. It seemed very strange to us since most ministers finish their studies with a Doctoral Degree.

We were told that the Archdiocese of Detroit was more interested in the vocation to the priesthood than the accompanying Degrees one earned. We went along with that. What were considered more important were the Degrees one received from additional studies in Rome, Italy, Louvain, Belgium or the Catholic University in Georgetown, Washington, D.C. As time went on, it became more and more important to have Degrees after one's name. The Seminary then became accredited, and even offered an abbreviated course for priests already ordained to receive their Master of Divinity Degrees. By the time that took place, I had already received a Master's Degree on the side from the University of Detroit from 1968 to 1971.

11. Praying With Migrants
In The Path Of A Tornado

I had another unforgettable experience during the summer of 1954. I was greatly influenced by the work done by one of my classmates from Saginaw. He was in charge of a summer program in the Saginaw Diocese of Michigan; they ministered to the migrants who came up to pick beets in that area. Most of the Mexican-American migrants were from Texas. They were brought up in trucks to the work the fields. Some of the migrants actually brought their whole families with them, kids and all. Picking beets was not easy. It was a job that called for a person who had a strong back, who was not subject to a sunstroke, and who would work for much less than the minimum wage. I recall reading about an experiment from one of the universities in Michigan in which they wanted to see if an ordinary student could endure the sun and pick beets along with the migrants. The majority of them could not!

I offered to participate in their Migrant Program in Saginaw for the summer. No, thank you! I don't mean the work in the fields but simply as a driver for the Spanish priest who would serve their spiritual needs. The priest in question, Fr. Talavera was from Spain and did not have a car nor a driver's license. I was given a car through the Migrant Program and was assigned to live and work out of St. Anne's Church in Pinconning, a little town near Bay City, Michigan. The Pastor, Fr. Bourget appeared so happy and relieved to see me when I arrived at the Rectory.

"Thank God, you're here!" He said with a smile. "We are having an awful time communicating with Fr. Talavera. We have to make signs and gestures just to get through to each other. That's when we're lucky! We need you badly to translate for us."

"I'm sorry", I said. "But I don't speak Spanish either. That's not part of my job, you know!" Well, maybe I knew a few words like "Tacos", "Adios!" or "Si, si". One could hardly converse that way.

"Well, what good are you?" He came right back at me.

"I drive him to the camps where the migrants are. When he needs to get around, I'm his chauffeur. That's what my contract says."

We all became frustrated! Fr. Bourget could speak English and French; so could I, but it was of little help; Fr. Talavera was limited to Castilian Spanish. What to do? We tried conversing in Latin, but it was obvious that our vocabulary was based on book knowledge and not on everyday conversation. We succeeded, but with great difficulty.

In the seminary I learned languages fast. So, I decided to learn Spanish as fast as possible. Communication could be a major problem! And it certainly was. Planning our day, going to the migrant camps, setting up meetings, scheduling Masses and discussion groups, training young ones in a religious education program, preparing couples for marriage and families for the baptism of their children and a host of other problems quickly developed.

The very first day I arrived in Pinconning I went to a bookstore and bought a Spanish/English Dictionary out of absolute necessity and desperation. Fr. Talavera's interest in English was not as strong as my desire to speak Spanish. The dictionary went with me everywhere. I was looking up words all day long. The good *padre* would pronounce the word for me if there were any doubt. I often pointed to a word in the dictionary in the middle of a conversation to make sure I was conveying the right message to him. Naturally, when he wanted me to understand something very important, he would do the same.

I had read somewhere that one needs approximately one

thousand words in a language to carry on a fluent conversation. That wasn't me! In the beginning, my Spanish was definitely broken and with a typical American accent. But I was not afraid to make a mistake! And I would ask the migrants for the word I was obviously trying to say. They were patient and happy that I was at least trying. It was such fun teaching religion to the children. My vocabulary was taken directly out of the book. The instruction book I used was a book of questions and answers. I would simply ask a question to the children. If they laughed I knew I said the wrong thing. I would ask one of them to say it correctly and slowly. The children felt good about helping me. These young, innocent children who had no formal schooling were my teachers. I loved it. We laughed a lot. Sometimes I would just open my mouth and start to say a word and the children were already laughing. I always looked forward to my job of teaching the children while Fr. Talavera took care of the adults.

After a period of about six weeks, I was already reciting the rosary in Spanish. Fr. Talavera and I would go together to one of the camps on Sunday afternoons, their day off. He and I would then separate and join a different group of adults gathered in one of the small cabins where they lived. The cabin was a one-room facility. Everything took place in that one room. It was their kitchen, their bedroom and their living room...with no toilet. I would guess the size of the cabin to be about 12 by 15 feet. Certainly not bigger!

On this unforgettable occasion, I was praying with about ten people crowded in one of those very cabins. While we were at least half way through the rosary, one of the migrants came up to me and said, "Padre, mira lo que esta veniendo hacia nosostros!" Translated, means: Padre, look what is coming toward us!" I knew this had to be something really serious, very serious, for one of these men to interrupt a rosary. I stopped for a moment and looked out the window. The frightened expression on my face impelled them all to take a look. Coming straight toward us about three hundred yards away was, without the slightest doubt, the awesome funnel of a tornado. It was tearing up everything in its path. Things were really flying around. Above the ominous black funnel were green clouds forming a circle around it. I had never seen green clouds before. We all had the same thoughts. We were in deep trouble. The end of our lives could come very soon! A couple of people started to make for the door.

"No!", I shouted in Spanish. "Don't go outside! You don't know which way the tornado is going. We will kneel here and pray. If we die, we die praying!" I have no idea where I got the strength to say that and with such authority. There was no time to think. We prayed. Did we ever! Every word was spoken as if it were the last word we would ever say in our lifetime, on our deathbed. The noise got louder and louder. We desperately tried to pray with more faith than fear. We were totally in God's hands. What was God's will? Would the Lord save us from obvious destruction? We would know shortly. I couldn't help thinking of the tremendous power of a tornado. I read once that a tornado had the incredible atomic power to disintegrate; or the force to drive a feather into a tree like an arrow; or the sound of a locomotive driving right through you. Or it could send us flying into the next county!

The following is what did happen. I had ten witnesses to testify to it. While we were still praying and the noise kept getting louder drowning out our words we looked at each other with an almost hopeless stare. Our eyes were saying goodbye, while our lips prayed with only a spark of faith remaining. To all appearances we were not long for this world. First there was a sense of being torn away from the ground on which the cabin rested. We then knew we were airborne. There was no doubt about it. We were flying...only we were not in control. I am sure

I was not the only one having images of being bashed into a tree or tossed like a baseball into a field. I am sure horrid thoughts plagued us all. We did not have the impression we were moving fast through the air...just moving! It was as if at any moment we were going to hit something real hard and very fast!

However, the noise started to subside giving us the possible glimpse of hope that the tornado had passed by. And we were still alive! At least for the moment! I then had the distinct feeling of descending. We were going down. This feeling was confirmed when to our surprise we touched ground. We expected a crash landing! Rather, it was an incredibly soft landing. It was a great feeling to have landed and still be alive. We finished praying then hurriedly dashed outside only to discover that the cabin was not in the same place as it was. We were moved, ever so gently by - what else can I say? - a Gentle Hand that must have reached down just before that dangerous moment and moved us away from the path of destruction. We were now several hundred feet from our original position. Did we really move that far through the air? Perhaps we only imagined it! We had to check it out. That was not hard to do. We found the original spot where the migrant family's cabin was prior to the tornado. A furrow about five feet deep and much wider was the result of the tornado's path as it made its way right through the place where we were kneeling. When speaking about it later, we all decided that the tornado itself did not treat us so kindly as it noisily passed by. Rather we were all in agreement that what happened to us was a miraculous event. The Source had to be a Power that had dominion over Nature. The Lord had shown us His kindness and mercy. We were marked for death. Instead, we were given new life and a deeper faith. We gathered together and, forming a circle of prayer we expressed a gratitude that came from the very depth of our soul. Tears flowed but they were tears of joy.

The next day as I read in the newspaper about the rash of

tornados near Saginaw Bay, Michigan, I realized that I was in one of them, the one that visited the Migrant Campsite. Reading about the amount of damage that occurred in that whole region again affirmed my faith and trust in God's Divine Providence.

12. First Love

While my faith in God was strengthened enormously that summer, I also experienced for the first time in my life the power of love. I am not saying that I had never loved anyone before. I loved my parents with all my heart. I loved my six sisters and my brother very much. In fact, the mandate of Jesus to love God with all my heart and soul and to love my neighbor as myself was not a problem for me. It was my very love for people that was the driving power to serve them in priestly ministry. I had been trained since I was fourteen to focus my energies on prayer, work and play. There was a place for each of them. Holiness and wholeness were very much alike. They both depended on a good balance between physical, mental and spiritual activity. My whole life centered on my studies and my preparation for the priesthood...which did not include a marriage partner. Romantic emotions and feelings had long been suppressed. In a sense, I felt immune, even invulnerable to a relationship with a woman. My life was so full that I had neither the time nor the interest to invest in such a relationship.

Well, life is full of surprises and so unpredictable. I met the secretary at St. Anne's Rectory the first day I arrived. I expected her to be older. She turned out to be one year younger than I. Each day I would greet her with a "Good morning" and a smile. When the Pastor was not in, and Fr. Talavera was not ready to make his daily rounds among the camps, I would spend a few moments talking to her. After all, we were nearly the same age and the two priests were considerably older. After a few weeks the conversations got longer. I enjoyed her company. After seeing her every day for over a month, the conversations became more and more personal. I wanted to know all about her: her family, her goals in life, her interests and whatever else I could think of on a given day. She was equally interested in my background, what motivated me to go to the seminary (I was afraid at that time to tell her about the voice!), my interests, etc. I had no idea what "falling in love" meant. I was twenty four years old but very innocent when it came to relationships, especially about a serious relationship between a man and a woman. But before I knew it, I was slowly moving in that direction.

I was growing sad as the days speeded by and I would have to leave Pinconning and the most wonderful girl I had ever met. (Not that I had any other such experiences.) I am reluctant to mention her name but her family name was very popular in the local community at that time. The time came, of course, to go back to the seminary. I returned to the seminary that Fall; every part of me was confined within the seminary walls, except my heart. My heart was still in Pinconning. I spent many sleepless nights going over the past events of that summer: the work with the migrants which was very gratifying, learning to speak a little Spanish, the incredible escape from a ravaging tornado, and especially the awakened feelings for a lovely, desirable friend.

I prayed a lot. We had to participate in morning and night prayers every day. But my prayers invaded the classroom, the study hall, and even the sports events. When alone at night I knew I had to bring this dilemma to a conclusion. It came during a retreat in which my spiritual life was at its highest point. I finally wrote a letter explaining everything I felt to my dear friend. She must have read it with tears in her eyes. I know I did! Several days later I received a letter from her. She was very unhappy about the decision she knew in her heart I had to make. Of the two loves, I felt my destiny was tied to the priesthood in a way that was greater than myself. It was as if I was drawn to the priesthood by a vocation that called out to me from the world beyond. Regardless of what I believed, it was a heart-rending experience. In spite of already saying goodbye, I still felt I had to call her on the phone to hear her voice once more and to clarify what I had written. We talked for a long time...and we ended as good friends whose time to take the "big step" had not come.

Near the end of the summer, before returning to the seminary, I asked Fr. Talavera and Fr. Murillo, a friend of his visiting from Spain if they would like to meet my parents. They were very happy to just relax and spend a day away from the migrant camps for the work was long and tedious. My parents had sold the store and moved further east but still in Detroit.

I realized I had to play the role of interpreter as I did back at St. Anne's; that is, once my Spanish was good enough. But this situation was much more complicated. My father was speaking to me in Arabic; my mother spoke in English. The two priests spoke only in Spanish. It turned into a hilarious comedy of errors. I wasn't used to switching languages that fast and often found myself speaking to my dad in Spanish and English to Fr. Talavera. They would throw their hands up in the air. It was getting more confused by the moment as this fun-fest went on. Eventually I settled down, got my languages in order and we had a wonderful conversation over a great meal. The meal was especially appreciated since I had a deep longing for my mother's home cooking.

13. 1955 - A Year Of Mixed Blessings

1955 was a year of mixed blessings. It was the year of final decision. We received the Order of Subdeacon. Within these ancient ceremonies, we took the Vow of Chastity and a promise of Obedience. There was no turning back! I was well aware of such a serious commitment. I had been in the seminary for eleven years before giving up married life under oath and dedicating my life to the service of others in obedience to the Archbishop of Detroit and to his successors. I had looked upon that day as a great challenge. In a world full of married people, it was not easy to be unmistakably different, to give up family life and worst of all, never to have children of my own. Since I came from a large family, the Lord would have to send me extra help.

In the Fall of the same year, I would be called to receive the Order of Deacon. This step took us ever so close to the priesthood. We could do almost everything a priest could do except celebrate Mass and hear Confessions mainly. Deacons preach, baptize, visit the sick, perform marriages, and conduct funerals or weddings without a Mass. These are all part of the purpose of the Order of Deacon: to give witness for Christ in the community.

Quite unexpectedly, two tragedies hit our family. My father died at the end of January. I was completely unprepared for such news. I took it very hard. When my brother came to see me at the seminary during class time I expected the worst...and got it. Only a death in the family could have us called out of class. It never dawned on me that my father would be called by God before my ordination. He was so proud to have a son become a priest and fulfill his own desire. I am sure he had thought about the time when he himself was removed from the monastery to get married and to raise sons to carry on a family name.

My dad was not at all offended when I informed him of my choice to leave the Maronite Catholic Rite and become a Latin Catholic. In the Roman Catholic Church the children follow the Rite of the father. I was born a Maronite, but I never attended the Maronite Church except for a wedding or a funeral. It was not part of my life. I was surprised when my father gave his approval - not that the seminary asked for it - because it was the only church he knew. What separates one Rite from another is basically the language and the music. The faith of both churches is the same: both believe in the Pope as the Vicar of Christ and as the head of the Church.

I have to admit that though I loved both my parents very much, I always felt more attached emotionally to my mother. I stayed close to her during the funeral and tried to help her through her grieving as much as possible. She was a precious gift that I wanted to take care of and at all costs. I simply could not let anything happen to her. I often imagined how proud and happy she would be on the day I became a priest. I would always take care of her. And thank God she was still around. A few of my classmates had also lost one parent before ordination. They managed as well as could be expected. So could I.

Three and a half months later, my dream burst in my face! I was walking in procession into the chapel with my class. As I made the turn down the corridor toward the chapel I spotted my brother Tony standing there. He looked very sad. I stepped out of the procession and walked toward him. He didn't say a word. I yelled out with a cry that tore my insides out, "No, No, No, No! Not mother!"

Poor Tony! The messenger's job is not easy when bearing bad news. He didn't say anything. He only nodded with a fatalistic dropping of his head. I could not accept it! For some reason males always try to be real macho, and to maintain poise and strength in the face of adversity. I didn't have any of that! I burst out crying as I never did before in my life. I didn't care if the whole world was watching. How could my life ever be the same! That day would go down in my personal history as the worst day of my life. I had reached the lowest point of darkness. Tony and I hardly spoke on the way home. We couldn't!

At the wake services we found out who our real friends were. Those kind souls who came to console us were a godsend to my sisters, my brother and me. They all expressed comforting words. Many of those who came had also lost one or both parents and understood full well how tragic it would be to lose both of your parents so close to each other...and so young. My father was 67 and my mother was 62.

The funeral ceremony was in English and at the local parish of St. Bernard. My mother liked Fr. Kerwin. He had a joyful disposition and she understood him better than any of the other priests. She insisted that when God called her some day, she wanted him to say the funeral. He did and his words helped a lot. At least we could understand him. My father's funeral, on the other hand, was at the Maronite Church where parts of the Mass were in Arabic, Syriac and Aramaic. The Homily was given in the most educated level of Arabic which they teach at the University. That level of Arabic is not understood by ordinary people. None of the family understood the homily. Not even my mother who spoke Arabic fluently. To tell the truth, I thought it was an insult.

I only broke down once while at home. I was standing alone in the back yard behind the house. We had just come home from the funeral luncheon for my mother and I looked around the yard where I spent many hours enjoying the company of my parents during summer vacation each year. While facing the fig tree my father nurtured and loved so much, something came over me and I realized I would never see my parents again in this lifetime. The thought of being an orphan overwhelmed me. My tear ducts opened and wouldn't shut down for a while. I then looked up toward heaven, and shouted silently but very seriously: " Lord, how could you do this to me? How could you possibly take these two precious people from me just when I am about to dedicate the rest of my life to your service. I am giving you my life and this is what I get? I think St.Teresa was right when she complained to you also. What she said was so true: 'No wonder you have so few friends. Look how you treat them.' "

Getting over the death of both my parents did not take place that day. It took time to reconcile with God over my hurt feelings. But time is a great healer. After a period of time, and later, after a serious study on the subject of "life and death", my understanding of the process and purpose of life here on earth sharpened greatly. In fact I came to fully accept my parents' transition to the spirit world. They had completed the mission God gave to them and it was reward-time for them. To hold them back for my sake would not be in their best interest or mine, even though it was only natural to want them present at my ordination. Actually, I believe with all my heart that they *were* present in spirit. I also considered the possibility that God was really protecting me and my parents from what could have been a horribly tragic situation if they held on longer. Thoughts flashed in my mind: "What if mother died the day before ordination or had a heart attack the very day I was to be ordained, or what if she or dad went into a coma on that same day, etc." As I prayed, I realized it was best the way it happened. In faith, I acknowledged once again God's Divine Providence at work. My parents were joined together in the hereafter as they were here. And they could watch over me from above. Still, once in a while, I do wish that the outcome had been different.

About a week before taking Solemn Vows, seminarians are required to make a retreat. The retreat is quite important because this step in accepting the Order of Subdeacon carried with it the

Vow of Chastity and the lifelong commitment of obedience to the Archbishop of Detroit and to his successors.

The vows were taken with some fear and apprehension because there was no turning back once you willingly made this commitment. The Vow of Chastity was a necessary part of a "priestly package" since the Catholic church in the west held to the tradition of an unmarried priesthood. I had always personally believed that priests should have a choice, but I knowingly and reluctantly accepted the challenge. We, as a class, were still young and confident that God's Grace would uphold us in time of prosperity or adversity.

Ordinarily the two weeks preceding the Ceremony in which we make our Solemn Vows was a time of elation and excitement. Each of us, scheduled to receive the Order of Subdeacon, waited in our rooms for the call to this important milestone along the way to the priesthood. If we heard a knock on the door, and were greeted with the call to Sacred Orders, we knew we were found acceptable by the faculty to take the step. Not all were called. Some were told to wait until a later time; others were discouraged from continuing in their pursuit of being ordained to the priesthood.

14. Off To Mexico -
An Encounter With Destiny

Summer vacation came quickly after receiving the Sacred Order of Subdeacon. There was some concern about the type of work a subdeacon chooses to do during the three months of summer, since we were now permanent members of the clergy. My choice was to study Spanish in Mexico. They asked for anyone interested in Spanish to apply and the Archdiocese would finance it. Since both my parents made their transition at this time, I wanted to get as far away as I could. Mexico would be fine! I needed to forget the horrible pain I felt in my heart.

Jim Sheehan, Dick Kropf and I were selected to study basic Spanish in Mexico City. We lived at the Diocesan Seminary called El Seminario Conciliar, located in a suburb of Mexico City called Tlalpan. I had an advantage over the other two since I spent the previous summer at the Migrant Camps learning Spanish every day. It was not easy for us to mix freely with the seminarians in Tlalpan since language and culture at first were a barrier to communication. I forgot most of the Spanish I had learned the year before. At St. John's Seminary back in the States, I was busy with Latin again. I had no time to practice the little Spanish I had learned.

In Mexico, learning the proper Spanish grammar and expanding my vocabulary helped me to remember what I had learned in the Migrant Camps in Michigan and to go beyond that. I finally began to speak Spanish correctly and more fluently. Between the classes at the Iberoamerican University taught by Jesuits and the fun talks we began to have with the seminarians in Tlalpan, I was feeling good about my level of communication in Spanish. The words were flowing more easily every day. I still needed more understanding when someone spoke fast to me. But I managed to get by fairly well even when I was alone with a group speaking entirely in Spanish.

Healthwise, the three of us were victimized by Montezuma's revenge. Everywhere I went, I carried a bottle of kaopectate. Near the end of the summer my body finally became accustomed to the Mexican style of cooking and the distinctive method of fertilizing their crops. Of course, we still had to be careful not to eat certain foods regardless of how appetizing they appeared to be. Tomatoes, lettuce and unpurified water were the biggest culprits to an American stomach. Every weekend the three of us would go on a trip to a different part of Mexico City or to one of the neighboring towns just to get a feel for Mexican customs and their way of life. It was paramount that we became more and more familiar with the culture of the people. That was one of the principal reasons for sending seminarians there - to learn Spanish, of course, but also to understand the Mexican culture more deeply. Ministry to the Hispanic Community depends for its success in good measure upon the ability to identify with and be sensitive to the pre-Columbian and present culture which has become a vital part of their life.

We are well aware of many races and cultures here in the United States, which is a melting pot of ethnic backgrounds stemming from every part of the planet. Each brings the richness of their heritage to America. As enchanting as these cultures may be, their ethnic and racial differences sometimes become the source of great conflict. Each country has its own history with its distinct moral values, ideals, religious or atheistic beliefs, and, in general, cultural practices. In this country, we have to keep an open mind or we will end up with perpetual, cultural hostility and bloodshed as found in Bosnia, Ireland or the Middle East.

So each weekend was a time of discovery and we were learning fast.

One weekend stood out above all the others; what I experienced affected me deeply...even to this day! It started out like any other weekend except that I was alone. My buddies from home, Jim and Dick, wanted to go to "Popo", the nickname for Popocatepetl, and its neighboring mountain Ixtlahuatl. If you have trouble pronouncing these words don't feel bad. Very few Americans can. The story of these two mountains/volcanoes is pretty much the same story as Romeo and Juliet. Popo was of a royal family and he loved a beautiful girl who was a commoner. They couldn't marry so they eloped and were never heard from again. They eventually became Popo and Ixtlahuatl. By the way, Popo is the highest mountain in Mexico and Ixtlahuatl looks like a woman lying down. In Spanish they call Ixtlahuatl "La mujer dormida" (The sleeping woman).

I decided not to go to the mountains with them that day. I preferred to fulfill two dreams I had for a long time. One was to go to the Basilica of Guadalupe in Tepeyac and the other was to actually see a pyramid. I had been fascinated by pyramids all my life. Both of these sites were included on a tour from Mexico City. So I went with a tour group of about 30 people, none of whom I had ever met before. Our first stop was the Basilica on the outskirts of the city. There was a lot of history at this Shrine dedicated to the mother of Jesus known to the Mexican people as Our Lady of Guadalupe. I could not help thinking of Our Lady of Consolation in Carey, Ohio. I thought to myself: "She sure gets around a lot!" I found the plaza and outside of the Basilica interesting but it was nothing compared to what was to come. Finally, the tour guide led us to the painting of Our Lady of Guadalupe. I have always seen life through the eyes of an artist, but when my eyes fell upon the image of Our Lady of Guadalupe I was utterly speechless! I had never seen anything more impressive or inspirational in my whole life. That was my immediate response. And it still is!

Its history is so extraordinary that it moved an entire country to become Christian. In 1531 Juan Diego was a peasant Indian who had just been baptized a Christian and he was going to church. He passed the usual way over a hill called Tepeyac. On one such occasion, there stood before him the apparition of a beautiful lady. She appeared to be from heaven. To remove any fear of her overpowering presence, she spoke to him lovingly like a mother to a child. Whenever she spoke to him she called him "mi hijito", meaning "my dear son", an affectionate title. She told him to go to the bishop and have him build a Basilica for her. Juan Diego was doubtful that a bishop would listen to him, but he obeyed the wishes of the Lady.

Poor Juan waited a long time for the bishop to see him. The bishop's secretary, a monsignor, kept telling Juan that he could convey his message to the bishop. But Juan insisted that he personally deliver this message to the bishop. Finally, he got to see him. The bishop then questioned Juan Diego as to the purpose for the visit. The Heavenly Lady on the hill of Tepeyac requested that the bishop build her a Basilica. The bishop must have smiled as he said to him that he needed some kind of proof that she really was from heaven. So Juan felt he had failed the Lady and did not go back home by way of Tepeyac but rather went to visit his sick uncle.

The next day while going to Mass in the morning as he usually did, Juan was again greeted by the Lady. He quickly explained the situation to her and she was not upset in the slightest. She said if it's proof the bishop wants we shall give him proof. She told Juan to go a little further and pick the freshly grown roses, placing them in his "tilma" which was a blanket used by peasants as a cloak. He gathered as many as he could. What was miraculous about the roses was that roses do not grow in that part of Mexico in December. Juan knew that and so he carefully guarded the roses in his tilma with both hands holding them as one would hold a basket. Again, sitting outside the bishop's office, he waited a long time.

At long last, he was told to enter the bishop's office. When the bishop asked Juan if he had brought a sign to prove that the lady who requested a Basilica was authentically from heaven, Juan lowered the tilma and the roses fell to the floor. The bishop immediately fell to his knees! Juan was surprised that the presence of the roses in winter time had such an effect on the bishop. What Juan did not know was that as the roses fell to the floor, in the very presence of the bishop and a few other people in the room the beautiful image of Our Lady of Guadalupe was being painted miraculously right on Juan's tilma. He was the last in the room to know. The painting and the roses were enough to convince the bishop to act without any doubt as to the authenticity of these heavenly visits.

Bishops and priests are usually the last ones to believe in extraordinary and miraculous events. We hear of so many phony and/or imagined miracles and apparitions and divine messages that we are very slow in accepting the truth of such occurrences. We have all been fooled at one time or another. We try not to be fooled a second time. And it looks bad for the church if sometime later the so-called healings and miracles were proven to be false. In that light, I can fully understand why the bishop gave Juan Diego a rough time.

Bishop Zumarraga was the bishop our Blessed Lady chose to have the Basilica built. He and his entourage believed Juan Diego and so he complied with the Blessed Lady's wishes. The Basilica lasted about 450 years as a place of worship with Popes and other great leaders visiting as pilgrims. Besides offering Mass there, millions have gone there with the hope of experiencing a healing. And there have been thousands of healings. Several walls in the original Basilica are literally covered with little images which are symbols of the type of healing that took place. For example a tiny image of crutches or eyeglasses, or a cane or a heart or whatever was the nature of the cure are hung on a wall. They are fervent reminders of the healings by God through the intercession of Jesus' mother. Whether healed or not, special honor and devotion continues daily at the Shrine of Our Lady of Guadalupe and throughout the Americas. She is, in fact, the Patroness of the Americas.

When I heard the history behind this incredible picture I was totally overwhelmed and drawn to the mother of Jesus all the more. The painting is truly a miraculous work of art. As I knelt for a long time in front of this powerful image of Our Lady of Guadalupe, I knew in my heart that I would spend as much of my priesthood as possible in serving her people. Without any words, I felt in my soul that my destiny was beginning to shape, and that I would indeed dedicate my life to serving the Hispanic Community. I had been waiting for a sign. And there it was!

Since Mexico City and the surrounding area are built on a lake, some of the buildings sink a few inches each year. When the Basilica of Guadalupe sank all of fifteen feet on one side, it was time to build another Basilica. The new one was completed around 1980. It is very well done, a worthy Basilica, but it does not carry the atmosphere of the old one. The old sinking Basilica still stands, but is off limits because of the obvious danger.

One last thought about the painting of Our Lady of Guadalupe. Scientists have tested the pigment used in the painting. With modern instruments, they can now break any element down to its basic molecular structure. There is no paint on this planet similar to the paint that created the image of Guadalupe. In fact, it cannot be explained adequately how the painting was done. Since a tilma is a heavy cloak used in winter, it is made from a very coarse material. I did a couple of paintings on burlap years ago. It was not easy painting on burlap because of the loose and rough condition of the burlap. I can't imagine

71

trying to paint on a tilma. The paint strokes would be even more difficult and sloppy with the colors seeping through the material. In fact it would be impossible to paint on it without many coats of gel to build up a smoother surface. None of the above was done. Scientists and artists to this day are puzzled as to how it was painted, since there are no specific brush strokes on the heavy material.

Also baffling is the fact that for over 400 years the faithful have burned many thousands of candles directly underneath the painting. There was no protection glass whatsoever in front of the painting, and yet the original painting was never discolored by the fumes from the candles.

The painting now has a glass covering. Not because of the candles so much as the senseless bombing by a very sick person about twenty or thirty years ago. (I am not sure of the date.) On that occasion, the whole altar was destroyed, but the painting of Our Lady of Guadalupe was completely unharmed.

The tour continues. We went on to the pyramids of Teotihuacan just outside of Mexico City. When we arrived at these famous archeological ruins the bus dropped us off near the Sun Pyramid. It was huge. Much larger than what I imagined. There were two pyramids about a mile a part with nothing but desert in between. When we got off the bus I immediately walked toward the Sun Pyramid. I was standing there facing the Moon Pyramid which was considerably smaller. Just then one of the ladies from the bus came up to me and asked, "Pardon me, but may I take a picture of you standing in front of the Sun Pyramid so that the people back home can get an idea of just how big it is?" I said that would be fine.

I remember seeing the flash of light from the camera when she took my picture. I then started to go and join the tour group. However, the most amazing thing happened! I said to myself, "What is this? What's going on?" I looked at my arms. They

72

were very dark. I then noticed I had only a loincloth around my waist. I felt my hair. It was straight and jet black. I kept saying to myself. "I'm a Mayan. How can this be? I am Jay Samonie. How did I get here? And how do I get back?"

As I was standing there in a state of complete confusion, someone came up to me speaking in another tongue, not Mayan. Nevertheless I understood perfectly and told him how to place a large block in place. The stone must have weighed several tons. It was moved in place with a sort of pulley system, something built like the metal bars of a child's swing. Where you would expect to see a swing, there were ropes connected to other ropes as we would use a series of chains. While one of the workers was pulling the outer rope several feet, the inner rope attached to the stone seemed to move about an inch. I remembered marveling at this make-shift pulley system. After a period of time, the block of stone fit perfectly in its proper place. It really worked!

I was actually doing the work of an architect supervising the construction of two rows of structures that eventually joined the two pyramids. A moment ago, there was nothing but desert between the pyramids. Now there were people everywhere. They all had their work to do. I kept them following the plan of construction, similar to "blue prints". Some of the adjoining structures were homes, shops, storage space or dwelling places for the priests. After a few minutes, I was a Mayan architect directing many workers. I forgot all about Jay Samonie. I was well aware that the workers were not Mayan and they spoke in their own language which I understood.

This did not happen in a mere fraction of time. I was well into this strange experience. I don't even know what to call it: deja vu, regression, a time-warp, a memory. Something was happening to this young seminarian who never heard of such things. I was never prepared for this! How could I? I was only groomed for the Roman Catholic Priesthood taking ordinary post-graduate subjects plus added studies in Theology, Scripture and Philosophy. Psychology was a branch of philosophy, but nowhere was the concept of trance, reincarnation, deja vu, regression and such topics ever mentioned. It was unthinkable. And here I was living the unthinkable!

After a full hour had passed, the tour guide was counting the group on the bus to make sure everyone was present. They were about to make the trip back to Mexico City when all of a sudden he noticed an empty seat. He asked whether someone had sat there. A lady spoke up. She said, "There was a young man sitting in that seat but he is nowhere on the bus right now." She continued. "I took a picture of him when we first got off the bus but I haven't seen him since." The tour guide asked if she would take another person with her and go back to the exact place where she last saw me.

The two of them went looking for me. They found me in the same spot where I was standing for her snapshot of the Sun Pyramid. They told me later my head was tilted to the right and I was standing up, but I appeared to be asleep or in a trance of some sort. First, they tried speaking to me. I did not respond. Then they yelled in my ear. It did not help. Then they began to hit me, beat on me, pinch me, slap my face...anything to bring me back to consciousness. Finally, after being continually pinched and slapped around, I opened my eyes. They both said I was speaking in another language. They had no idea what it was. Nor did I when I realized after a few moments that I was Jay Samonie again. I was absolutely stunned. I did not know what to say when I got on the bus. They all applauded the two ladies who found me, but I was afraid to mention what I experienced. I figured they would take me to the psychiatric ward instead of the main office of the bus company.

While returning to Mexico City on the tour bus, however, I thought I would take a chance to verify my sanity. When the tour guide, who was apparently very knowledgeable, asked if there were any more questions, I raised my hand. Remembering the role I had while in trance, I asked whether the Mayan Indians built the pyramids. The tour guide said, "Well, I guess you missed that whole talk I gave on the construction of the pyramids! No, the Mayans did not build the pyramids. The natives of Teotihuacan actually built them. That's why they are called the Pyramids of Teotihuacan. They only brought the Mayans in as *architects*." I nearly jumped out of my seat. Without knowing anything at all about the history of the pyramids, that was precisely what happened. I was on a roll!

So I thought I would ask the other important question. I had to know!!! Was this all imagined or was it real? I asked the guide if there were any theories or even a possibility that there might be some structures buried beneath the sand in the area that joins the two pyramids. The tour guide did not respond right away. Then he said, "You ask some very interesting questions for a guy who missed my entire commentary on the pyramids," he commented. "Yes, there is a very real possibility. Just recently two archeologists were here taking soundings and they believe there is *definitely some kind of construction* in that exact area. The sands of the desert simply covered them up after so many centuries. As a matter of fact, they are going to begin *excavating* next year." I never felt so good! The two questions were right on target.

Maybe I did have some kind of real experience of the past somehow. I neither understood it nor could I explain it. So I did not share what happened with my buddies who returned that evening from the mountains. Nor did I talk about it with anyone for a long time. How could I? Who can possibly believe this kind of talk? Maybe in the nineteen nineties but not back in 1955.

There is a sequel to this trance-experience or whatever it was that happened to me. In 1975, exactly twenty years later, I conducted a tour to Mexico. I made sure that the tour included a visit to the pyramids. I had not seen them for twenty years. And I never heard or read anything about them during that time. You can imagine how excited I was just thinking about the excavation and what actually did show up under the tons of desert sand. Again, the first thing I did after getting off the bus was look for the same location in front of the Sun Pyramid where I stood before. The sight was overwhelming! As I looked straight ahead in the direction of the Moon Pyramid, I saw that the two rows of stone buildings were completely excavated. It was identical to what I had seen there twenty years ago while they were buried under sand.

This was another turning point in my life. Amazing that they both took place on the same trip! First, I decided to dedicate my priestly ministry to work with the Mexican Apostolate (as we called it then); secondly, I felt, in a sense, compelled to study about paranormal events. I hoped that some day I would come up with some answers as to what occurred at the pyramids in Mexico.

15. The Life Of A Deacon

Summer vacation was over. It was time to get back to the reality of seminary life. In less than three months, I was scheduled to receive the Sacred Order of Diaconate, empowering me as a deacon of the church. Six months later, I would graduate from St. John's Theological Seminary as a candidate for ordination to the Priesthood. In the scholastic year 1955-56, the life of a deacon was not nearly as eventful as it is today, that is, in the nineties. Deacons now take a year of Internship in one of the parishes. They learn on the spot how to apply what they had been learning for many years. They have opportunities to preach, baptize and do all the things previously mentioned. There is no better way to learn a new job than by a "hands on" program, just as computer users are taught. When a deacon gets ordained to the priesthood today, there are few surprises. This system results in better preparation and a more efficient application of priestly duties.

Back in 1956 with ordination came a host of surprises. Some of us before ordination only rarely set foot in a rectory where the pastor lives. Even if we made a short visit to the Parish House, we never had any idea what priestly life was like. In order to identify with priestly ministry, it would be necessary to live among priests for a while. Not just during Christmas or Easter vacation, but rather, living right on the premises of the particular parish all year. That way, one get's a first-hand view of a priest's response to situations on a day-to-day basis.

During the last year of seminary life, I stayed at the home of my oldest sister, Marie, during Christmas and Easter vacations and on certain free days. She happened to be a member of St. James' Parish in Ferndale, Michigan, just north of Detroit.

Although a deacon's life was actually not that active in those days, I did help at the Easter Vigil Mass on Holy Saturday. I was the commentator explaining from the pulpit those unusual annual ceremonies. The ceremonies, still in Latin at that time, desperately needed explanation. That was a big night for me. Besides helping at Christmas, there I was at St. James' Parish again able to assist the priests in a practical way. However, I had trouble getting there. While we were at supper eating fish on Holy Saturday evening, a bone got caught in my throat. It lodged sideways. It would not go down; I tried eating bread to no avail. So they took me to the hospital.

The doctors would surely know how to remove the bone. Not quite! The one doctor was not successful in reaching it, so he called for additional help. There were now three of them trying to reach the bone; they could barely see it deep in the throat. They tried different instruments. Nothing worked. I would start choking each time they tried. Time was moving on. I needed to get to the church very soon. Besides the fact that they expected me at church, my throat was hurting. I was choking and coughing trying to make it go down. So while the doctors, about ten feet away from me, were consulting one another what to do, I said a quick prayer to St. Blaise, Patron of throats. Immediately, I felt the bone dislodge itself and move harmlessly down my throat. I told the doctors I was fine. They examined me once again and remarked that they must have gotten it out after all! I didn't argue and left them in their innocence.

I do remember one Sunday when I happened to be at the Mass Msgr. O'Brien, Pastor of St. James Parish, was celebrating. The old Monsignor always had trouble walking. And negotiating steps was even more difficult. At communion time he was coming down the steps with a very large ciborium filled with hundreds of hosts. One of his feet gave out, causing him to stumble. He then missed a step and fell on the floor in front of the altar which in those days faced the back wall. I saw white wafers flying all over the sanctuary. They went everywhere. The problem was that in 1956 lay people couldn't touch a host since the church had not evolved sufficiently yet to have Extraordinary Ministers of the Eucharist. Nor could I, as a deacon, touch a consecrated host either at that time. So someone went over to the Rectory to find another priest to help pick up the hosts. It was awful. The priests were on their knees picking them up while the people watched in shock. They had never seen anything like this. (I didn't either!)

Then comes the question: "Are the congregation going to receive the same hosts that were on the floor?" They did indeed! Years ago we were not as afraid of catching a bug, a germ, a virus, aids, or one of countless infections we are aware of today. So everyone went to communion as usual. We all felt sorry for the Monsignor; he was kind and gentle. But his days of going up or down steps without a rail were over.

16. The Final Preparations For Ordination To The Priesthood

As with all Sacred Orders, the call was given indicating that the faculty of the seminary believed that my classmates and I were called to the priesthood. The call or vocation by custom was given by a knock on the door. We were all accepted. Before taking the monumental step of dedicating our lives in total commitment to the priesthood, we made a retreat. That retreat, particularly, was the big one. There was no turning back. It was for life. In those days, that is, in 1956, a priest never even thought about the possibility of leaving the active ministry; certainly not with the church's blessing. It would be extremely rare to receive the approval of the church.. Our commitment was for life. That was made very clear to us. However, following the Vatican council, in the late sixties, laicization (leaving the priesthood and becoming once again, a layman) was not uncommon. The church had opened the door for clergy and religious to leave with dignity.

During my retreat before ordination, I took the initiative myself to ask that mysterious voice to assist me in making the ultimate decision of my life. The *voice* was always comforting and assuring. And spoke with authority as if the message were straight from heaven. *But no help was given.* I took long walks alone, hoping to receive some encouragement to take that final step. *No voice!* Believe me, there was a great internal struggle going on within me. I first had to remove the anger and disappointment over the loss of both my parents which happened at the most crucial time in my life. That was not easy. I prayed, I wept...at long last, I chose to take that step to which my whole life was moving. It had to be my destiny! I had too many mystical encounters to ignore the continual guidance afforded me. By the end of the retreat the decision was made: I believed with all my heart that I was called to the priesthood of Our Lord Jesus Christ.

I was ordained a priest on June 2, 1956 at Blessed Sacrament Cathedral by Cardinal Edward Mooney. There were thirty of us from the Archdiocese of Detroit. The big dream finally became a reality. The Cathedral on Woodward Avenue in Detroit was completely filled with many standing. And it was by invitation only. Two thousand seats was hardly enough to contain the many relatives and friends we had.

The Ordination Mass was magnificent! The Latin added a certain mystique to the ceremony. The music was outstanding. A few memories are still very vivid in my mind. Candidates to Holy Orders were officially called forth one at a time. Our answer was "Adsum!" In English it simply means "Present!" but in this ceremony there was contained the thought of being fully present and aware of this sacred undertaking and ready. Quite ready! How can any of us forget the moment when the Cardinal Archbishop then placed his outstretched hands over each one of us individually, and without words spoken, invoked the Holy Spirit to confer on us the power of the Priesthood of Our Lord Jesus Christ. Meanwhile the choir was singing the beautiful words taken from Sacred Scripture: "Tu es sacerdos in aeternum secundum Ordinem Melchizedek," that is: "You are a priest forever according to the Order of Melchizedek." While the choir continued singing, each priest present came up to us as we knelt and also placed their hands over us as a symbol of the power we shared and as a mark of solidarity in the service of Christ. There were several hundred priests present. Each one supported our empowerment into the priesthood. Tears flowed freely as I knelt before the Lord offering him my entire life. Nothing was held back! I was His to command. Death itself could not separate me from the God who gave me life and chose me to receive the Sacrament of Holy Orders. I was happy and proud to be called a servant of God. I prayed only for the grace to fulfill my lofty promises.

I embraced the priesthood that was part of my family legacy. It was as if I represented a priestly caste. My family tree on my father's side which is fully recorded in the Catholic Encyclopedia goes back to the seventeenth century.

The name Samonie is not the actual name on my birth certificate. It was Jacob Laba Assemani; later, the name Jacob Joseph Samonie was written over it, with the original name still visible. My original middle name Laba is Arabic for St. Jude, a Patron of Lebanon. In the early nineteen hundreds when my father came from Lebanon to the United States, many relatives with the same last name came from the same town of Hasroun. They changed their names at the Port of Entry to names like Semain, Semanie, Simony, Samonie or kept the original name Assemani. They could neither read or write English very well, if at all!

The name Assemani (in Arabic: Al-Semaani) achieved great notoriety in the Middle East. The following is a quote from the Catholic Encyclopedia, page 794:

"It is the name of an illustrious Maronite family of Mt. Lebanon, four members of which, all bishops, distinguished themselves during the 18th century in the East and in Europe. For their zeal, learning, and unbounded attachment to the Roman See, they were held in great esteem by the popes, who conferred upon them many well-merited ecclesiastical dignities and offices.

"Oriental (Middle East), but especially Syriac studies, owe more to them than to others; for it was through their research, collection of manuscripts and voluminous publications that Syriac Studies, and, in general, the Middle East History,

82

Hagiography or Lives of the Saints, Liturgy, and Literature of the Middle East Churches were first introduced into Europe. Therefore, they can be justly regarded, if not as the creators, certainly as the most illustrious pioneers, of modern oriental Middle East Studies.

"The four Assemanis are the following: Joseph Simon, Born in the mountains of Lebanon in 1687 and died at Rome, January of 1768. In 1703, he entered the Maronite College in Rome to study for the priesthood. Soon after ordination he was assigned to the Vatican Library. Pope Clement XI sent him to the East for the purpose of collecting manuscripts which he did, successfully, visiting Cairo, Damascus, Aleppo and Lebanon. In 1735-38, he was again sent to the East and returned with an even more valuable collection .

"On his return he was named the Titular Archbishop of Tyre and Librarian of the Vatican Library, where he devoted the rest of this life editing and publishing the most valuable Syriac, Arabic, Ethiopian, Armenian, Persian, Hebrew, and Greek manuscripts, all treasures of the Vatican." Joseph Simon Assemani, my uncle with about five greats in front of the word uncle, was not only a great man of the cloth , but also great in the academic and scientific world of his time. He wrote extensively. He published in his lifetime over one hundred and ten volumes on various topics.

He was very well respected by Popes and Kings and was, by far, the most famous name in a long line of Bishops of the Maronite Catholic church.

Following him was his brother Bishop Josephus Aloysius, born in Tripoli in 1710 and died in 1782 in Rome. He worked with his older brother in the Vatican Library and was also a prolific writer.

Archbishop Stephanus Evodius (or Awwad) was born in 1707 and also died in 1782. He assisted in the Vatican Library but was also a member of the Royal Society of London. He has authored many books as well.

Bishop Simeon, grand-nephew of the first and second Assemanis was born in Tripoli, Lebanon, 1752 and died at Padua, Italy in 1821. In 1785, he was appointed Professor of Oriental Languages at the Seminary of Padua, and in 1807 was named Professor at the University of Padua. His works are also well known.

There was a fifth uncle who lived after that article was written in the Catholic Encyclopedia. His name was Bishop Louis. He was born in Lebanon around 1860 and died in 1950. He is the one to whom I wrote a letter when I was in high school. To my knowledge, he is the last of the Assemani Bishops. Bishop Louis' brother was the Superior General of the Franciscan Order of the Black Friars of Lebanon.

Joseph Simon Assemani was so well liked by Pope Clement XI, that before he died the Pope established a "Seat of Learning" for any direct descendants of Joseph Simon. I was an eligible descendant to study at the College in Rome for my last four years of study at the Major Seminary. However, I chose not to pursue that direction. Instead I studied Spanish and worked with Hispanics most of my priesthood.

There I was, a descendent of a long line of bishops, entrusting my life to the same Lord that endowed these church prelates with the zeal and vigor of serving God in the priesthood.

During the Ordination Ceremony, our hands were then anointed with holy oil called Chrism blessed on Holy Thursday. Chrism was used in the Sacraments of Baptism, Confirmation and Holy Orders (the official name for Priesthood.) A cloth bound our hands together as in a gesture of prayer. In that part of the ceremony we were given the faculty to offer Mass, to bless and to forgive. Priests' vestments were placed on us for the first time and we celebrated our first Mass together with the Cardinal. It was truly a day to remember. All the studies, all the sacrifices, and all the stressful situations we endured along the way were worth it, after all. I felt the presence of my parents but I still longed to see them and to hug them and, yes, to congratulate them.

The next day I celebrated my first Solemn Mass as the principal celebrant. It is customary to celebrate the Mass at your home parish. At that time, St. Bernard's Church was my home parish. I was very excited and felt privileged but I was also concerned about doing it right. A Solemn Mass in those days included two other priests, one who would function as a subdeacon and the other as a deacon. I figured they would help in the event I got confused. As it turned out, everything went well.

After that first Mass, there was a reception for me. When I got to the Hall, I was overwhelmed to see hundreds of people lined up to receive my blessing. They waited patiently since it was considered a special grace from God to receive the blessing from the hands of a newly ordained priest. I was truly humbled when a very elderly man I did not know knelt down before me and asked for my blessing. He appeared to be in his nineties and he was asking a twenty six year old youngster for a blessing! He then kissed my hands that were consecrated at the Cathedral. I was deeply edified by such faith especially by a older man who obviously lived many more years than I, and who, I am sure, had acquired much more wisdom as well.

Everything went well at the reception until I got up to say a few words. I promised myself that I would not mention my parents; I knew that the very thought of them would make me too emotional. So I spoke in general terms. Then I started thanking all the wonderful people who shared in making the banquet such a great success; I thanked my family who arranged the banquet...and then I slipped and mentioned my mother and father who were not present, and I broke down. I couldn't speak and I felt very foolish. At last, I recovered my composure and continued, avoiding that delicate topic that made me so vulnerable.

17. My First Assignment

I received my first assignment as a young assistant in Ypsilanti, Michigan. Fr. Bill Mooney was pastor, and the first assistant was Fr. Jerry Krieg. I was automatically second assistant. Rank was everything in those days. I enjoyed the two priests immensely. Fr. Mooney was one of the funniest men I had ever met in my life. He was funny to look at (I mean that as a compliment!) He was pudgy and truly comical. It would not be considered funny if someone always had a cigarette in the mouth, but Fr. Mooney never took the cigarette out of his mouth, even when he was speaking. As he spoke the ashes were continually running down the front of his suit. Watching the ashes trickle down was humorous enough. He was also a genius at making you laugh with an unlimited supply of jokes. It was nearly impossible to keep a straight face listening to him even before he finished a joke. What upset me was that I would tell him a joke. He hardly cracked a smile. The next day he would actually tell me my own joke and he would have me genuinely laughing. At my own joke, no less!

One day I entered his office and told him that I had a problem. I told him the Tokay wine was too strong for me. I explained how "the congregation started to look a little blurry" by the time I got to my second Mass. This was the problem. In 1956 Catholics were not permitted to eat or drink anything, not even water after midnight if we intended to receive communion the next day. Naturally, since I was the second assistant, on the bottom rung, so to speak, I was given the last two Masses. That meant that I would be saying the ten o'clock and twelve noon Masses. Having an empty stomach and drinking wine at both Masses had a real effect on me. I told the Pastor about it. He said, "Tell me exactly what you do at the Offertory of the Mass when you pour the wine into the chalice."

"I simply pour the wine in the chalice till I empty the cruet." I said.

"Well, no wonder, ya darned fool! You don't have to drink it *all*!" he explained laughing. From then on, I poured a very small amount in the chalice. The people no longer looked blurry!

I really liked being in Ypsilanti. The people were warm and cooperative and I was beginning to find a new ministry for me at Eastern Michigan University which was located in the Parish. I had some very enlightening discussions with the college students and I was hoping to become their chaplain. But that was not to be! After only three months everything changed. I received a letter from the Archbishop's office transferring me to the inner city of Detroit. Within a week, St. Boniface was to be my new home. It was situated next to Tiger Stadium on the lower west side of the city. It seemed that the Assistant Pastor collapsed one day through bad health and stress. They found him on the floor. He needed a rest and a change. So they swapped us. I went to St. Boniface in Detroit and he went to St. John's Church in Ypsilanti. They also wanted me to work with a community of Hispanics in the area. I was amazed how quickly our lives could be changed around...like pawns on a chess board.

From the moment I began working among the Hispanic people, I always felt a sense of belonging. However, my ministry was to all the people of St. Boniface. And I did not avoid any group in the Parish. I loved visiting the children in school, working closely with the Maltese and Hispanics, and I reached out to the rest of the parish with no less zeal.

My first job was getting along with the Pastor. He was a tough guy to live with. He was the type of person who was continually checking up on you and taking notes. He would write down every mistake you made, from leaving the newspaper in the wrong place to forgetting lights on, not closing a door and countless other insignificant things. At the end of the day just before supper, we would be sitting down *relaxing* (I use that word loosely). Fr. Joe inevitably would take out his famous "List of Errors" and read them off one by one. I always felt as if he were examining my conscience instead of his. I was far from perfect but overlooking a couple of simple things or making a few minor mistakes was not going to change the parish or the world. But this was a daily ritual.

I began to wonder if perhaps the Assistant Pastor before me was overcome more by a stressful life living under those conditions than because of poor health. After several weeks of this daily pattern, he was starting to get on my nerves. I decided to do something about it. Two can play that game! I carefully watched him for the next few days, making a mental note of any slip-ups on his part. By the end of the week, I got what I was looking for. While we were sitting in the living room waiting for supper, he began his usual tirade against carelessness. True to form, he took out his "List of Errors" and started to read each error very carefully and clearly. He wanted to make sure I understood "the charges."

I listened attentively. When he finished I then said "I have something to share with *you* also." He looked at me inquisitively as I pulled out a slip of paper from inside my suit coat. It was the last thing in the world he expected. I read off his "misdemeanors", such as leaving the safe in church open one day. Naturally, I emphasized how dangerous that was because we had all the sacred vessels kept there; it would be tragic if someone stole them because of his carelessness; a basement light was left on and he was the last one to be down there; he did not lock the back door twice that week. And there were several other items. When I finished I said "When you get your act together, I'll take care of mine! Fair enough?" He got up off the couch and started walking in my direction. He said, "Get up!" I thought he was going to try to deck me. I was ready to duck. Instead he said, "Now, you're a real man! I like you." And he shook my hand warmly. From that day on we became the best of friends. No more lists, no more complaints or tirades. From that time on, we worked well together and had a very productive ministry. He didn't even mind when I went to the baseball or football games at Tiger Stadium, which was only a couple of blocks away. If any parishioners complained about me spending too much time there, I told them I was taking a census of the parish. A couple of people actually believed me. After all, Tiger Stadium was definitely within our parish boundaries. The truth, of course, was that I didn't want to miss a Lions' game during the incredible championship years of Bobby Layne and Joe Schmidt.

18. A Tragic Fire -
The Death Of A Heroic Priest

A couple of years later, we had a priest staying with us. There was a lot of room; the Parish House had at least five bedrooms with a private bath. Fr. Adam Joseph came to us from Cracow, Poland. He had been a professor at a University in Cracow and was also a parish priest. He was not afraid to get in the pulpit and speak openly against the Nazis. Soldiers came in one day during Mass and took him to a Concentration Camp where he was ill-treated and tortured. At one point he was chosen for experimental surgery on his stomach without anesthesia. The Nazi doctors wanted to see how much pain a human being could endure before losing consciousness. They removed a portion of his stomach. My biggest surprise was that he was alive to talk about it! After two years in the concentration camp they sent him back to his church.

After a few months he began to criticize the Nazi Regime again. The parishioners knew that this time they would kill him outright or torture him to death. Some of his devoted parishioners managed to take him almost by force to a train leaving for Switzerland. It was not easy for them to convince him to leave the country, but they did succeed. They dressed him up like a woman, wearing the popular babushka. One of them accompanied him to safety. From there, he made his way to America. Another surprise was that his English was almost perfect. When he came to St. Boniface Parish looking for a place to live, he was already teaching Theology at the University of Detroit. How he negotiated that position I'm not sure.

The Pastor, Fr. Joe Bruck, like many Michiganders, was

accustomed to go down to Florida for a post-Christmas vacation. While he was there in 1958, I was witness to a terrible tragedy. I had gone to bed one evening only to have a bad dream that there was a fire and I was smelling smoke. The scent was becoming stronger every moment. Then I realized I was awake and still smelling smoke. I jumped out of bed and saw that the smoke was coming from the door across the hall. That's where Fr. Joseph's room was located . I quickly opened the door and what I saw was absolutely unbelievable! The door to the Polish priest's room was wide open, the entire room was on fire, and in the middle of the room was Fr. Adam Joseph standing there burning to death right in front of me. He mumbled, completely dispirited, "Please help me..." as he fell to the floor either dead or dying. I tried desperately to enter the room but I couldn't. The door was completely surrounded by fire. Just then a fireman came up to me and told me to get downstairs immediately. The smoke, starting at the ceiling was coming down fast. It was just above my head when I made for the stairs. The fireman had a lot of equipment on including an oxygen mask, but he could not get in the room either. He called for some fire extinguishers as I made my way downstairs. Someone had seen the fire from outside the building and called the fire department. They got there quickly.

The Parish House, as I said, was very large. On the other side of the house lived two elderly ladies. One was the cook and the other the housekeeper. I went up the back stairs only once when I first came to St. Boniface. So I did not know that area very well. When I came downstairs during the fire I did not see either one of them. I told the firemen on the first floor that there were two ladies upstairs on the other side of the house. He said that there wasn't anyone up there. He was beginning to patronize me, "Father, why don't you just drink a little coffee here and relax for a moment. Everything is being taken care of."

I heard enough! I grabbed a napkin off the table, placed it over my nose and dashed upstairs. One of the firemen shouted at me to come back. He yelled loudly, "There is no one up there. Come on down!" I paid no attention to him.

On the second floor, the smoke was already about three feet above the floor causing total darkness in the rooms. I was on my hands and knees. I made my way to where I thought one of the beds was. I was right! There was somebody still in bed. I shook her and she awakened, getting out of bed immediately. That was the housekeeper. I asked where the bed of the cook was. But this was no time for directions. She told me to hold on to her and she would take me there. The smoke was about bed level. If the cook inhaled it she would surely die in her sleep of asphyxiation. We got there just in time. We awakened her and dragged her out of bed at the same time. The smoke was not more than two feet above the floor. We were crawling as fast as we could toward the only flight of stairs on that side of the house. We were now only a few feet away from the top of the stairs when a quick decision had to be made. I couldn't hold my breath any longer. I took a breath, inhaling smoke. I could not exhale. I was literally passing out. I was being asphyxiated. In that split second before losing consciousness, I let go of the housekeeper's hand and threw my body in what I hoped was the direction of the stairs - nothing was visible - and I was right. My body came tumbling down the stairs. The fall woke me up. Just behind me came the housekeeper, her body falling down right behind me. Gravity was working in our favor. We coughed a bit but were out of serious danger.

They were all happy to see us both alive, but we didn't waste a moment telling the firemen that there was still one of the ladies up there. Protected with an oxygen mask, one of them ran upstairs to get her. We presumed she was lying on the floor near the stairs. He came down empty-handed. We were shocked that we did not save her. Just then someone came in the back door telling the firemen to rescue a lady up on the terrace of the second floor. What a smart move she made. The cook was accustomed to sit out on the terrace quite frequently in good weather. She knew exactly where the doorknob was and she made a quick exit instead of heading for the stairs. She was saved after all!

Fr. Adam Joseph was rushed to the hospital. He never regained consciousness. He died in the hospital. The cause: asphyxiation from the fumes. His body was burned badly after he fell unconscious to the floor. My heart went out to him. Imagine surviving the terror and torture of a Nazi Concentration Camp and then dying in a peaceful setting where there was no war, no attack, no violence...only faulty wiring, which triggered a sudden fire, according to the Fire Inspector's Report. The ladies and I were being treated for any effects of minor asphyxiation. We stayed with Fr. Joseph as long as we could. By the time we got back from the hospital, it was almost dawn. Since the Parish House was considered unsafe until the entire wiring system was replaced, the ladies made provisions to stay with relatives until further notice. Besides, the smell of smoke pervaded the whole house. I knew it was late, but I did not realize just how late it was. The ladies and I were up till dawn, feeling weak and totally exhausted. We were fully aware that we barely escaped the jaws of death. The fire could have taken our lives as well, but strangely enough, fear set in only after the whole ordeal was over.

About 8:00 am, I received a phone call from one of the Bishops. He was not kind in his choice of words to me. "Do we have to read about the fire in the newspaper? Why didn't you call us?"

"I nearly died in the fire and I am feeling very weak." I said.

"You are supposed to report any such damage immediately.

You know better than that!" He was actually reprimanding me!
"I nearly died in the fire!" I repeated more loudly.
"You were not following procedure. We don't want to be
the last ones to hear about a fire!" He continued.
"I was asphyxiated and nearly died!" I shouted. Now I was
angry! "Are you deaf? I am lucky to be alive. What do I care
whether you hear about it or not? Are you listening or shall I
hang up?"
I finally got his attention. "Oh, are you all right? I'm sorry.
I didn't realize it was that serious."
"It was serious enough to take Fr. Adam Joseph's life!" I
reminded him.

We were now communicating. He recommended that I stay
in a house we owned that was inhabited by the maintenance man
and his family. There was one unoccupied bedroom. He said if
it was satisfactory I could stay there until the rectory was
completely repaired, wiring and all. If I did not like staying with
that family he would make other arrangements. It was fine. He
also told me to call the pastor in Florida, inform him of what
happened and tell him to stay there until the rectory was ready.
The Archdiocese was aware of the Pastor's poor health and
heart condition.

For almost a month I kept having nightmares. I would wake
up perspiring and re-living the same scene: Fr. Adam Joseph is
standing in the midst of flames and asking for my help. Night
after night I could see the pitiful look on his face when he knew
the end had come and the fire would consume his very life.
After about a month the nightmares tapered off until I no longer
had them. I was ready to see a psychiatrist if they had
continued.

A few months after the fire, Fr. Bruck was transferred to St.
Joseph Church in Trenton, MI. It was a sad parting. He treated
me more as a co-worker than as an assistant. I know there was

a tear in his eye because he could not look at me face to face when I was making my farewell.

19. My Ideals Of The Priesthood - Challenged

I was still at St. Boniface, but my life was turned around again. The Pastor that followed Fr. Bruck was very challenging and the situation got worse as time went along. The picture of what I did *not* want to be as a Pastor was being demonstrated every day. I owe this second Pastor a debt of gratitude for permitting me to witness what a priestly ministry should *not* be. I was only there about a year and believe me, that was long enough. I understand that the average stay of assistants that followed me was also about a year. All seven of them!

This same Pastor (I choose to withhold his name) was possessed with the idea of controlling everything in the house, including me. He wanted to control my life, my time, my ministry. According to Archdiocesan policy, each priest was strongly encouraged to take a full day off. The very nature of a priest's daily schedule usually demanded more than eight hours a day. Most priests worked and lived in the same building. If a typically hard-working priest did not get away from that situation at least once a week, he could become obsessed with his work or experience "burn out." And his priestly ministry would suffer greatly. It was both healthy and necessary to have a change of scenery each week. My day off was Wednesday. I always showed up wide awake and fresh to celebrate Mass the next morning. I spent every day off with about five or six classmates, all priests. Sometimes there were eight of us that spent the day together (especially if we were looking for two foursomes for golf!) At any rate, we would go out to supper, and since there was so much to talk about, we often stayed out late. We sometimes ended the evening by attending the Opera, a Musical at the Fisher Theater or a movie.

The very first week with the new Pastor, I came in about 11:00 pm on my day off. I was surprised to see the light on in the living room. There was the Pastor sitting on a couch waiting for me.

"Do you know what time it is ?" he screamed.

"Yeah, about eleven. Why?" I said calmly.

"Priests should be home in bed by ten o'clock!" He said pointing at his watch.

"Where did you ever hear that nonsense?" I came back defiantly.

"My mother told me that!" He replied as if that would end all arguments.

"Then, do what your mother tells you. My mother never told me that!" I scooted upstairs and ended the conversation abruptly.

In the following weeks I deliberately stayed out longer than ten every time. He waited each week, complained each time, and convinced me to come in even later. I was an adult male. I was going to take as much time as I wanted on my day off. At other times, I followed policy; on my day off, my time is my own!

After about a month and a half, the weekly confrontations finally ended, and I could go straight to bed for a well-needed rest.

On another occasion, I was in the basement with a group of Hispanic parishioners. We were planning a big celebration in honor of Our Lady of Guadalupe in December. The twelfth day of December is the day usually set aside for the commemoration recalling the apparitions to Juan Diego and the construction of the Basilica in her honor. I was sitting with the officers of the Guadalupe society. We faced the other members and also the door that led to the first floor of the Rectory. During the meeting, I happened to notice the Pastor coming down into the basement. He rarely did that. He looked around and saw that there were at least thirty Hispanics at the meeting. What he did next was unbelievable. He went to the switch and turned the lights out on us. We were in complete darkness. I told everyone to calm down. I slowly edged my way in complete darkness to the light switch, and there was light again! Most of the members thought it was a momentary light failure. I knew better and so did a couple of the officers who saw the whole thing. But we didn't say a thing about it.   I know the Pastor deliberately did it because he didn't think the Hispanics supported the parish sufficiently. In fact, he admitted to it later. There are other stories about this man that are much worse. Any one of these incriminating stories could have ended up in a lawsuit against the church. I no longer care to share them; he has died since. Let him rest in peace! Nevertheless, his behavior had a profound impact on me.

Unfortunately, my first appointment at St. John's in Ypsilanti turned out to be a temporary three-month assignment and here I was at St. Boniface in my first full assignment as an assistant, where I learned what kind of priest I did not want to be. I was hoping for another Pastor like Fr. Bruck who could give me a good example of dedication and a loyal commitment to a productive priestly ministry. I discovered that priests were fully human and had the same weaknesses and frailty as any human being. I had higher expectations than that. I was certainly given a good start in Ypsilanti. Thank God for the inspiring priestly example I received in Ypsi. I'm glad that came first.

20. My First Encounter
With Metaphysics

In 1959, I was appointed to All Saints Church on Fort street in southwest Detroit. I have the most beautiful memories of my life as an assistant working under Fr. Fred Borck. He was an elderly priest almost completely bald but he retained a boyish appearance. He also gave me an example of a loyal and devout priest joyfully serving the Lord. He was generous in spirit and fair in his function as Pastor. I really liked him. We took equal turns being on duty on Sundays, hearing confessions, and there was a fair division of all the other responsibilities that comprised priestly life.

I especially loved one of my responsibilities; it was part of my job to attend the high school athletic activities and to teach the tenth grade. I was into sports big time. I had played practically every sport at one time or another. The All Saints high school basketball team had just won the All State Championship a couple of years before I got there. They beat Austin when Debusschre (later an NBA star) was playing for Austin. The newspaper article, commenting on the game the day after, spoke of the Tiny Tims against the Giants. It was a fact that there were only 27 students in the senior class and they were very small for basketball, but they were excellent ball-handlers. Austin was a huge high school in comparison. The paper also made an astounding statement: the Tiny Tims of All Saints did not make a single mechanical mistake during the game. Two years later that championship game was still fresh in the minds of the students and of their parents. They still spoke and acted like champions.

They were still winning games and when they played their

greatest rivals from St. Gabriel's Parish, the game was sheer madness. The noise level and the cheering on both sides was worth the price of admission. There was always excitement right till the last second. I am glad my heart was young then. The pressure was enormous. I always blessed the boys before the game and told them to just play and do your best. The outcome was not that important. But the emotions were telling them and me something else. It was very difficult to lose a close game and walk away perfectly calm. It took real discipline. Only a seasoned player could do that.

Their baseball team was not bad either. They played their hearts out on the field. But baseball never reached the feverish pitch of excitement as did basketball. Nevertheless, I tried to attend every game regardless of their position in the league. I realized how important it was for young people to have the support of the parish and especially their spiritual leaders. And they did!

Teaching the tenth grade was not accidental. The principal and the teachers all agreed that the toughest class in the entire school was the tenth grade. I don't know if that was because of the specific personality of that whole class or if all tenth grade classes were the toughest. I accepted the challenge although I had never taught a required class in high school before. I was used to simply making a brief visit to all the classes just to get acquainted with them and also to help remove any fear of coming to me for counseling should they ever find themselves in that position.

Sometime during that first summer before I began teaching Religion, which was a regularly scheduled class, I met one of the parishioners of All saints. Her name was Mrs. Pope. What a nice catholic name, I thought to myself. We used to have interesting discussions. One day she asked me what I thought of graphoanalysis. I said "grapho" what? She explained that the

101

science of graphoanalysis or graphology, as it is also called, was based on the premise that handwriting was brain writing. She said she had studied all twenty booklets written by a man named Bunker. (I thought that name was very appropriate also.) The way we think was the way we write. She said it could be proved.

I realized then what she was talking about. About a year before, a good friend of my sister Jenny, named Ann, was present at a family gathering. She was going around asking for samples of writing. She came up to me and asked politely if I would mind writing a few words for her. I asked what was the purpose. She said she studied different styles of handwriting. She had me write: "Tall men tell tales. Red rivers run dry," and a few other sentences plus my signature. So I did. I said that I sometimes write in a different style depending on the circumstances. For example, if I am taking notes I write considerably different than writing a letter. Or if I were taking a test or writing only for my own information. She said "fine! Try writing in every style you use." I filled the whole page with samples of my handwriting.

Later she came back to me while I was in the middle of a card game with some relatives. She startled me and everyone around me with some interesting comments about my personality. She claimed it was just from the handwriting. But I complained that she already knew me. Or maybe my sister Jenny told her a lot of things about me. She insisted that was not true. As a matter of fact, the two of us had never had a discussion before. I had never spoken to her alone and I had only seen her on one occasion before. Yet what she said about me was extremely accurate. She gave in detail aspects of my life that she could not have known on her own.

Ann said she belonged to a group of professional handwriting analysts. They were always looking for a good specimen of handwriting to bring to their monthly meetings. She wanted to take the sample of my handwriting to their next meeting. She simply needed my permission. I said it was all right but not to tell them I was a priest. She said she was not going to tell them anything at all about me. That would spoil the whole effect of their research. I didn't believe a word of the whole matter. I kind of humored her. She seemed so sincere.

About two weeks later, the group of professional handwriting analysts mailed me the results of their monthly meeting. The report was six pages long, and it was complete with many details of my personality. They usually examined four or five samples of handwriting and gave a thorough report about each person. However, at that particular meeting the analysts spent the entire meeting on my handwriting alone. Ann said that was very unusual. And she kept her word as she promised by not participating in the discussions about me because she had already met me. After they completed their investigation and the conclusions were drawn up, Ann then told them that I was a clergyman. They could not believe their ears. They said they wanted to meet me in person.

I agreed to attend. There I was at their next monthly meeting. I felt like an animal in a cage. They were all staring at me. What they were probably doing was comparing in their minds what they expected me to look like or how they expected me to act...according to my handwriting, of course. At last one of them broke the ice by asking me a question, and we began to have an interesting conversation together. They were expecting a person who made a career in music, astronomy, science, art or philosophy. But a Roman Catholic priest! No way! My mind was too open, in their opinion, to be a priest. I was definitely a non-conformist according to their findings. They were delightfully surprised and amused. They said I could have been successful at anything I wanted to be.

While we were engaged in conversation, I could not help thinking about what they had written. When I was about twelve years old, my parents bought me a painting set. My first painting was a numbered painting. It was awfully easy to follow. You simply fill in each well-marked spot with a particular color and the picture is finished. It's almost like filling in a coloring book for children. This gave me no satisfaction. I vowed never to do a numbered painting again. And I never did. Since then I have painted over three hundred original paintings. And I had never taken an lesson. How could these total strangers possibly know about my artistic nature?

I started playing the piano at about age fifteen. Up to that time we could not afford a piano; finally my parents found one for fifty dollars - not in the best condition - but all the keys worked. I immediately went downtown to Grinnell's Music Store and bought a ninety-page book of piano music. I did not know one key from another so I also purchased a cardboard strip that is placed above the keys and identifies each note. That same day I was able to play the entire book of ninety pages. Since then I read notes and I can also play by ear. I have never taken piano lessons. Did my musical ability also show up in my handwriting?

As far as astronomy goes, when I was nine years old, I could walk outside and, without looking up, point to and name all the constellations of that season. I used to study the stars all the time. It got me in trouble once in a while. I loved to lie on the grass and stare up at the skies. Oftentimes, I would fall asleep out in the field and my parents would be looking everywhere for me. Once they even had the police searching for me. I could not figure out why everyone was so upset. I thought they knew where they could find me.

My interest in astronomy has never lessened through the years. I loved science and all its branches, especially astronomy, the science of the stars. I wanted to know what the latest theories were regarding creation of the cosmos and especially the star system we live on and planet earth that faithfully has continued its orbit for billions of years. I was fascinated by stellar nurseries, the cosmic conditions in which stars are born. I wanted to know what makes things work and grow, and why there was such a variety of life forms on this planet. I was forever intrigued by the systematic body of knowledge of the material world gained by empirical observation and experimentation. The laws by which science derived their conclusions excited me, but the source of these laws was even more fascinating.

The same is true with philosophy and all the various branches of philosophy. My personal library at that time was filled with books on science and different philosophies. In the seminary we limited our philosophy to St. Thomas Aquinas and a few other selected philosophers. However, I was often found in the library reading about philosophers and theologians that were not on our approved reading list, such as Descartes, Hegel, Kierkgaard, Bultmann, Nietzsche, Karl Barth and others. I wanted to know what they were all saying not just the favored few. However, I never expressed my personal views in class. It would not be wise if I wanted to continue in the seminary. Anyway, I didn't feel the need to defend what I was merely exploring. I simply wanted to know more and to expand my view of reality.

I still questioned how the graphoanalysts could know so much about me just from my writing? I was thoroughly baffled by their accurate evaluation and insight. But after a time, I lost contact with them and put this whole matter aside. I have to admit I almost became convinced that their major premise was correct about handwriting being the expression of brain writing. I wasn't quite ready to give assent to it.

So when Mrs. Pope defined and explained the Bunker System to me, I realized she was talking about the very same thing. She encouraged me to read about it; it was a big undertaking with each of the booklets containing about fifty pages. So I did! It was easy reading and there were a lot of samples of handwriting that took up most of the space on each page. From the outset I was determined to show that Bunker's material was a lot of bunk. In 1960 this kind of talk was off the wall. Cuckoo! Weird! I kept telling myself to keep an open mind. Don't prejudge! Fine, I said to myself, I'll check it out. I then began to read and to test at the same time.

I first checked each item, such as, the slant of the writing, the loops or lack of loops in the letters "h" or "t" and the loops below as in the letters "g", "j" or "y". Everything meant something. The way you dot the small "I" or cross a "t". I went through all twenty books. I still wanted to prove that the system was totally false. How could this nonsense be true! Yet from the very beginning, every time I tested out a letter and its meaning, it turned out to be accurate. On myself and others. Whenever I received any correspondence by mail I tested out the handwriting and compared it to my knowledge of the person writing it. Again, it was amazingly accurate. How could this be - I kept asking myself. I continued to apply the principles and found myself slowly becoming a believer. a reluctant believer!

21. Exploring The World Of Metaphysics

None of this information was ever presented to us in the seminary. My studies were based on the teachings found in the Bible and on the facts or, at least, the "accepted knowledge" of our time. Theology and Science seemed to be a trustworthy foundation of belief but, all of a sudden, I found myself moving slightly off dead center. The foundation of my belief experienced a little tremor. I thought to myself: For years I had a hard time believing everything I read or heard about in the religious, scientific, philosophical, psychological and historical fields of knowledge. But I had no other acceptable information that told me otherwise. I stayed with my traditional beliefs but I began to question.

If this system of graphoanalysis works because there is an integral functioning between our body and mind, then how far does that go? It could give credibility to other systems that treated the body and mind as a single unit such as Biorhythms, in which the physical, the mental and the intellectual activity functioned best or worst on certain days of the month. In fact, pilots in Japan and Germany are not permitted to fly on critical days (in which they are most vulnerable); Palmistry, the art of determining aspects of one's destiny and character from the lines on the palm of the hand, a practice going back to the fourteenth century; Reflexology, a system developed around 1920, of massaging specific areas of the foot or sometimes the hand in order to promote healing or the relief of stress in another part of the body; Iridology another system that also found acceptance around 1920. One could supposedly identify the health condition throughout the body by examining the iris of the eye. I had only read about these sciences before, but I had never given any credence to them.

Down deep within me I knew there was a space that had to be filled. There were too many unanswered questions. I believed I was starting to ask the right questions. To change my mental power-base, I needed stronger convictions, built out of passion and personal experience. Anything less than that was not sufficient to remove the mental shackles of limitation. I had a great desire to think freely, creatively. I obviously wasn't ready. Einstein's premise kept repeating itself in my mind when he said "Each person sits in the prison of his or her own ideas!" I needed personal experience. I wanted to explore for myself the mysteries behind the body/mind connection.

I didn't waste any time. I began the school year with the tenth graders by having them write out their names, supply information about their families, and name a career they would like to pursue as an adult. I merely wanted to get more samples to test against the principles of graphoanalysis. I now had a lot to work with. First I separated the "talkers" and "trouble-makers" in the classroom and surrounded them with the more quiet and cooperative students. All was done entirely from their handwriting. I did not know the behavior of these students. This was my first personal encounter with any of the students. It proved to be successful.

Next, I wanted to demonstrate to the class how they could train their memory to function in a superior manner. If I succeeded, I was willing to share my secret with those interested. I had studied the famous Roth Memory System. It's a very simple process of enhancing memory through association. I asked the students to give me thirty words. Each of the words was written on the blackboard for all to see. Naturally, they went to their dictionaries to hunt for the strangest, oddest words they could find. The only requirement was that it had to be an noun. Verbs were not permitted!

Then I turned my back to the board and proceeded to name all thirty words in order. To show how versatile that memory system was, I asked them to call out a number from 1 to 30 and I would give the word that corresponded to that number. Then I added to their shock by giving all 30 words backwards. By this time they were sufficiently impressed. They had agreed before this memory experiment that I was permitted two mistakes and no more. As it was, I correctly remembered all of the words.

After placing the students in a seating arrangement according to their handwriting, which really worked, and leaving them stunned with the memory demonstration, the tenth grade became a very easy class to teach. The other teachers marveled at the change in their behavior. They wanted to know what I did to accomplish that. "Ask the students," I replied.

Several things happened that were worth noting. About a week after I had made a good study of each student in the tenth grade, the principal, Sr. Mary Arthur, came up to me and asked what I knew about this one student. She gave me his name. I stared at her for a few seconds, wondering if I should tell her what I discovered about him from his handwriting. He had been new at the school. No one knew him well. I said, " I have some information about him but it is not good and I don't know whether I should share that with you." She wanted to know anything at all I knew about him, good or bad. I then related to her that just from his handwriting alone it showed that he was capable of violence. He could actually kill someone. She then told me that the police were called in that afternoon; this same student stabbed a boy in the back with a compass. Both boys admitted it was over a very minor thing.

At any rate, it didn't take long for word to get around the school that I was involved in knowing a person's character through their handwriting. But I had support. They knew and liked Mrs. Pope who was deeply involved in school activity.

And she interpreted handwriting also. Besides, her son was a basketball star.

One day, a senior student asked if she could make an appointment with me. We set up the time for her to come to the Parish House. She was considering going into the convent and wanted some counseling concerning her choice of Religious Communities. After we finished the session, she place an envelope on my desk. I asked what it was. She said that was the handwriting of one of the seniors in school. "Tell me whose it is!"

I said, "Now wait a minute! I never claimed to be able to pick out a particular person out of a group, just by looking at a note written by one of them." That was quite different than simply making a study of handwriting.

She did not back off. "Study it then and tell me who wrote it." I did not promise I could do it. "I'll try," I responded rather weakly.

Each day I made it a point to talk to the seniors at lunch time to get to know them better. After a week, I broke it down to six possibilities. I called in my "challenger." She verified that it was one of them. After another week, I selected two possibilities. She agreed that one of them was correct. At that point, I admitted these two students were so much alike I couldn't distinguish which one could have written it. She insisted I try again. I did, and chose one them. I said it's only a slight difference, but that would be my choice. It was the right one, and the person who wrote it verified it. I was more amazed than they were!

The head or president of a seminary is called a Rector. I was at the seminary one day visiting the Rector, a classmate of ours. I was there with five other classmates; we had just finished playing racquetball there. Somehow, the conversation turned toward this "weird business" of handwriting and what it

110

revealed about a person. They took it as a joke, of course. I had only mentioned handwriting analysis in passing. But just for fun they wanted me to demonstrate how it worked. They were well aware that I knew their personalities and character traits, having been in the same class for years and then spending our days off together. So they came up with this great plan. It happened to be the same challenge I got from the senior class. So, just for fun, they each wrote something down on a slip of paper and put it in a hat. Instead of detecting the writer of just one note, they somehow got me to agree to match each note with the right person. Although we were close friends, I did not know their style of writing. I had no idea. But all I needed to do was fit the note to their personalities, which I did know well. To my surprise and theirs, I got them all correct without much trouble. So Fr. Ozog, the rector says, "I have a note on my desk from one of the twenty-five professors here at the seminary. "Whose writing is it?"

"Whoa", I shouted. "I don't know them all that well."

"Let me say that you do know this one fairly well," he assured me. He showed me a type-written list of the names of every priest on the teaching staff. I knew at least a dozen of them quite well. I looked at the writing. It only took about ten seconds to identify the writer, and I was correct. They were all surprised again. "How did I do it?", they asked. This time they were serious. Their skepticism had turned to belief. I said, "Judging from that particular style of handwriting, it had to be the most cultural person on the faculty. And one who whose field was probably English and Literature. I only know of one person like that on the staff here". This incident with my own classmates (and worst critics,) gave me a lot of confidence in the Bunker System of graphoanalysis. (I still did not like the name "Bunker"!)

111

22. The Dark Night Begins

I am not going to say much about my next assignment except that it was another situation in which I was demoralized by the example of the Pastor. Granted he had chronic malaria which he contracted during the war years as a chaplain, but that did not explain his continual erratic behavior. The first assistant and I did not know from one day to the next what to expect from this man. He changed his mind frequently, even within the hour and never gave us a clue as to what was coming next. My position on the staff was in this order: first the Pastor, then his mother who lived close by, then his sister who was also the cook, then the maintenance man who was his brother-in-law, then the first assistant, and finally me. That was the order of authority. I kid you not.

The same Pastor continually tried to turn us against each other. Coming back from a day off, the other assistant told me word for word what he said about me. Naturally, none of it was worth repeating. Conversely, when he came back from his day off, I filled him in with the damaging statements made about him. We stayed together on this and would not let him come between us. The rest of the memories there were not any better. The people in the parish, as in my other assignments, were wonderful. I never had a problem with the communities I worked with. My main problem was the guy at the top!

I was re-assigned again! I went from the proverbial frying pan into the fire. My next appointment was not much better. I was sent to a parish in southwest Detroit. It was historically a Hungarian parish. When I arrived, the neighborhood was changing rapidly. Every time a Hungarian family moved out, the space was immediately replaced with a Latin-American one. As in my other assignments, part of my ministry was taking care of the Latino Community. It was forever a source of conflict with pastors and my appointment there lasted five long years. After about two years of fighting over my assigned duties, I had to get one of the Bishops to write a letter to the pastor affirming my assignment to the Hispanic Community as well. There was now one notable change: Half the week I would work with the Hispanics and half with the rest of the parish. That now meant that I was working under this man only three days a week. Thank God for that!

I could not begin to put in writing just how bad it was living in those conditions. This Pastor topped them all. He was the loudest, meanest man I ever met. How could this happen to me again? I do not wish to judge another human being. Jesus mandated us to love our neighbor, which is everyone. And so I did love this man in a spiritual way. Of course! But his actions, no! Whether he was aware of how badly he came across with the people, with Fr. Istvan Bali, a very elderly priest also assigned there and with me, I do not know. And whether he was conscious of his explosions of anger and violence or of his obvious expressions of racial prejudice, again I am not sure.

I felt like I was a prisoner. I pretty much had to stay in my room most of the time. On my day off, I was out of there as soon as possible. I was always in trouble with this man no matter what I did. Fr. Bali would come up to me quite often and say in his beautiful Hungarian accent: "The Pastor is mad again...with you. This is black eye for you!" He loved that expression. I heard it so often that once in a while I would run to a mirror to see if I really had a black eye. Fr. Bali was a saint living there for so many years under this same man. Unfortunately, there was no other Hungarian parish, and Fr. Bali's command of English was very poor.

In the midst of living under such tension and stress and trying to survive in a very depressing atmosphere, I had to make a decision similar to Hamlet in his "To be or not to be" soliloquy. I made a decision to face life. I was determined that what I went through in the last twelve years (in three depressing appointments) was for a reason. I would not back down.

First, I was almost forced to stay in my room unless I had an appointment, since the Pastor reminded me more than once that all the furniture in the living room was his personal property. I was never welcomed to sit there unless he personally invited me to join him. So, being in my room a lot, I took up several hobbies. I bought an organ. I could play or practice almost any hour, day or night, without disturbing anyone. All I had to do was put on the ear phones. I played whenever I could and learned to read notes with a much greater confidence. I started to play the guitar also. Since we were now saying Mass in the homes as well, I learned about fifty songs to play. When I had a home Mass, I took care of the singing, the guitar music and the Mass itself, whether in English or Spanish.

For my studies, I firmed up my Spanish, and began to learn some Italian. The languages were close, so it was not too difficult to move from Spanish to Italian. I pursued my studies in science and astronomy, read a great deal on a variety of other subjects, worked puzzles and, in general, kept my mind very busy. I also started painting again. In my so-called "captivity" I found satisfaction in the learning process. I was learning something new every day. It became fun.

Again, I loved the people I served. It was my greatest joy. But there was something down deep in my soul that was crying out for help. Why was I given assignments that were so demoralizing? What was I supposed to learn from such situations? Did God happen to know what was going on? I was ordained a priest to serve people. I was far from perfect. But when I was a seminarian I dreamed of working hard with my brother priests in solidarity and cooperation. We could conquer the world if we stayed together. I had always looked up to older priests with great admiration. They had paved the way for us young ones. They had the true missionary spirit, forging ahead and building new parishes around the archdiocese. It would be a privilege to work along side these great men. I knew these fine priests were still out there working with an undying zeal. And some of my Pastors were outstanding in the exercise of their authority and leadership.

Nevertheless something was missing. Maybe it wasn't the negative influence of a few of my Pastors, after all. Maybe it was me...or a combination of both! Something that was lacking finally emerged one night while I was walking around in church. The church and rectory were connected and it was no problem walking through the hallway to the Lord's House to say some night prayers before retiring. The worse my living situation got, the more I was over in church asking for Divine assistance. Without blaming anyone for the darkness that seemed to surround me, I knew that I had to find a new way to communicate with God. Somehow, in the same way in which I had my struggles with certain Pastors, I was also struggling within myself for understanding and internal peace.

I realized, first of all, that my meditations were becoming commonplace. They lacked a vitality that inspired saints and other dedicated followers of Christ. Either I was too distracted to talk to God or my method of praying needed help. One way or another, my attempts at meditation were becoming less effective. And the example around me was anything but inspiring. I prayed for guidance. Sometimes I would walk for hours around and around the church pleading for some direction. The dim light of votive candles gave me just enough light to make my way through the aisles without stumbling. Night after night I would walk. At one point I yelled out loud in church. Does anybody up there care? Are you deaf? Will you please show yourself, assert yourself, tell me that you are real? I was shocked that my thoughts became verbal! I felt very alone in this world unable to share my innermost feelings about the meaninglessness of it all. I seemed to hit rock bottom, perhaps to the place where Kierkegaard called the "Angst". The Angst was a German word for the ultimate pit of anxiety in which faith is momentarily gone and there is utter darkness and despair. One could only go up from there!

Each of us has our own concept or image of God. Our personality and our self-image have a lot to do with it. As the saying goes, "We do not see the world as it is, we see the world as we are." It is, if you will, a mirror of what we see within us. And so I believe it is the same with our thoughts about God. Each of us has a unique relationship and concept of who he is and who we are.

Years ago, as a child, I thought of God as a very ancient and wise man sitting on a throne. I believe the idea was planted in my head by one of the nuns who was trying to give young children a way of looking at God. The intentions were good, but the image stereotyped God as one of us, only a lot smarter. It took a long time, a very long time before I could image the Father as anything but a very old man. The trouble with that is, of course, very limiting. In theology, that would be called *anthropomorphism* or, freely translated, making God into our image.

Through the years, I heard many definitions of God, some emphasizing what He can do, being Omnipotent or what God knows, being Omniscient, etc. Some definitions compare human nature and Divine Nature, putting God in an entirely different category. But God is not a *thing* to be studied nor is God a *what* with a Divine Nature. God simply cannot be classified. To classify God is to limit Him. Even calling God Father or referring to Him as a male, is very limiting. God must be beyond gender. Or we have reduced the Infinite Divine Spirit to someone like us with a physical body, a male one at that. Yes, Jesus took on a male body; but that was necessary if he wanted to enter into our three-dimensional world to be seen by us and convince us of the reality of a spiritual world. In my opinion, calling God *Father* established *relationship* rather than the essential nature of the Divine Creator.

God Is would be a perfect definition of God. After all it was God's own definition of Himself to Moses: *"I am Who am!"* The meaning is clear: God is a God of the Eternal Now, not of the past and not of the future. Neither the past nor the future exist in God. In God's life there is always the present moment. That is why the church and the bible refer to God as the *God of the living*. All Divine Attributes are contained in the God of the living, and much more. God is everything. There is nothing outside of God. If there is anything at all that is actually separate from God, then we have just created another god. God is all. The fact that we think we are separate from God does not in the least prove that we are. Only in our minds exists the thought of separation. God Power sustains everything that is.

The present moment is like an open window, making it possible to see and communicate with God. That precious moment that links us to the Eternal Lord of the Now is called a Holy Instant.

St. John in his First Letter, 1:5, says: "God is Light and in Him there is no darkness at all. According to the New American Bible Light refers to God's Truth and Goodness. Darkness would be those who live in error or in ignorance. Although God dwells in each one of us, we may not be aware of His Divine Presence through ignorance. Most of us live in the past. Almost everything that occupies our minds are about something in the past. What somebody said or did to us, a bad golf shot, or a real

117

good one, a sickness in the past, etc. There nothing wrong about considering the past; we simply don't want to live there. We have to let go, to move on, to learn from the past. A baseball player can never reach home unless he lets go of third base! Nor can we ever arrive *home*, where God lives unless we let go of the past. The same is true of the future. We can dream, plan, desire but only in the present; the future does not exist yet. We can't live or hide there either.

After weeks of walking around in church at night, often desperate and pleading on my knees for help, I desired more than anything to address God through the present *window, the now*, where Truth dwells. What can I do to change this deplorable situation, Lord? I let go of some unpleasant memories that were depressing my attitude, I did not want to escape to the future, so I focused on the present moment...the window of direct communication with the Divine Helper. It felt good to stay in the present.

A few days later something totally unexpected happened. I happened to be into a bookstore in Lincoln Park and as I walked past a certain section, a particular book caught my attention. It was called "Yoga in Ten Lessons", a book written by a Benedictine monk, Fr. J. M. Dechanet, who saw the advantage of a people in the West practicing yoga with Christian values. His approach is therefore called "Christian Yoga". His intentions were not, as he stated in the preface of the book to Christianize Yoga, but rather simply to adapt certain Yogi disciplines to his spiritual life. Fr. Dechanet also quotes Carl Jung who stated that, "The West will have to create its own Yoga, Yoga built on Christian foundations." The theory was that if a person meditated daily Yoga-style, the Lord would make himself present to the person who is sufficiently fine-tuned spiritually through meditation. It is believed in Yoga that, "When the student is ready the Master will be waiting!" I recalled reading about Buddha that under the pipal or Bo tree, he experienced an emancipation of spirit. It was at Buddh Gaya near Benares. From that time on he became known as Buddha "The Enlightened One". He was rewarded because he never gave up. I was determined that I too would not give up. I would meditate every day until the Lord manifested his presence in some way or I would die trying.

I studied the various positions of yoga and became rather proficient in the performance of them. I found the Lotus position was more appropriate for me in deep meditation than on my knees. I also learned that Hatha-Yoga which is usually called just by the name "Yoga" was a preparation for meditation. It conditioned the body to be more receptive, more attentive; it elevated the mind by focusing the mind's energies, and lastly, by raising the vibration level of the meditator.

I believed that the Lord was answering my prayer when he put me in possession of that book. The timing was good. The book sufficiently inspired me to be filled with hope and determination. One of the qualities I have demonstrated all my life was determination. Once I became convinced, I wasn't going to quit easily. I became more and more proficient in performing the postures or "Asanas" and breathing exercises or "Pranayamas". Among the many postures possible, I was especially faithful in performing the headstand in the middle of the floor. In fact, at one point, I used to say: "I am on my head in the morning before most people are on their feet." There are five pathways in Yoga that lead to union with the Creator. Hatha-Yoga: health; Bhakti-Yoga: seeking truth; Juana-Yoga: knowledge of the real and the unreal; Karma-Yoga: selfless work, and Raja-Yoga: meditation, leading to liberation or freedom. It is not difficult to see the great value in the five varieties of Yoga. For the Christian, the paths are similar; the difference is in the names. The beatitudes of Jesus, the teachings of the church, the spiritual and corporal works of mercy and the weekly homilies from the pulpit all offer a path to God but in Christian terms.

I kept the same goals that I always had. But I wanted to pursue a path that had worked for others who were very serious and had the passion to storm heaven demanding some kind of response, to seek enlightenment above all other values, to distinguish what is real and what is unreal in the eyes of God, and ultimately, to embrace the Truth. I desired to have the readiness and pre-disposition of a student entering the school of spiritual growth.

I made sure that understanding accompanied my daily exercise in Yoga postures. My daily meditations always began by giving thanks, praising God, clearing the mind and learning to focus. The deep breathings were equally important. I meditated faithfully. I asked the Holy Spirit to guide me throughout this spiritual journey. Meditation was prime time, along with Divine Guidance.

Nothing happened for the first few weeks. I thought of that as normal. After all, this was no ordinary adventure. I was not the one in control. I was making every possible effort to maintain balance physically, mentally and spiritually. Physically, by being very careful what I ate, avoiding fried and fatty foods when possible. I exercised regularly on my days off. I was a bowler, skier, golfer and played racquetball. Mentally, I tried to remain as positive as possible, always expecting the best results. And I read many spiritual books during that time. When I was getting my Master's Degree at the University of Detroit, I still recall vividly what Fr. Alfred McBride told us in a discussion about mystical experience. His ideas were almost identical to those of Thomas Merton who wrote a very inspiring book "The New Seeds of Contemplation". This latter book had impressed me more than any other concerning growth in the spiritual life. I must have read it about three times and I shall continue to read it. Merton wrote a book entitled, "Seeds Of Contemplation" early in his monastic life as a Trappist. However, near the end of his life when he had explored quite profoundly and lived for many years the contemplative life, he made some very interesting comments on meditation and shared these insights in the "New Seeds of Contemplation."

Both of these great teachers: Thomas Merton and Al McBride, came to the same conclusion when they spoke about an authentic mystical experience or true communication with God. This was a very important point.

McBride stated very clearly that the most we could do to prepare for a mystical, spiritual or cosmic experience was to set up the conditions for the *possibility* of having such an experience. We could not *make* it happen! He repeated this over and over; he then emphasized that if we caused the experience to take place it would be an action of the ego and not of a Divine Power. He went on to say that we could be completely deceived by the beauty and excitement of something cosmic, for example; but unfortunately, it would be the result of a wild imagination at work without making the slightest contribution to one's spiritual growth. And, in my opinion, Merton would be in complete agreement.

I did not want to waste my time with the possibility of deception. I continued to meditate and resolved to wait until something authentic occurred to me. If nothing happened, so be it! But I don't give up very easily. I would still wait. Wait I did! After a year...still no results. I began to wonder if I was practicing *Meditation Yoga* correctly...and was my motivation and determination supported by the right attitude and the right theology. I did harbor a few doubts about what I was doing. And did I still believe that Divine Providence would step in at any time and exert a spiritual transformation, thus justifying the

121

countless hours I was investing in my quest? I got a little shaky for a moment but I did believe. Again, I waited. Still there was no response. If something extraordinary was about to present itself, I wanted to be on the receiving end. Two years went by.

Nothing happened.

Three long years, then four, passed by and I was still meditating every day and going through the Yoga postures, sitting in the Lotus position every day...and waiting.

Still no results!

Should I throw in the towel, so to speak? Was it time to call it off, admit it didn't work? This practice of meditating and waiting for the Master to take some action was a grand idea, but maybe that's all it was...just an idea. The dilemma increased as time went on. By this time I had invested a notable portion of my life in this enterprise based on an ancient premise that supposedly worked in the past. *Will it work in the present age? Was it merely an empty dream? Should I quit now and admit defeat?* I didn't like that word "defeat" any more than I liked the word "failure".

No! I was not going to stop! Nothing was going to make me stop. It was all or nothing! Where there is passion and commitment, time is irrelevant. I was going for it. I reiterated my intent: I would continue meditating until a Divine Intervention took place, until I received some kind of enlightment, or a visible sign or a truly mystical experience. Only death could stop me.

What may not be apparent during this period of my life is the complete lack of understanding on the part of any of my colleagues. Even with a Spiritual Director whom I admired a great deal. I was never able to successfully initiate and participate in a discussion about mystical or metaphysical experiences. These subjects were simply not well received. We were trained in a fixed Theology.

To talk of a different way of praying such as using Yoga would be to deviate from the accepted path. It would immediately be suspect! The official prayer book of the church and therefore of the clergy was the Breviary. It was a great book but it was only a book. It did not increase the possibility of praying more creatively or with a fresh imaginative approach. To speak of having a spiritual experience the night before, could sometimes bring laughter from fellow priests. It was really understandable. We as priests have all witnessed at different times some parishioners who were not in full command of their senses speaking of such visits from above, or hearing a message from God, or claiming to be a modern day prophet, or someone with a firm belief that God had chosen him or her as a locutionary or spokesperson to deliver messages to the world or a particular sect. Most of this kind of communication is really strange, ridiculous - even comical. However, when an authentic experience is revealed, it sometimes gets the same treatment. That's what happened to me. With or without support, I was willing to walk alone.

23. A Glimpse Of Light

In 1968, five years later, I was transferred to St. Bernadette Church located in Southeast Dearborn. I had written a letter late in 1967 to Cardinal Dearden, stating several reasons why it would be a practical move to place me in residence at St. Bernadette Church. There, I could work full time with the Latino Community and further develop a team of co-workers to handle the fast-growing Hispanic population all over the southwest area of Detroit. The first draft in establishing what we then called a "Latin Ecclesial Team" was completed on November 22, 1967.

Three other priests and myself were making every effort to coordinate the ministries of priests assigned to Spanish-speaking parishes. Another serious problem facing us was the loss in number of priests that spoke Spanish. There were no replacements. Teamwork was important and a Director was necessary to get the team started. I was officially appointed Director by Cardinal Dearden. Upon completion of my six month special assignment, I was expected to show some concrete results; namely, that the formation of a team of priests could adequately provide for the spiritual welfare of the many thousands of Spanish-speaking brothers and sisters.

Before my six months were up, I had put together a team of seventeen people: Five priests, five Mexican Sisters from Tlalpan and seven lay persons. We met three times a week, prayed together, and studied together. We established Bible Circles in Spanish called "Comunidades de Base". We were happy with the results, but we knew something significant was missing. It came to us during prayer one evening. In the Acts of the Apostles in the New Testament, the Apostles realizing their limitations, created the order of deacons to handle the economic and social problems people had to cope with on a daily basis. We wanted to do the same thing; namely, to confine ourselves solely to the spiritual well-being of our people. We would have to let go of the other aspects of ministry by placing lay people in charge. Laity would be serving laity and with a much wider range of resources and skills.

We had a lot to learn! We wrote to twenty-nine Spanish-speaking organizations in Detroit; we requested two delegates from each organization to attend a meeting. The letter stated our purpose. We prepared a hall with seating for fifty-eight delegates and waited. The meeting was a complete failure. No one showed up! We prayed over it and came up with a new plan. Each of us on the Ecclesial Team took the names of a few organizations. We gave up on the letters. We now insisted on personal contact in every case. This time nearly every delegate showed up.

I conducted the meeting, explaining our intentions and their role as participants. I discussed the role of each officer and then took nominations. Gus Gaynett was selected as Director, and Joe Lopez as Assistant Director. Other officers were also chosen. Then we wanted to come up with a name for our organization. I broke them up into five groups. We preferred a name that was also an acronym. After considering many possible names "LaSed" was accepted by everyone. LaSed means thirst implying also the hunger of the Hispanic people. The letters L-A-S-E-D also carry the meaning Latin-Americans for Social and Economic Development. LaSed was born. I inducted the officers. We congratulated them and then the Ecclesial Team, including myself, left our positions at the head table and turned LaSed over to the officers.

Gus Gaynett, Joe Lopez and I appeared before a Committee representing the Archdiocesan Development Fund. We applied for starter-money to purchase a building and open an office for LaSed. They gave us $40,000. LaSed began slowly, then turned into a very large and successful organization. We planted the roots of a truly blessed organization that to this day continues to assist Hispanics in every way. They help get them jobs, lodging, a driver's license, education, classes in English, programs for the elderly, for youth, plan activities and a host of other helpful services.

Early in 1969, immediately following my six-month assignment, I was appointed Pastor of St. Bernadette Parish. Being only twelve years ordained, I was, therefore, the youngest Pastor in the Archdiocese at the time. The Cardinal also placed me in charge of another parish nearby, called Our Lady of Mt. Carmel. It was a little Italian Church with an elderly priest whose health was extremely poor. So, I was responsible for the operation of both churches. There were two separate parish councils with the appropriate commissions and committees, and financial reports. The entire administrative operation was doubled.

That wasn't so bad but when I had a Mass every Sunday in St. Bernadette Church at 9:30 am, followed by a Mass in Italian at Mt. Carmel at 11:00 am and then return to St. Bernadette for a 12:30 pm Mass in Spanish, it was somewhat cumbersome and sometimes confusing. I occasionally would be talking Italian to the congregation at the Spanish Mass; the Mexican people just stared at me with no emotion, not hinting in the slightest that I was in the wrong ball park. Then I would catch myself and switch back to Spanish. If, by chance, I would somehow slip into Spanish or even say one word in Spanish at the Italian Mass, hands would be flying all over the place. They would all be yelling very loudly, "Parla Italiano!" "Italiano!" That caught my attention very quickly! I saw clearly demonstrated before me the old saying about Italian people talking with their hands. And they were not shy! Since my Italian was not nearly as good as my Spanish, I began to write my homilies out in Italian so that I would never slip into Spanish again.

I was pretty busy at this time. I continued as Director of the "Equipo Pastoral" or Pastoral Team, as we then called ourselves. St. Bernadette Church remained as headquarters since I was now its Pastor, but the focus of activity to the general Hispanic community became the former bank we purchased as the Center for LaSed.

Following a Detroit synod, the Archdiocese of Detroit was divided into twenty five segments which were called Vicariates. Each Vicariate consisted of between 10 and 15 parishes. Each Vicariate had the responsibility to choose their own Vicar who would conduct their meetings and be a liaison to the Cardinal's office. St. Bernadette was situated in the Southwest Vicariate which consisted of about 12 parishes. There was a lot of lobbying going on to put the best man in the position of Vicar. It was politics and very similar to the action behind the scenes while campaigning for candidates vying for public office.

The Vatican Council ended in the middle sixties. From then on, the Church moved forward almost in giant steps compared to the pre-Vatican adherence to ancient traditions. The Council sent out the message very clearly that it strongly recommended, and in some cases, mandated that lay people become more involved in the inner life of the church. Also, that Bishops should work more closely with their priests. One way of accomplishing that goal was to establish a system in which the Bishop would be current in his contact with priests and the faithful in general. Thus, the Vicariate system came into being.

Each parish in the Vicariate was invited to send delegates to the general Vicarate meeting. The church was coming alive with new ideas as a result of Pope John XXIII's openness to change and the progressive recommendations of the Vatican

Council, approving this kind of participation. Surprisingly, every parish in our area sent delegates. They were there to vote. Each parish had a maximum of four votes. By the end of the meeting, there were two priests that survived the many names submitted: Fr. Stan Borucki and myself. He was a fine priest, a little older than I was at the time, and very popular - not just among the Polish Community. The delegates decided to have the final vote the next time they got together, and at the same time, begin their first official Vicariate meeting.

A month later, during the night before the election of the new Vicar, I was awakened during the night by a loud thumping sound coming from some empty gift boxes I had left in the corner of the room. It wouldn't stop, so I got up and went over to that corner and opened each box. There was nothing that could cause the noise. I put the boxes back as they were and went back to bed. I said with deep faith, "If there is anything evil in this room, in the name of Christ, begone!!" The noise continued. I presumed it was all right to go back to sleep. It wasn't easy with the continual thumping on one of the boxes. But I was tired and I did get back to sleep. No sooner was I unconscious when in a very lucid and vivid dream I saw my mother coming toward me in a quick step. I ran toward her and when we met I hugged her and lifted her off the ground. I was so delighted to see her. I was aware that she had died fifteen years before this and I said to her. "Did I die?" She said, "No, my son. I just wanted to be the first one to congratulate you."

I said, "For what?"

"For being elected Vicar of the Southwest Vicariate," she replied.

"The voting is not until tomorrow night, and everyone believes it will be close." I told her.

"That is true," she said. "But I want to congratulate my son who will be elected Vicar."

I decided to ask her about the noise. "Did you make that thumping noise in the corner by the boxes?"

She smiled. "Of course!"

"Why? I came right back.

"Just to get your attention," was her answer. "I must leave you now, my dear, but I am never far away," She hugged me one last time and was gone.

My eyes popped open and I did not have the feeling that I was dreaming. It seemed more real than when I was awake.

Of course, I did win by a very narrow margin. Over one hundred delegates were there. As the votes were being tallied, Fr. Stan and I switched back and forth as the leading candidate. It was ever so close. When it was all over and I had barely won, I expressed gratitude to those present, and I could not help thinking of my mother's visitation the night before, and her confidence in knowing the outcome.

At that first meeting, we voted in the other officers. Then we came to an impasse. No one would run for the position of Religious Education for the whole Vicariate. Everyone claimed they were too busy. To resolve the issue, three of us volunteered for the job; namely the two nuns, Sr. Kathy Peatee and Sr. Anne Dunn along with myself. These two Sisters of the Immaculate Heart of Mary Community were already on my staff. So the three of us simply expanded our programs to keep the entire Vicariate informed. We also established a Center in the school building of St. Bernadette. Parishes in the Vicariate had easy access to the Center which was filled with the most current books, articles and slide presentations, ready to be borrowed and used as teaching aids in Religious Education. We worked hard at it and earned the respect of the parishes we served.

Lastly, I was still getting my Master's Degree at the University of Detroit. I entered the program in 1968 and received my Degree in 1971. The Degree was called Religious Studies which in reality was Biblical Theology. It qualified me, if I so wished, for becoming a teacher or a Director of Religious Education as a full time job. I really did not need another job. Being Pastor of two separate parishes, carrying the responsibilities of a Vicar, continuing as Director of the Pastoral Team for the Spanish-speaking and writing term papers for every class at the University, not to mention the thesis I had to write, were enough to be called full time. So what did I do? As usual, I added more work by taking on the job of Co-Director of Religious Education for the whole Vicariate. I was living on a race track, rushing from one place to another, from one meeting to another. And there was no let-up.

24. At Last...The Awakening

During this whole time of super-activity, I did not cut down on the commitment I had made in 1964. My daily meditations and prayer life continued as usual although it was becoming increasingly more difficult to maintain. But I gave my word and I refused to back down. It wasn't until November 17, 1970, six years later, that I received my first response, which was more than I even hoped for. Beyond anything I could have dreamed up or invented! Nothing I had ever experienced before prepared me for the impact it made on me. Nothing could ever erase the memory of it! What happened to me was so extraordinary that every sacrifice I had ever made up till that moment, every inconvenience I ever endured and every dark night in which my soul was troubled - all of that - was completely insignificant and unimportant compared to what I experienced that day.

I was walking through the aisles inside the church of St. Bernadette, as I was accustomed to do. It was in the early evening, just before supper, but already dark outside. As I was walking toward the altar, a ball of light about seven or eight feet in diameter appeared between me and the altar. I could not see the altar behind it. The light became so brilliant that I was afraid of being blinded, but knowing that it was no ordinary light, I kept staring at it. Then all of a sudden I saw a most heavenly, dazzling, magnificent figure inside the ball of light. He was even brighter than the light surrounding him...which I couldn't imagine possible. He looked at me with a soft, gentle smile. I was not afraid. But in his presence, I realized how imperfect I was. How sinful, compared to this Perfect Being. It was practically impossible then, as well as now, to put into words what I was experiencing. I rarely ever got teary-eyed or emotional, but it seemed that these mystical experiences had opened up a totally new channel of sensitivity within me. I was trained to remain in control. Yet in the presence of such greatness I could not help myself! I wept with tears of joy that I met in my lifetime the One to whom I had given my life. I dedicated my whole life to Him. I gave up having a wife, children, and grandchildren. I limited my talents to the service of others in his name. He was my Master. The One to whom I prayed for the grace to be faithful until my dying breath. There was no question in my mind who it was that visited me. Not a single doubt entered my mind. I automatically fell to my knees. I was not worthy to stand in his presence. I did not know how to act. I simply said, "I love you...but I feel very unworthy." The tears began to stop and my soul was filled with a peace that went beyond anything I had ever experienced. Even after my Lord had vanished, I was still on my knees for a long time, trying to comprehend the indescribable enormity and grandeur of what I had just experienced. It belonged to another dimension. The gravity of that moment was not suited to the world in which I grew up.

I had read about what mystics referred to as the Christ-Consciousness. They all speak of it as an unforgettable experience. I am certainly in agreement. I have never forgotten what I saw and what I felt. I knew that kind of experience didn't happen often. How fortunate that it even happened once in my lifetime. It not only made life worth living. It was a privilege to be alive on the earth and receive this Visitor from the Heavenly Realms. Needless to say, I could hardly keep my feet on the ground. I had the feeling that I was flying the rest of that day.

In the graduate courses of Biblical Theology at U. of D., they used the word *discontinuity* to refer to a Divine Intervention. This occurred when there was an interruption or discontinuity in the normal course of events. God's Power being at work alters the outcome of the event. Throughout the Bible there are many instances in which Divine Intervention changed the course of Salvation History. For example, when Moses and the Hebrews crossed the sea to flee from the Egyptian soldiers and achieved freedom, that was a discontinuity. And when Jesus entered this world through a virgin birth and later rose miraculously from the dead on that first Easter, God's Power was at work.

The Lord certainly altered the course of my life. I now had first hand experience that the Presence of God is a reality. That Jesus is truly the Prince of Peace, one of his many titles. Was I deceived? Not at all! There was much more to come. That was only the beginning. I waited six years and now the Lord was about to take the initiative. In my wildest dreams I could not have produced what took place in church that day.

That same night I went to bed filled with excitement. I managed to get to sleep, but in the middle of the night - at 4:00 am to be exact - I was suddenly awakened as if someone shook me. It was quite unusual for me to wake up during the night unless the phone rang. I generally slept through the entire night from sheer exhaustion. On that particular occasion, I found myself very alert and fully awake, lying there at 4:00 am in complete darkness. After a few moments, I saw a light coming toward me. First it was point of light then it became larger every second. There was no doubt that the light was moving closer and closer.

When it came within about ten feet it took the shape of an eye, with the eyelid made of what looked like embroidered gold. It was an extremely clear image in the total darkness of the room. Light emanated from the image itself. As it continued to get closer and closer, the jet black pupil kept getting larger. When it reached me, I was in a sense, pulled into the eye. Then

I continued to gain speed and went through a tunnel. I saw the night sky at the end of the tunnel. When I came out of the tunnel, I looked around and I found myself out in space beyond the earth and the moon. Believe me, this was not the result of reading too much science fiction. I never read such books!

Here I was floating in outer space without a space suit on and not sure how I got there or why I was there. While I was pondering the situation, a hand reached out to me, and a *familiar voice* said "Do not be afraid! I will guide you." I did not look at the one who spoke. And it did not seem to be the time to ask. I was thrilled to be accompanied out in space by someone who spoke with such confidence and self assurance. This much I knew: I felt completely secure with the guide who offered to show me the way. He held my hand firmly and we started traveling rapidly. We were moving at astronomical speeds beyond comprehension. We went beyond our galaxy into the far reaches of space. The guide pointed out different nebulas, galaxies, planets and other interesting cosmic phenomena. It was by far the longest trip I had ever made and without doubt the fastest. After the cosmic experience, we returned pausing just above the rectory. While I was brought back very slowly into my bedroom, I could see my body lying there asleep. The guide very gently put me back in my physical body. As soon as he did, my physical eyes opened and I was looking at the ceiling. I turned to the side and looked at the clock. It was exactly 5:00 am. One full hour had gone by. We covered a lot of territory. I then looked around the room; no one was visible to me.

That added greatly to my already exuberant day. I was very excited later that morning when I awoke and got up, body and all. If someone told me he or she went through a tunnel last night and traveled through the cosmos at phenomenal speeds for a full hour, I would question that person's sanity or veracity.

How could anyone believe such a story? *How could I even believe it?* And yet I actually experienced it! On the other hand, I would be foolish if I denied having a real experience in which I was fully awake. And this was a very moving experience filled with emotion which I viewed undeniably with my own eyes. Nor would any average, sane person who was, without question, awake, deny the experience of the senses. I was so excited that I was whistling and humming tunes for the rest of the day. I could hardly contain myself.

The very next night I went to sleep without any trouble. Again, at 4:00 am I was awakened. This time I saw many points of light that reminded me of many stars moving in a circle. The "stars" banding together then took the shape of a magnificent, royal crown, which was composed, to all appearances, of the most sparkling and radiant gold I had ever seen. There were precious jewels at different points and in key areas on the crown itself which was several times larger than a full moon in the sky.

I was very curious. I asked "What is the meaning of the crown? The guide said "It represents all of Reality. It is God's Kingdom. All that exists is represented here."

"Am I somewhere on that crown, too?" I had to ask.

"Of course," he replied. Then the crown which at first was distant, began to move closer. It increased rapidly in size and zeroed in on one single area of the crown to the extent that we were literally surrounded by jewels and precious metals. Finally, after enormous magnification, there was a portion of a precious gem directly in front of us. "You are right here!" He emphasized. Then the crown began moving back slowly to its original position. I could then see where I was on the crown. It was an exciting moment! This time I had not left the room. Everything took place while I was lying there wide awake. I looked at the clock. It was 4:45 am. Naturally, when I got up for Mass later that morning I was again in ecstasy. And for that

135

matter, all day long!

There was no way I could have manufactured such experiences. I neither had the knowledge, nor the desire, nor the ability to conjure up such magnificent images. In spite of all that was happening, my day to day living did not change. I continued my meditations as usual. They were far more advanced now compared to my early meditations six years before. At times I had to set the alarm clock so that I would not be meditating well into my next appointment or meeting or whatever was on my schedule. I preferred to meditate at night when I had no other items on the agenda. But often I was too tired to wait until bedtime. The morning was best. If that was not possible, then I waited till evening.

The next night I was again awakened at 4:00 am. This time I was shown a beautiful lotus flower. It was stunning to look at. It was surrounded by what I could only describe as a Divine glow. It was also preceded by points of light that eventually resulted in the image of the lotus.

I said with confidence this time: I know what that is, "All is one and all reality is contained in this symbol."

"Yes! That is right."

The lotus expanded as did the crown the night before. It magnified to the cellular dimension. A particular cell stood out among all the others around it.

"I presume that is myself." Correct again, I was told.

Then I was given a further explanation and meaning of the lotus in my life. The guide said that just as the lotus had its roots in the mud, so to speak, and the flower rose above the water facing the brightness and life-giving energy of the sun, so was the work I came to do in this life. It was the purpose for which I was born.

I said I didn't quite understand.

The guide added further information. He said I came to serve the poor and the lower classes of society and to give them hope. They needed encouragement and support and to know that the power and grace of God has never left them. That God's love shines on them even when they feel they are in darkness. Like the lotus flower. They were represented by the soil under the water - hidden from the sun. They needed to know that the sun or God's grace was nourishing them as well. Helping to bring light to those in darkness was part of my mission. When the image before me vanished, I noticed it was almost 5:00 am.

I couldn't sleep right away. I kept thinking about what was said to me. Actually, my guide shared a lot more than is written here. Interestingly enough, the instructions given to me prepared me for my future priestly ministry. In fact, about eighty percent of my total ministry was working in the inner city of Detroit where hope was sorely needed. Where families with low income are generally found. That thought gave meaning to an otherwise odd list of nine parishes to which I was assigned. The highlight of that explanation was fulfilled more than ever when I was appointed Pastor of Most Holy Trinity Church, serving over 30,000 of God's poor that came to us for help each year.

The next night I was fully awake at exactly 4:00 am. This came as no surprise. This time when the star-lights formed a circle at they did before, I was drawn into that circle and went traveling through the tunnel again into outer space. The faithful guide was there. Taking me by the hand, we were moving beyond light-year speed. We slowed down and I thought we were back home again. Not quite. It was a planet but not planet earth. I looked around as we were making a quick entry. There was some green areas, but the outstanding color that I recall was light brown - a rich tan color. When we came closer, all I could see was desert and some foothills in the distance. I did not see any mountains. We stood on the sand of this planet. Only then did I notice some human activity. There were people much like ourselves there, but their life style was much more primitive and simple.

I asked the guide if they could see us. He assured me that they could not.

"Why are we here?" I asked. He expected my question.

He tried to keep the answer as simple as possible for my sake. He said there are many such planets throughout the universe. This was only a sample. It would be arrogant to think that this whole universe with billions and billions of galaxies and each galaxy having about 100 billion stars would all be created for one, tiny, insignificant, fragile, almost unnoticeable planet called earth. To think that only one average star, our sun, among the trillions of stars, is the only place to find life - is nothing short of ridiculous! The human race has a lot to learn.

There was much more said. The clock was a little past 5:00 am when we returned to Dearborn, Michigan, U.S.A., Planet Earth.

What happened to me on those few nights was far beyond the expectations I had in mind when I first began my quest. I was grateful that it only took about six years to start getting results. I was ready to go all the way - that is - until my last breath! The one factor that I would not allow to change or weaken within me was being serious. A commitment that was not serious could never stand the test of time or the lack of support or understanding from my closest colleagues and friends.

These nightly visits were not over yet. The very next night after traveling through the universe again, I was awakened at 4:00 am. The time never deviated. I was greeted by a new experience. The guide was present and I was being instructed once more in matters I knew nothing about.

The following night I received another visit, and another the next night, and another. The 4:00 am visits and instruction did end...after forty consecutive nights. That is correct! I had a mystical, spiritual, or cosmic experience every night for 40 nights in a row. Some nights after being awakened, I would just lie there while being instructed with a much more profound yet simple theology than I had ever known. Part of that instruction was a clearer understanding of God's action in the world. I do not feel it is necessary to repeat what happened each and every single night, but I will go over the last one which was nothing short of amazing.

On the fortieth night I was awakened at the usual time. All at once before me was a large round stone. It was about a foot thick and reminded me of the Aztec Calendar I had seen in the Archeological Museum in Mexico City, except that there were two huge pegs of wood, one connected to the top and the other to the bottom. Although my room was in complete darkness, naturally at 4 am, everything, as usual, was very bright and clear. A picture came alive in the circle of the large stone, much like watching a movie on television. As I watched - this time in silence - I was shown the important events in the life of a particular person. It quickly covered his life from early childhood to manhood ending in his death. The events were logically connected and sort of summed up the values and direction of that person's life. Needless to say I identified with that man. It was a very early civilization. I was unable to focus on that period of time. And I did not want to interrupt the flow of the images by asking anything. If I were to guess, I would probably say that it was Lemuria.

I thought it was all over when the screen/stone went blank. Not quite! The wooden pegs remained in place while the stone turned completely around so that the other side of the slab was now visible. Then followed another lifetime, this time I believed it was in Atlantis. The scene came alive. Again, the salient

139

moments in that person's life were played out, from teenage years to old age. I identified with the man in question as I did before. Each of these special events were making a point, bringing out certain important factors in that person's life - what was earned, and what was lost. The bottom line was either spiritual growth or the lack of it.

That was followed by another lifetime. Same format - showing the events that had the greatest impact on a certain man's life. I identified with that life each time. The lives seemed to follow history. After the scenes from Atlantis, there followed a life in Egypt, then China, then Greece, Rome, France, England and so on. I believe there were fourteen different lifetimes presented to me. Each time the stone slab slowly turned around, it introduced another incarnation.

I will share an outstanding scene of the fourteenth and last of the lifetimes given that night, since it seemed to relate to my present life. The young man was not very religious and his adult life was not much better. He was a professional artist and apparently achieved renown in his lifetime. When he was on his deathbed, he wanted to see the painting he did of the crucified Christ. The image of Christ was brought to him. Staring at the painting he spoke the following words as he drew his last breath, "The next time, I will give you everything." Uttering those words, he expired. At that moment, my guide made his one and only comment: "That is why you chose the disciplined life of a priest, giving up everything to serve Christ completely." I was shocked that he made such a statement. However, about a year after that incident, while visiting the famous Prado Museum in Madrid, Spain, I saw that very painting and my soul was electrified at the sight of it. Goose bumps covered my skin!

After the last lifetime, the large stone, serving as a screen, immediately was gone and left me in darkness. I did a second-take as I looked at the clock. It was 9:00 am!!! Five full hours

140

had gone by and I hadn't moved a muscle. I was so entranced by what I was witnessing, time seemed to stand still. I was grateful that I did not have a morning Mass that day. Was that a coincidence or was that planned? Either way it happened at the right time and day.

On the forty first night, I was not awakened at 4:00 am. One could not help thinking about the biblical number 40, the number of days that Jesus and well- known prophets spent in the desert being tested and/or purified before they began their public life. The Israelites on the run under Moses took 40 years to become purified as a whole nation. Is that what was happening to me? Was I being purified and instructed for something special that was yet to come? I had no idea.

Surprisingly, about a week later I had another visit during the night. Then another a couple of weeks later. After that I had one once a month for about five months. As unexpectedly at they began, the 4:00 am visits at this point ended.

25. A Brief Reflection On The Kingdom

The images of the kingdom were so clear and so beautiful, I could not stop thinking about them. I had to make some adjustments in my basic theology of what the kingdom actually was. As a youngster I learned that after we die we go to heaven or to God's kingdom and live happily ever after. I believe that as a child I thought of heaven as a fixed place of eternal happiness. I only knew we would love God and be very happy.

Through the years I began to think of heaven as the fulfillment of all our dreams and a lot more action. Several distinct images of God's kingdom helped me to realized that there was no single way of demonstrating what heaven is like. Jesus compared it to a mustard seed: "The kingdom of God is like a mustard seed which someone took and sowed in his field. It is the smallest seed of all, yet when full-grown it is the largest of plants. It becomes so big a shrub that the birds of the sky come and build their nests in its branches." It is not static; it is ever growing, changing, expressing. Anything that does not move or grow is dead. Jesus continues: "The kingdom of God is like yeast which a woman took and kneaded into three measures of flour. Eventually the whole mass of dough began to rise." The kingdom is ever expanding, extending love to encompass more and more. St. Thomas once defined love as "Diffusum est." That is, love is diffusive of itself. Always reaching out. A reality in motion. To believe that heaven is a place in the clouds where people play violins or just sit there and listen to music all day is really boring.

Marie was my oldest sister; I loved her very much. Not long before she died she wanted to know what to expect when God called her to the next life. I said, "Well, first of all, what do you think heaven is?"

"Heaven is a big cathedral and all the people are in it."

"What are they doing?" I asked.

"They are attending Mass. The angels are singing and God is at the altar."

Going along with her scenario, I asked again, "Are Jesus and the Holy Spirit present?"

"Oh, yes. Jesus is the one saying Mass; the Father, who looks very old, is sitting on a throne behind him; the Holy Spirit is a dove flying above the altar."

I said, "Fine, how long is the Mass?"

"Maybe a couple of hours," she answered.

"What happens after the Mass is over?" I wondered...waiting anxiously to find out how her scenario was going to continue.

"I don't know. I never thought about *that!*", she replied in frustration.

I said, "Marie, we are talking here about eternity. Forever. Non-stop. I mean millions of years. I am saying that Eternity lasts a lot longer than two hours, if you know what I mean."

I was saying to myself that if she enters eternity with those ideas she will be shocked and incredibly surprised! Not that I have all the answers.

Finally, I said, "Marie, we need to talk." We then had a wonderful discussion about afterlife. We talked about being active in the kingdom, helping each other out, assisting others who die suddenly in accidents, through sickness, heart attacks and the countless other ways people move from this dimension into paradise. In heaven, you could have your hundreds of questions answered. (I know I have a lot of questions to ask!) You can learn through libraries or schools; you can explore the universe; you can be with your family; you can discover and experience true love and true happiness. You can do most anything.

"I would like to work with children who die and are confused and need someone to comfort them. It would make me happy to teach them and help them to adjust to life in the spirit." I was amazed at her insight, and so quickly.

"I am sure there will be many opportunities for you to do that and much more." I assured her.

Marie died in 1980 not long after our talk. I pray she is doing just what she desired. I am sure her first two hours went by quickly...

Heaven is filled with action. Anyone who thinks it's going to be dull and uninteresting is in for a big surprise. It will surpass your dreams and your wild imagination by leaps and bounds.

But heaven is not something only to be achieved in the future after we die. We can speak of heaven in the present tense. The Master did.

"The kingdom of God is *within* you."

"Blessed are the poor in spirit, for theirs *is* the kingdom of God."

"Blessed are those persecuted for holiness sake, the kingdom of God *is* theirs." Everything appeared to be in the present tense. I understand it to mean that we can have a taste of heaven, a moment of heavenly bliss right now. You might even say that we can choose heaven or hell right this moment. Many people consider this life *hell*. And for them, it probably is. Believing God is distant or doesn't care is hell. Someone suffering in a Concentration Camp could easily equate that with hell. On the other hand, a person like Victor Frankl found peace and happiness in a Concentration Camp by seeing it differently, by a change of mind.

Sometimes Jesus' words are in the present tense and sometimes they are future. In the Lord's Prayer, we say "...thy kingdom *come*, thy *will be done* on earth as it is in heaven..."

which indicates future. It makes sense when put in the right perspective. In God's Kingdom, His Will is obeyed perfectly, and we want that to happen while we are here on earth - which obviously has not taken place yet. In this world God is sometimes mentioned only as a swear word! Or a word found only in the dictionary. Many millions of people living today have no thought about God's kingdom or God's will from the moment they rise in the morning till they are fast asleep. Nor are they concerned with it. From where we stand God's kingdom can only be viewed as future. Looking at reality from God's viewpoint, a spiritual viewpoint, there is only the eternal *now*. And it is present to a person who has insight and awareness. St. Peter reminds us that we are "partakers in the Divine Nature. Not tomorrow, not after we leave this earth. Right now, through prayer, desire and right action heaven is yours for the asking. Why wait? God is not far away, nor is His kingdom. Since we live in two worlds, this one and the world of spirit, we can choose at any time to be there in spirit. When people are worshiping on Sundays, there is a great peace that pervades the church, whether they are singing softly, listening, or singing loudly with body rhythm and hand-clapping. People respect each other and offer signs of peace with each other. Their spirits are uplifted (especially if they hear an inspiring sermon), and they experience a little bit of heaven. That's why some people attend religious services every day. The veil between heaven and earth gets thinner every day.

26. Exploring And Expanding
My Perception Of Truth

I had to make a retreat. There was no way I could possibly figure out what was happening to me while working the five jobs I had previously mentioned. I needed to take time out. I spent a week at Colombiere which was a former Jesuit Seminary that closed because of the lack of vocations. However, it was a popular place for retreats. They had great meals, a private room, a swimming pool and about 400 acres to walk around in. I enjoyed walking outdoors and letting my mind go free.

While I was there I reflected on an incident that had happened to me at Holy Cross School where I used to visit the High School Religious Education Classes. The year was 1967. At that time I considered myself to be a very open-minded priest. I told the students that they could ask any question they wanted. They should never fear that they would be rejected for asking a foolish question. Asking questions was an important part of learning. A few of the students asked some general questions about the church and the Bible. I answered their questions without any difficulty. Then one of the boys got up and asked what I thought of reincarnation. I answered abruptly, "That, of course, is a lot of nonsense! Next question."

"Wait a minute," he fired back. "You said you were open-minded. You didn't even explain what it was and why you called it nonsense. I was serious when I asked the question." It was one of the few times in my life when my dark Lebanese skin blushed. I got noticeably red. And deserved it. This young high school lad caught me promising one thing and saying another. Recovering slightly from my embarrassment, I said, "I'm sorry I responded like that! I'll try to find out more about reincarnation and give you an answer next week."

After a couple of days, I had forgotten all about the incident in class. I believe it was on Wednesday that I was walking through a book store and as I passed a certain section, one of the books caught my attention. I thought: "Oh, oh, another book is practically jumping off the shelf!" The word "Reincarnation" was written on it and it was the biography of Edgar Cayce. The name of the book was "There is a River" by Thomas Sugrue, a Catholic layman writing about the very subject I needed to research. Naturally, I bought it! And devoured it! Once I got into that book I couldn't stop. I couldn't believe that a person so gifted as was Edgar Cayce actually was living in our time and on American soil. "Was this guy for real?" I wondered. I easily finished the book before the next class.

When I asked the student who had questioned me about reincarnation to stand up, I wasn't sure what I was going to say. I did not want to give him the impression that from a single book I had read, it was all right to believe in reincarnation. On the other hand, I could not say that the church fully approved of it. I had never seen any official church statement on that subject. I was not even sure of the reason why he asked the question in the first place. I simply explained the meaning of reincarnation and added that it was a subject worthy of study. I let it go at that. I neither praised it nor condemned it since I was not quite sure what I myself believed.

When I was alone in my room and with my own thoughts, I did find the book of Edgar Cayce's life fascinating. He spoke profusely about reincarnation and karma...and it did make some sense. I wanted to know more, but I got caught up in other things and put the whole topic aside for a while. Maybe another time. I had to take care of this life right now. I didn't have time to worry about some other lifetimes; that is, if there *were* any others.

Then I recalled the experience I had in front of the Sun Pyramid near Mexico City. I had to face some hard questions. Was it possible for the human spirit which cannot be destroyed and will live forever to take on another body and still retain one's identity? Was Cayce the only person who talked about reincarnation? Was it contrary to Catholic Doctrine? Was I walking on dangerous ground by reading about a subject rarely spoken of in the middle sixties? If I died which body would I have in heaven if I had more than one here on earth? Why didn't Jesus talk about it? Was there anyone who had all the answers?

I had made a decision by the time I returned to the parish. Since no one in my circle of friends seemed to know anything about the practice of a Yoga-style meditation and the possible results, I found myself alone in the study of birth and rebirth. I was also extremely curious to find out if there was new information in print on the mystery of life after death. Oh, I read the old Catechism cliches "We were created to know, to love and to serve God in this world and to be happy with Him in the next." But that didn't even approach the real issue.

I wanted some facts, some documented evidence based on my experience or the experience of others. I spoke about all the activity that takes place in heaven, but now there was another important question to address: What happens to us when we leave this body? For good, that is. I had left my body several times during the forty nights I was awakened...but came back. I wanted to know: We are individualized spirits created in the image and likeness of God. Is it possible to have a physical body here on earth, then have a spiritual body in heaven and somehow have another physical body again, never losing our identity? Could we possibly come back here to do some unfinished work called karma?

I began a new quest...a quest for understanding. I bought

some books on metaphysics. I read everything I could find on the subject of reincarnation and its companion karma. The more I read the more I became convinced that we had been sheltered for centuries here in the West. Among other things, I discovered that three quarters of the human race believed in reincarnation. That was my first surprise! Then I found out that others had memories of past lives. Many others! In recent years it was becoming fashionable for bookstores to have a whole section on past life memory. Some books outlined the whole history of reincarnation and offered a list of famous people who accepted it. I also discovered that there was a huge difference between *reincarnation* and *transmigration*. Many people confused the two concepts. Reincarnation is always the human soul being born into another human body and experiencing unfinished business, called *karma*..much like the Christian concept of purgatory, only the purging of the soul takes place in this world rather than in the afterlife. The soul is and always will be a human soul. Transmigration, believed only by a small contingent of humanity, and confined usually to the less educated, believes that we may come back into another species if we fail to live a good life; maybe as a dog or an insect. In those countries, there is grave concern for taking care of, quite possibly, grandpa or grandma who is now a fly or a cat. For this reason, they kill no living thing except vegetables. And so, vegetarians dominate in these territories. But the reincarnation of a human soul fulfilling its karma in another lifetime as a human is, quite frankly, more accepted than I thought was possible. Henry Ford was one of them. Plato was another. The list was long. Among outstanding Christians were St. Clement of Alexandria, Origen, St. Gregory of Nyssa, St. Francis of Assisi, St. Bonaventure, Duns Scotus, Archbishop Passavalli, Cardinal Mercier and Thomas More. In the pre-Christian era were Pythagoras, Virgil, Apollonius. Some of them maintained a strong belief in reincarnation, others were at times ambiguous, such as St. Augustine, Aristotle and St. Justin, martyr.

Poets seem to soar beyond the confines of a single lifetime on earth and focus on the immortality of the human soul and its brief experiences here. I was astounded to know that the following adhered to the concept of rebirth: Emerson, Poe, Longfellow, Tennyson, Thoreau, Whitman, Gibran and O'Neill. I have always had the greatest respect for Carl Jung and Aldous Huxley, men of our time; they endorsed rebirth as well. I have no proof but I have read in a book by David Christie-Murray that "Pope Pius XII (1939-1958) seriously contemplated the official recognition of the doctrine." Two current books found in almost every bookstore are "Life After Life" by Dr. Raymond Moody, and "Embraced by the Light" by Betty J. Eadie. Both of them throw a lot of light on afterlife.

The Bible has several texts that seem to support the concept of reincarnation. One of them is found in John 9:2 in the New Testament, when the Apostles asked Jesus about the man born blind, "Master, who did sin, this man, or his parents, that he was born blind?" It could be argued that if it was the man, he must have sinned in a previous life to have been born blind in this one. If it was the parent's sin, they incurred karma which is a counterpart to reincarnation.

After Jesus was transfigured on the mountain before Peter, James, and John, they were sure that Jesus was the Messiah. Coming down the mountainside, they "put the question to him: 'Why do the scribes claim that Elijah must come first?' (To announce the coming of the Messiah?) In reply he said: 'Elijah is indeed coming and he will restore everything. I assure you though, that Elijah has already come, but they did not recognize him and they did as they pleased with him. The Son of Man will suffer at their hands in the same way.' The disciples then realized that he had been speaking to them about John the

Baptist."

How does one explain the answer the Apostles gave to Jesus when He asked them: "Who do people say that I am?"

"Some say you are John the Baptist, Elijah, Jeremiah or one of the prophets." Interesting response to his question. We have to give the people some credit. All three of those prophets were associated with the Messiah. They had no idea who the Messiah could be or about his background, but John announced the arrival of the Messiah. That was his entire life work. Elijah was supposed to have gone directly up to heaven while he was still alive in a fiery chariot only to return to announce the coming of the Messiah. Jeremiah was believed to have taken the Ark of the Covenant and hid it in a cave - to be brought forth when the Messiah came. The people were at least in the right direction. But they were quick to believe that people came back into another life.

I am not trying to prove anything here. Whether reincarnation is a reality or not does not matter to me. And whether I have had true deja vu experiences from my own past lives or if I somehow, unknowingly, unwittingly tapped into someone else's lifetime, does not matter. All I know is that I *truly had* these experiences. How to accurately define what they were may never be known. On the other hand, the emotional impact of such experiences was very powerful. I cannot forget them; I cannot ignore them. I will never deny what I truly experienced in the awakened state. My memory and my sense of integrity will not allow me to reject what was real. To interpret them is another matter. To build a platform of beliefs based on my experiences would be conjecture. I do not want to deal in conjectures. I desire only to seek the truth.

While all of this was going on in my life, I, to this day, have maintained my belief and acceptance of official Catholic teaching which are paramount to the Catholic Faith. The issue is that I do not see any contradiction between what I have experienced and what is Catholic Doctrine. The fact is that the Church has not made a thorough study of the theory of reincarnation. There have been some priests who condemned it outright in the course of time just as I did. But to make a judgement on a theory older than Christianity and supported by some of the greatest minds that ever lived, is premature. Most of all, it would be difficult to prove or to disprove "beyond a reasonable doubt" a theory to which the majority of the human race accepts and to which millions of people support through personal experiences. This was a shocking revelation to me. It did not prove anything, of course. Nothing that demands proof from the eternal realms beyond death can be clearly demonstrated in this physical world. But it helped me to realize that reincarnation was possible in the eyes of many. And that there were good reasons for that possibility.

27. Direct Contact

In the Spring of 1971 I went to Spain with two friends. All three of us spoke Spanish and went to places most Americans never visit. We traveled to the churches where John of the Cross and Teresa of Avila were honored, and to the Shrine of James the Apostle in Galicia.   It was also part of the trip to visit the famous Prado Museum in Madrid where I had seen the painting of "The Crucified Christ" on a previous trip. On that trip the hair on my arms stood out and goose bumps covered my body when my eyes fell on that painted image.

My Patron Saint is St. James the Greater. I had a relic of St James in a cross that I cherished very much. I wanted to take that relic with me to Spain where he is the Patron Saint. I could not find that relic. I looked everywhere and no sign of it. I finally got in bed, exhausted. I prayed to find the cross in the morning. When I woke up, I reminded my guides "Don't forget about that relic. You have to help..."I stopped in the middle of the sentence! Looking at my suitcase with the clothes packed in it, I noticed something on the very top of the clothes...the relic. I was grateful once more.

We arrived in Madrid, Spain, and so it was natural that one of the first places we visited as tourists was the Prado Museum. About half way through the guided tour we were led into a large room with one huge painting that took up the entire front wall. The tour guide began to relate the history and meaning of the painting. There I was standing in the middle of the room which held about fifty people. As soon as I directed my attention to the painting in question, I immediately went into trance. I guess that is what you would call it.   I was actually painting that same picture. Everyone in the painting came alive and were posing. I was the artist, directing them to stand in a certain spot. I was well along into the painting when suddenly someone apparently bumped into me while backing up. It was enough to knock me down. As I was going down my hands broke the fall. It was somewhat painful but my hands and arms prevented me from hitting my head on that marble floor and possibly cracking it open. My subconscious - or whatever - saved the day. I was actually unconscious until I hit the floor. Let me say that it was a rude awakening. My traveling buddy, Tom, came running toward me when he saw me on the floor . He didn't know what to make of it and neither did I. I couldn't answer his question when he asked me what happened. I told him that I was just standing there with the rest of the folks, listening to the tour guide when suddenly I was the artist himself completing this huge painting. Interestingly enough, the artist had included his own portrait in that picture. I couldn't help wonder if I ever looked like that.

After I explained to Tom what happened, he asked who painted it. I said I didn't know. So we both went up closer to the painting and saw the signature. It was a Spaniard and a rather famous name. I would rather not mention that name here. (To me, the name was not as important as the experience itself.) It dawned on me at that very moment, that two different psychics on two separate occasions had told me I was that artist. The two of them did not know each other. I did not, of course, place much confidence in the words of a psychic, but it sure hit me hard when I realized that they both named the artist that produced that painting. I was really starting to get concerned now. Why were these things happening to me? That was the second time I went into a trance state - and I didn't even know what a trance state was! (And I still don't.) Then I had to reconcile my 4:00 am visits which offered fourteen incarnations that were supposedly my past lifetimes.

Instead of resolving my quest of pursuing truth through meditation, the trance experiences and the last of the 4:00 am visits caused me more confusion. What was I supposed to believe now? Up to that time I had received a limited academic education. That was the normal process of education in the United States for the priesthood. I had no other tools with which to examine the concept of life and death other than that provided by a metaphysical or empirical point of view. By experience! The information offered in the seminary or at the University of Detroit did not even approach the subject. I wanted to know because I was experiencing something not found in books recommended by proper authority.

I could not resolve this dilemma. I had always been a model student and priest. I believed in the principle: "Roma locuta, causa finita", which is Latin for "When Rome speaks, the discussion is finished." I respected the word of my superiors and the established teachings of the church. What do I do?

The answer came unexpectedly, as usual. I was visiting Mundelein College in Chicago the following summer. I stopped to see a couple of nuns who were studying there. While at supper, we were discussing the possibility of communicating with one's spiritual guides. Since I seemed to have already tapped in on some form of communication I thought I would follow the recommendations one of them had read in a book. When I returned home, I meditated now with a specific purpose in mind. Could I establish an ongoing conversation with my guide who had visited me forty nights in a row and then some at 4:00 am? I would try. And did. And tried again. Finally, there was a communication established! Slow at first, then picking up speed to a normal conversation.

I was surprised again! I started out asking questions right away. I had a lot of questions. What had happened to me did not so much give answers but raised a lot of questions. I now felt free to converse. I asked first of all about the visitations during the night. Why at 4:00 am? What was so special about that hour? These guides (there were often two or three) were pretty smart in giving proper assistance. Instead of simply telling me the answer, they made me work for it. The answer could be found in a book called "The Yoga of Light", they told me.

"Fine", I said. "Where do I find such a book? I doubt if the regular book stores would carry it." They named the store where I could purchase it. It was called "The Mayflower", a store specializing in metaphysical books. When I finally got time to go to that store, I walked in and saw books everywhere, from the floor to the ceiling. There were several rows of books. Some books were piled up on the floor. Obviously, there were too many books for the size of the store. The books that were on a shelf did not appear to have any order by title or category. So I went to the desk where there was a young girl apparently in charge. She was reading a popular magazine, chewing gum wildly. I said politely, "Do you have a book called "The Yoga of Light"? She said she didn't know anything about the books. So I asked, "Is the owner in today?" She replied that he had gone somewhere that morning and was expected sometime later . She did not know when exactly.

I thought to myself: "Okay, guides, you got me here. There is no way I am going to go through thousands of books trying to find the one you mentioned."

"Go straight ahead to the third aisle." They said with confidence. I did.

"Turn to your right!" I did that, too.

Their last statement. "Take three steps, stop and turn to your right." I did just that. And there it was staring at me in the face: "The Yoga of Light" It was the only copy on that shelf and probably the only one in the entire store of more than 10,000 books. This incident helped me to place more trust in my guides. They had not failed me.

I was still seeking an easier way out. I again appealed to an alternative: "Why do I have to read that book in preparation for your answer?" They emphasized again that I would not be able to apply what I was learning unless I fully understood it, internalized it and owned it. They were not "Answer People". They were spiritual guides. Their work was to groom me at a pace that kept me balanced and spiritually healthy as I moved forward. This was the first of many books they recommended. And they only named another book when they felt I was ready for the next step.

The guides were very conscientious in their role as counselors. They apparently were careful that I received the greatest spiritual benefit from their recommendations. And I did. I recall once asking them if they knew what numbers were going to come out in the lottery the next day. They said they did.

"Fine," I replied. "How about some help here?" They quickly reminded me that they did not deal in material matters. I said, "How about winning to raise funds for the church and for the poor?"

"No deal!" They repeated. They then cautioned me about asking such questions. They knew, however, that I was only testing them. But their point was clear and I never pursued that line of thought again.

I got serious again! I inquired whether these guides were responsible for waking me up for forty nights in a row and instructing me with cosmic and mystical experiences. They replied in the affirmative.

Were they the ones who led me into the seminary by means of *the voice* that did an incredible job of getting me to the seminary and encouraging me each year to stay there?

They were indeed! Where does Christ fit into that picture? They described themselves as his helpers.

"Why didn't you help me when I needed you the most after my parents death?" Making the decision to be ordained was certainly the most important decision in my life up to that time. "Where were you?"

"We were right there beside you, but we were not permitted to make that decision for you. Our role was to get you there. The final decision was yours. And you chose correctly."

Five times I asked an explanation of the vision the four of us children had back in 1937. Each time they said I was not ready. I asked in the early seventies - middle seventies - always with the same answer. I wondered when I would have sufficient awareness to comprehend the vision. If it was so profound why did we as children have it in the first place. To be at peace, I let go of it mentally.

My guides occasionally referred to me as a *mystic*. It was not easy for me to accept that title. My concept of a mystic is a person who is holy, receives unfused knowledge and/or infused contemplation, and obviously has mystical experiences as a natural and normal result of sublime meditation and an extraordinary prayer life. Did they make a mistake labeling me as a mystic? That's what I asked. Their reply was that I should re-think why so many miraculous events accompanied my presence and why was I so gifted with experiences about which an average person can only dream about or hope for.

I slowly accepted the fact that I was rather frequently given rare experiences. That my prayers after years of aridity were answered in a framework far beyond that which I could not even wildly imagine.

In humility I thanked God for the joy and the sorrow, the sickness and the health, the satisfying moments as well as those frustrating ones that form character and strength. Without those horribly difficult assignments I had in my early years as a priest, when the cross was quite heavy, almost to the breaking point, I would never have been so motivated to pursue Truth and thereby discover the direct action of God's Love and Providence in my life. In a way, I became *grateful*!

In the course of time, I read many books, some of them recommended by my guides. Others, I simply found on my own in bookstores. I would usually check with the guides to see if they approved of a particular book I bought. Not all were acceptable. The guides warned me about some New Age material on the market. Some of the authors distorted the truth while others were not even close to the truth. A sincere reader who did not have proper discernment could be lead astray in their well-meaning quest. I was fortunate to have good helpers. I believe, through the years, I have received several hundred answers to questions I did not know at the time and many hundreds of comments on a wide variety of issues. I have them all recorded on tape and also transcribed on paper, but I have been strongly advised not to share them publicly. At least not up till now.

I talked with several priests concerning my experiences. They were totally unaware of what I was talking about. They never heard nor read about such things. I even went to a priest who was known for his advanced spirituality; I was sure he had similar experiences. He had no knowledge of what I experienced. I was both surprised and disappointed. Even with his very rich background in spirituality, apparently he and I had entered different realms of communication with Divine Guidance. Neither was better than the other. They were simply different paths toward truth.

28. Experience Is Knowing

I have always been interested and fascinated by pyramids - even as a child. Since my youth, I managed to collect many pyramid-shaped pendants or medallions. One of my dreams was to actually go to the pyramids in Egypt. The memory of the ones in Mexico never left me. Since the trance experience in Mexico, I read whatever I could find about pyramids.

While at St. Michael's in Pontiac, I was awakened one night at the usual time, around four in the morning. Upon awakening, I thought I had to go to the bathroom. I got out of bed and, out of habit, was walking toward the bathroom... but it wasn't there! I was wide awake, not sleeping. I knew the difference. I also quickly realized that I was in a different place. Just where *was* I? I kept questioning myself. As I kept walking, I noticed a little light about twenty feet further. As I approached the wall, I found myself looking at hieroglyphic writing. I said to myself: *Good heavens! I'm in a pyramid! Is it Giza?* I was not sure what my next move was. I could barely see, but it was just bright enough for me to pass through a narrow hallway into a larger hall.

What I saw in that hall were the most colorful, vivid and radiant murals. They depicted scenes of the gods acting upon the earth. It looked like a fresco just painted within the hour. I have been to many museums. Nothing compared to the brilliant colors and larger-than-life scenes on the wall. While I was admiring the painted walls, I didn't realize there was someone else in the hall. He was dressed in a long garment similar to a cope, studded with precious jewels. He reminded me of a High Priest of some sort. Then his face kept changing. It must have changed a thousand times. It was almost continuous motion.

One face after another, covering every race, culture and creed. He looked stern and serious, young and old, male and female, until, finally his face changed no more. His final appearance reminded me of a Middle East person. Dark, olive skin, completely bald.

"What are you doing here?" He inquired. He was serious. I told him I was not sure. I didn't even know *how* I got there!

He looked at me straight in the eyes, and asked "Do you know what room this is ?"

"The Hall of Initiation" I replied hesitantly. I don't know where I got that information.

"That is correct. Do you know what happens here?"

Again, the answers came to my lips. "Those deemed worthy are initiated into the White Brotherhood."

"Is that your wish?"

I did not answer right away. Then I slowly said with assurance, "I now believe that is why I am here!"

He said "Lie down." Which I did. There was no table to lie on, but I leaned back and found myself lying down in mid air. It seemed quite natural at the time.

He lifted both hands very slowly then stretched out his hands over my body. My body started to shake - as if I were shivering, although I knew at the time it was pure energy penetrating my whole body. I remained lying there immobile with the sincere feeling that I was being *transformed* by a tremendous power. When it was completed, I felt myself returning briskly to my room. I was back in my physical body but conscious of my body still shivering somewhat. I couldn't sleep for a long time, considering the impact of what had just happened to me.

The next day I questioned my guides about the incident. I asked if that was the pyramid of Giza. They said no. The pyramid I entered was of such exciting and lively colors because it belonged to another dimension. Later, I was told that the initiation took place in the sixth dimension, to be exact. They said it was a real experience. I said. "Please explain..." Here's what they said:

"In 1956, you were ordained on earth into the priesthood in the three dimensional world, but now you have been blessed from on high into the White Brotherhood. You are in good company." After reflecting a long time on their words I looked up the references to the Resurrection and the Ascension of Jesus, as they recommended. In Mark 16: 5, the women went to anoint the body of Jesus. Upon entering, they "saw a young man sitting at the right *dressed in a white robe*." He told them Jesus has been raised up. He is not here.

Again, at the time of Jesus' Ascension as recorded by St. Luke in Acts 1:1, *two men dressed in white* told the disciples: "Men of Galilee. Why do you stand there looking up at the skies? This Jesus who has been taken from you will return, just as you saw him go up into the heavens." Members of the White Brotherhood also conversed and comforted Cayce often in his walks behind the A.R.E Center.

I made a trip to the Cayce Foundation at Virginia Beach, Virginia called The Association for Research and Enlightenment. They simply referred to it as A.R.E. I made the trip with two other friends who were also seekers of Truth and open to metaphysics because of some personal experiences they also had. I had to see for myself if there really was such a gifted person alive in my lifetime.

Edgar Cayce died in 1945 when I was only fifteen years old. He spoke profusely about the Essene Community who lived in Palestine around the time of Christ. Not many people believed there was such a community. Cayce predicted that absolute proof would be given two years after his death. In 1947, exactly two years after Cayce died, the Dead Sea Scrolls were discovered in the caves of Qumran proving beyond doubt the

162

truth of his statements and confirming the description he often gave about the social and religious life of the Essenes. I regret that I had never met Cayce. The belief system of my teenage years did not permit even the remote possibility of an encounter with him.

The workshop we signed up for was mainly about the ancient Egyptians. People came from all over the United States. It was exciting and comforting to know that we were not alone in this matter. Those who attended were well educated, refined persons who were also seeking the truth of what had happened to them.

The lecturer based his quotes on the 15,000 Readings that came through Edgar Cayce. I said *came through* Mr. Cayce because all of the Readings took place while Cayce was completely unconscious. Almost every topic you can think of was covered in the Readings. He was extremely accurate in diagnosing sicknesses or conditions of a person and giving remedies to resolve the situation or heal the sickness. He only needed the person's name and birth date. His eyes were never open during a Reading. There have been many books written about this phenomenal man who is known as the world's greatest psychic. If interested, begin with "There is a River" by Thomas Sugrue, "The Sleeping Prophet" by Jess Stern or "Many Mansions" by Gina Cerminara.

While I was in the recording rooms checking my tape recorder in between lectures at the A.R.E., I backed into another participant of the workshop. Most people meet with a handshake. We, on the contrary, met by backing into each other and almost knocking each other down. We both apologized then looked at each other's name tag. We discovered that we were both from the Detroit area. That led us to become good friends. She was a nurse and her husband was a thoracic surgeon and chief of staff at Bon Secours Hospital on the East side of Detroit. When we returned home we began a study group based on a book that came through Edgar Cayce while he was unconscious. It was called "The Search for God". The book was excellent for persons starting on the path of meditation and spiritual growth. Along with a group of about seven people, I learned many things that have contributed to my own personal development.

29. Communication Through Dreams And Rescue work

Among those gems of wisdom that came out of the Cayce Readings was the importance of dreams. He once said that there were two ways to communicate directly with God: through meditation and through dreams. Since I had received excellent guidance through meditation, I decided it was time to explore guidance through dreams as well. I asked my guides to help me to remember my dreams and to interpret them for me if I had difficulty understanding them. They agreed.

Again, I was very serious. I wanted to know if God was still communicating through dreams as He did in the Scriptures. In the Old Testament, we find that Daniel was referred to as the man who could interpret dreams and solve problems through dreams. Joseph, one of the sons of Jacob was sold by his brothers to an Egyptian. Joseph gradually worked his way up to become the Pharaoh's right hand man by interpreting dreams. In the original Christmas story, Joseph was told to take Mary as his wife in a dream by an angel, then later he was told in a dream to leave Nazareth and head for Egypt. The angel informed him that Herod wanted to kill the child Jesus. In another dream they were told when it was safe to return to their homeland. There are many more references to dreams as the dimension of communication directly with God or with one of his messengers. The word *angel* means *messenger*!

Besides still being active directly or through angelic guides or meditation, was God also communicating to us through dreams? I am referring to spiritual dreams. I would make every effort to find out. My guides wasted no time. I began to remember dreams the very night we agreed to work together.

Sometimes I would have two or three very clear dreams the same night. Every year I filled an entire book with dreams and their interpretations. I would always try to interpret the dream first. If I was not successful or if I were completely stumped I would ask for help. A perfect analysis and interpretation of every dream came quickly when my guides helped. There was no hesitation. They knew exactly every point in the dream that had significance. The majority of the dreams were spiritual. Occasionally I was warned in a dream - about things not so spiritual - such things as a flat tire or engine trouble, in which case what I dreamed happened to me exactly two weeks later. Every detail happened as I dreamed: the exact time in the evening, the freeway, the street where I had to get off because the engine was flashing red, smoke was pouring out of the hood, and the car was stalling. In both the dream and the reality two weeks later, I ended up at a gas station about two blocks past the exit. The car died there! My Associate came and picked me up.

The second time, I dreamed of a flat tire - the right front tire - so I went out and bought a new tire, the best tire they made. I wasn't going to get caught this time. However, after two weeks I found that brand new tire flat when I went to my car that morning. I put on a spare and went back to the same tire company to check it out. The mechanic was baffled. He said there was absolutely nothing wrong with the tire. The message, in the final analysis was not about the tire at all. My guides were simply reinforcing the idea that the future could be foretold and that dreams in particular, may pertain to the past, present or future. No harm was done; I simply learned a lesson. Occasionally I was given information about certain future events. I never doubted my trustworthy guides. And they were never wrong!

I was working with dreams very effectively and they were

a source of spiritual growth for me. About that same time, I was then introduced to what was called "Rescue Work" by my guides. It made a lot of sense. Helpers on the other side are ready to welcome those who have passed from this life to the next. It would be helpful to them if the persons dying could be prepared in some way before their transition. For example, as a priest, I could talk to souls ready to leave their bodies, do a bit of counseling and remove as much as possible the shock of finding themselves on the other side. This was all new to me. So, I made arrangements with my guides to do this kind of work during the night. My plan was to use my sleep time productively. I could serve others even while I am sleeping.

The first night after we made an agreement, I was suddenly awakened with a horribly loud noise. It was an accident on the road. I was there seeing a man dying. He was lying on the seat of the car with his head tilted back. I was surprised to be there, and more surprised that he could see me. I was wearing my priest's garb. I asked if I could help him. He said he was not Catholic. I replied that it didn't matter. I continued: "Would you like me to pray with you?" Without hesitation he said "Yes, please!" We prayed together; I asked him to tell God he was sorry for anything he had ever done to offend his conscience. When I was finished, I immediately found myself back in bed wide awake. I was stunned! I had made my first rescue service to a total stranger about to make his transition. I went back to sleep but not right away. It took time to come down emotionally.

No sooner had I gotten to sleep when "Pow!" Another accident. This time I am standing in front of a lady, dying out on a highway. There were two cars involved with two fatal injuries. I ministered to them both; one was Catholic the other was not. It didn't matter to me in the slightest. I was happy to serve them in their last moments here on earth. When I finished, I was back in bed wide awake again. When morning came I was exhausted. After all, I was not used to working through the night! For the next three weeks I was awakened one or more times each night. I would go to sleep like everybody else. Then, "Bam!" I am out on the street offering spiritual help. Sometimes I found myself in the hospital administering a sacrament and/or a prayer to someone about to die. I seemed to be especially drawn to someone who was praying for help. After the three weeks, I consulted my guides. They were not surprised. I admitted that I could not continue this overly active night ministry. We called it off by agreement. I said if I am healthy and strong enough when I retire I would consider continuing Rescue Work. From that point on I limited myself to the work at hand...during the day.

Rev. Jay J. Samonie

Fr. Jay's parents: Jacob and Mary Samonie
Above: His sisters Marie Hellow and Jennie Latiff

Family Photo - Fr. Jay's siblings in bold print. From upper left: **Jackie** and Craig Cebulskie, Mary Ann Samonie (Anthony's wife who died in 1997), **Rose** and Philip Semain, **Anthony** Samonie, Bottom row: **Lillian** Simony, Fr. Jay Samonie, **Elizabeth** Nader

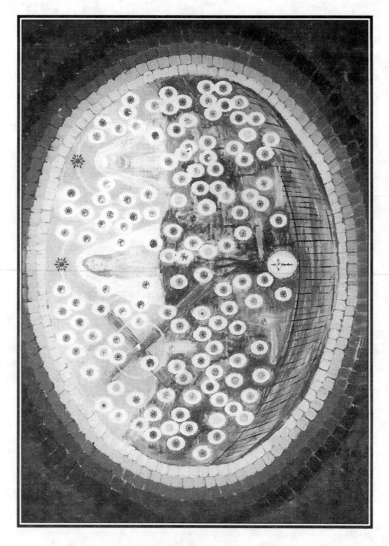

Vision Shared in 1937 by four Samonie children: Anthony, Rose, Elizabeth, and Jay (who later painted it in 1974.)

30. Teaching Mind Development
And Stress Control

In 1972, I received a call from a representative of the Assignment Board for Priests. He stated that they wanted me to accept the appointment as Pastor of St. Michael's Church in Pontiac. I told him I was quite busy with several projects at St. Bernadette's and would like to stay on where I was. Then I received a call from the regional bishop requesting the same thing. I figured it was time to leave St. Bernadette church and finally I accepted the appointment. A curious thing happened at that time, unknown to me. A couple of Arabs from Southeast Dearborn made an appointment with Cardinal Dearden. The Cardinal was surprised; but he received a greater shock when a whole bus load of Arabs came to the meeting arranged with him. The Cardinal himself told me this: he asked them to explain the purpose of the meeting. They told him they wanted to keep Fr. Samonie at St. Bernadette's. He asked why, since they were Moslems. They had their own imam. (priest). They responded that they did indeed have an imam but that Fr. Jay was their Pastor. The Cardinal heard from them about my struggles at the City Council meetings defending their rights and siding with them against the city in general. He related to me how impressed he was. Nevertheless, he emphasized that I was already reassigned. There was no turning back. He felt badly but the decision had been made. Needless to say, I was surprised at the whole incident.

Not long after my appointment to St. Michael's in Pontiac, Rita Hopkins encouraged me to take a Course called the Silva Method of Mind Development and Stress Control. We had just completed a meditation with a few other people and were discussing various new programs on the market. She recommended the Silva Method to me as a very good program to help build self-image and as an excellent introduction to metaphysics.

I took her up on it! From the very beginning, I notice two things that made the Silva Method interesting to me: the first was that it not based on conjecture, but that it was scientific. Every technique used in the course was validated by empirical evidence or scientific instruments. The second item that impressed me was that it was free of charge to clergymen. The founder, Jose Silva, was an outstanding, active catholic layman who attended Mass regularly. He welcomed clergy of all religions and their input concerning the program.

The Lecturer, Ken McCaulley, had to be on his toes in class. I asked a lot of questions. Every new concept that was introduced was accompanied by at least one or two questions I had to ask. I challenged practically everything in the Course. However, the explanations given by the lecturer were excellent! He was a gifted instructor, and knew his material very well. I was impressed. I was also grateful to Mrs. Hopkins for putting me in contact with a program that was going to make a noticeable change in my life.

While at St. Michael's, I was visited more than once by the Lecturer Ken McCaulley. He said that with my background and knowledge I would make a good Lecturer of the Silva Method. I was honored but I felt much too busy to spend an extra forty hours teaching while continuing my daily responsibilities. The Basic Course took four days or two full weekends at ten hours each day. Mr. McCaulley did not give up on me. I was finally convinced to take the Lecture-training Program in Laredo, Texas. Interestingly enough, there were two other persons from the Detroit area that also signed up to be Lecturers. Both were nuns! I couldn't quite figure it out, but we almost gave the impression that the Silva Method was a Religious Course sponsored by the Catholic Church. Nothing could be further from the truth! Any appearance to that effect was purely coincidental. In fact, ninety-nine percent of the Lecturers were lay people, and, by far, the majority were of mixed religious persuasion or had no religious affiliation at all!

After two weeks training, we returned home and I began teaching under the supervision of Ken McCaulley. I taught in homes from the start. One of my first classes in the Silva Method was to a group of teachers in the local Public School System. I was a little apprehensive teaching a group of teachers. I would soon find out whether my personal belief that I could teach well was real or imagined. I finished the Course and it was time for an honest reckoning and evaluation. The teachers were impressed with the lectures and said they were amazed at my teaching skills. I was surprised and greatly encouraged to continue as a Lecturer in the Silva Method. I saw nothing I taught in conflict or offensive to my convictions, to Catholic Doctrine, or to any religious or moral standards as I understood them. The Silva Method was simply a Course in self-improvement. I taught the Course over sixty times in a period of about sixteen years. Through the accomplishments of my teaching, research and success in the field of mind development, I earned a Doctorate in Metaphysics or Mind Sciences called Psychorientology.

31. Wisdom From the East

Many people have had mystical and cosmic experiences; some have written about them. Yet I never met or read of any experiences similar to mine. That is, until I met a genuine Buddhist monk from Sri Lanka. One night as I just got to sleep, the phone rang. It was Ken McCaulley. He apologized for calling so late but he stated that he was well aware of my desire to meet a Buddhist monk. Well, now was my chance. The famous Eastern Master Mahinda who had been teaching and lecturing all over the world for the last twenty years was giving a lecture at the very moment in Ken's SMC Center. He would be finished by midnight and agreed to spend some time with me afterwards. It was the only opportunity to visit Mahinda as he was leaving town the next morning.

I was not going to pass up this opportunity. I dressed as quickly as possible and drove down to the Center which was located on Gratiot and Nine Mile, about forty minutes away. I got there about ten minutes before midnight. Mahinda was just finishing his talk. After a few last comments were made and everyone had left, it was almost exactly the midnight hour. The two of us sat and chatted. We talked about some general issues concerning the concept of God, the world, the purpose of life on this planet and many other issues of common interest.

When the appropriate moment arrived, I started speaking about my forty nights of mystical, spiritual and cosmic experiences. He listened attentively. Once or twice he interrupted to add a clarifying description to what I was saying. After the first time he made a comment, I thought to myself that he was very kind and surprisingly accurate. The second time he spoke with comments so specific that what he said could only be known by someone who had been there, someone who was speaking from experience and not guess work. I became very excited, knowing that he knew! I was not alone! I cannot explain the thrilling and exalting feelings that ran through me as I related the whole experience to him. When I was finished, he made some startling comments. First, that he knew precisely where I was in the realm of spiritual growth. He explained how one's readiness and achievement prepared a person for a visitation appropriate to his or her level of awareness. The Religion of the Master or the Teacher responding, would depend on the religious convictions of the recipient. Mahinda pointed out to me, that being a Christian, my encounter would naturally be with Christ in the "Aura of Light." A devout Buddhist would most likely be visited by Buddha. He also did not express any element of surprise while hearing of my out-of-body experiences as well as the instructions I was being given. It was all part of the same package, so to speak. One item surprised the monk! He was amazed that I achieved that level of awareness without a teacher. He said that in India a student generally had to follow a Guru or teacher around for at least 10 years before they began to get genuine results. He added, that being a Westerner, I was truly an exception to the rule, and pursuing the path I followed with undying passion was almost unique in the Western world. Then he made a statement that brought all thoughts within me to complete silence. He said he had traveled the world over, and met many members of the clergy, most of whom were outstanding. But there was no doubt in his mind that I had achieved an awareness as high as any clergyman he had ever met. Another statement of surprise! He knew exactly what my next step was. I knew what his answer was going to be, but I asked anyway: "Will you share that next step with me?" As I presumed, he stated that I did not ask a proper question.

My question was improper because each of us has to find our own niche, our own path, our own place in the sun. We both knew that! He did share this much, however. He affirmed that if I were to continue on this same path, I would be given the next phase of enlightenment within the next five years. He would speak no more about it. He tossed the proverbial "ball" elegantly and with precision back into my own lap. After all, it was *my* quest! This Buddhist monk represented the only person I had ever met on this planet who also experienced similar phenomena and who understood my dilemma as a priest living in the West. I was far more impressed that he understood than I was by his compliments.

Believe me, I do not wish in any way to place myself above anyone else. As I said, we all have our own path to follow. Mine is not better; it is simply different. If you want to be impressed, I believe we are all humbled by the example in the Scriptures of the widow's mite. In the Gospel according to Mark (12: 41-44) it reads: Taking a seat opposite the treasury, Jesus observed the crowd putting money into the collection box. Many of the wealthy put in sizable amounts: but one poor widow came and put in *two small copper coins worth a few cents*. He called his disciples over and told them: "I want you to observe that this poor widow contributed more than all the others who donated to the treasury. They gave from their surplus wealth, but she gave from her want, all that she had to live on." Jesus immortalized her generosity. He placed her far above most of the human race in the spirit of giving.

A more modern scenario would be a young widow with several children - she may be far superior to us all in the pursuit of commitment, sacrifice and yes, holiness, because of the passion in which she fulfills her purpose: to raise and educate her children to the best of her ability with the limited income and resources available to her. I bow my head with profound respect to these women for such a perfect demonstration of responsibility and single mindedness. We are all on a journey pursuing our goals. We are not in competition with each other. Each of us can do something the other cannot. No one can walk in your shoes. Everyone is contributing something unique to life.

Each of us has a mission to accomplish in our lifetime. If there is work yet to be done, we are given the opportunity to accomplish it. I spoke of the time when I was spared from leaving the earth by means of a tornado; there were also other instances in which I escaped death quite miraculously. A few years before I was assigned to St. Michael's in Pontiac, I was driving to Chicago with a classmate of mine, Fr. Joe Brady. We drove his father's car, which, at that time, was better than ours. We were on the freeway about half way to Chicago. It was winter time, but the roads were clear and we were driving at the proper freeway speed. Without warning we suddenly drove over a patch of ice that caused the car to be completely out of control. I was behind the steering wheel at the time and I made every effort to regain control without success. There was a huge ditch by the side of the road and we were heading straight for it. Joe and I looked at each other - the meaning was clear. The situation was hopeless and did not allow for words, but my mind was saying: "I'll see you in the next life, my friend!" Just before the tragic moment was about to take place and catapult us into the next life, I managed to pray the expression I am accustomed to in the presence of danger: "Jesus, Mary and Joseph!" Certain death awaited us. But that's not the way it ended! As we approached the area of the treacherous ditch, we happened to hit a guard rail - a very small one at that - which was not visible at the time.

We hit the guard rail with the full force of the speed and weight of the car. We then turned completely around and the back of the car hit the same guard rail equally hard; that caused us to spin and threw us back on the road. We were now in the correct position and direction to continue driving. I touched my face and chest to see if I was still alive...in the flesh. We both gestured with a sigh of gratitude. Looking at the car from the outside, both the front and the back of the car were damaged heavily. The bumpers absorbed the full impact, and the car, incredibly, was still driveable! We continued on to Chicago, took the car to a garage and had it fixed while we spent the weekend in the windy city as planned. For a few brief moments we thought we would be entering the Kingdom of Spirit. Instead we arrived at the loop in Chicago. Neither of us was injured in any way except perhaps financially - getting the car repaired. We knew then that we had more work to do. Our time had not yet come!

Not long after that incident, I was driving Rachel Hessen - a close friend of our family - to the airport. We were on the freeway a few miles short of the airport. The traffic suddenly came to a complete stop. We were the last in a long line of cars. I happen to look in the rear view mirror and I saw a car speeding toward us. It was not slowing down. I screamed: "Ray, we are about to get hit. Brace yourself!" We anticipated the worst and we got it. The car ramming us had to be doing freeway speed; it jolted us very hard and we went smashing into the car in front of us; then the same car that made the first strike, hit us again. This time, with full impact. My beautiful new car looked like an accordion. I checked body parts one a time: legs...okay; arms...okay; neck...no whiplash!

"Ray, (that's the way she spells it) are you all right?"

"I think so," she said. "Wait a minute! I think my instep is fractured!" She was wearing heels. That was the only injury. When we both got out of the car squashed to almost half it's normal length, people looked at us with amazement. We were amazed, too! The man who hit us and started a chain of accidents, was quite intoxicated. He was unhurt, of course, and quite oblivious to the lives he almost sent into the world of spirit. Thinking of God's Divine Providence once again, "Thank you" repeatedly poured out of my mouth.

Once again, I received an affirmation that we only leave this world when our mission is complete, and not before then...regardless of what the circumstances look like.

32. Experimenting With New Principles

After about a year in Pontiac, my associate and I decided to put up a fence around the back yard. It would give us some privacy to sit out there and read, given the time on a pleasant day. And so we did. I had never tried my hand at farming, but I went and bought some starters for tomatoes and some seeds for cucumbers, radishes, carrots, and other vegetables. When it came to corn, I wanted to try an experiment. I had bought a tiny six-inch pyramid. It was made of firm cardboard that folded. The dimensions of this tiny pyramid were the same as those of the Great Pyramid in Giza, Egypt.

According to Dr. Thompson, an expert on the Great Pyramid, the shape of the pyramid itself is a cosmic form and affects objects in it. Perishable food will not rot, only dehydrate. If you have ever smelled a rotten egg, it would send your nostrils reeling! That doesn't happen in a pyramid-shaped form. Eggs and tomatoes dehydrate. Perhaps that is why mummies are dehydrated.

It also has some interesting properties according to Dr. Thompson: seed placed under it are energized and grow bigger and better. That was my corn experiment! I placed twenty kernels inside the tiny pyramid and twenty outside of it. The next day I planted them side by side. One row energized and the other not. The old saying "Knee high by the fourth of July" turned out to be a joke! On July 4th, every single energized kernel became a stalk easily above the knee, more like up to the *hip*! The other twenty had several barely up to the knee with some kernels not taking root at all.

It was strange looking at the two rows, one looked almost sickly, and the other utterly amazing. My brother Tony claims to be able to use the same safety blade for shaving twenty times longer when place inside a pyramid form. If there is any truth to the pyramid theory, how did the ancient Egyptians acquire such *knowledge*, thousands of years before Christ?

The yard produced vegetables for us all summer. At the same time, it helped to keep our food budget down! One day at table, Jim and I were discussing the possibility of getting a dog, now that we had a fenced-in yard.

I said "Let's use one of the programs taught in the Mind Development class." We then visualized some one calling us and offering us a dog. It usually took anywhere from one to twenty-one days for the program to manifest in our life. One week later, I got that call. One of our parishioners had a puppy and wanted to offer it to us. I said "Fine! We would be happy to have a puppy." I was going to add "What took you so long?" I thought I better not. We already named the dog before we got it. We called the dog "Chris", short for Christian, whether it was male or female. Chris happened to be female.

The dog was half African Besangi and half bird dog. What a hunter she would make. Besangis are raised in Africa specifically to kill rats. They can smell them out and kill them in a bloodless manner. Add the bird dog instincts to Chris and you've got a hunting-dog-plus on your hands. We were plagued with mice in the old parish house at that time. But not for long. Chris killed about ten of them in a few days. She would kill a mouse then drop it in the middle of the floor. It was then up to us to dispose of it. Soon the word got out among the mice...and we never saw another mouse in the house for the next five years of our ministry there.

One day while at dinner - it was just a couple of days after Chris arrived - we heard Chris moving around quickly as if playing with something. It was a mouse. She would place a paw on its tail just like a cat would in the movies. Then she would release it. The mouse ran for its life. Then she would grab the tail again. Finally, she got tired of playing. She then gave the mouse a right hook - that's the only way to explain it - and killed it instantly. This breed knows precisely where and how to strike its victim. She looked at us as if to say "Clean up this mess!" and walked away.

On the negative side, from the time we got the dog, she had a misconception of what a bathroom area was. She thought that the whole house was one big bathroom and the yard was to be preserved immaculately. After a week of doing a mess on the carpet, she kept Jim and I disgustingly busy. So we decided to do something about it. I suggested using a system devised by Bea Lydecker when training animals. Jim Agreed. I held Chris' face in both hands and looked at her eye to eye. As I gave the command to keep the house clean, I also visualized it as clean; then I said the yard is the place to go to the bathroom, visualizing a bush, a tree, the grass, whatever. I said "We will give you two weeks to make the change. If you continue to mess up the house we will have to get rid of you...and we're considering getting a cat."

I gave that one command and it worked. From that very moment Chris never once made a mistake again. Even when we were both out and came in hours later - with her bladder ready to burst - she still waited till she got in the yard.

One last thought about the dog. As a joke, when I wrote my weekly article for the Parish Bulletin, I mentioned that Fr. Jim and I now have a young girl living with us. Oh boy!! I did not expect such a reaction! We received many calls and letters deploring the behavior of priests today. Most people were shocked and even scandalized. The next Sunday in the Bulletin and from the pulpit, we had to explain that Chris was a girl puppy, and a cute one, mostly brown, with white dots and some black, a full integrated healthy dog. The tongues stopped waggling!

While at St. Michael's Parish in the early seventies, I learned very clearly what "change" does to certain people. There were six parishioners, all active, well known, and members of the Parish Council. My Associate, (We no longer used the word 'assistant') Fr. Jim Wysocki and I endured the most vicious attacks from these same people who were determined to discourage us to the point of leaving the parish. They insulted us openly at meetings. At one point I threw one lady out of the Council meeting when she used some perverse and vulgar language against us. Their opposition did not diminish. My initial reaction was to tell them off, announce publicly from the pulpit the nature of their offensive behavior, and declare them officially removed from the list of registered parishioners. And wiped off the earth, if possible! Of course, I did not do that.

Fr. Jim and I prayed for direction. We wanted to maintain a proper Christian attitude toward them. I decided to use a technique which I had taught in the Mind Development classes: to solve the problem with a positive attitude, by mentally inviting them to re-consider and help us build a Christian Community together. Each evening I sent them messages mentally telling them they were welcomed to be on the same team, working in a united effort to accomplish our goals. Then I meditated on the goals we established at the Council meetings. I also envisioned a happy, active Christian Community praising God, growing in a united spirit, and working in peaceful cooperation. I could see the whole parish forming a circle of unconditional love with the symbol of Christ in the center. Then I invited each of the six persons to become a part of that group. I would say something like "Please join us. You are very welcome...but if you choose otherwise, that's all right." I did not want to force them to change.

At first, I pictured St. Michael's Community all holding

hands in a huge circle framed within a rectangular mental screen. After a few days, by itself, the image and the frame became circular. After about ten days, with no deliberate action on my part, I began to hear music. Everyone started to move in rhythm. We were dancing! I kept asking the same six people "Please join us. And to the others, "Make room for them, please!" In the Mind Development Course, we were recommended to repeat the respectful invitation each day for twenty-one days. As if on schedule, about three weeks later, one of the six came up to me and apologized for the rude treatment they gave me and my Associate. He now wanted to work with us. He did indeed, and went on to become the Council President. We accomplished a great deal together. His sister also was on the Council and one of the six people who resisted change. She, too, felt bad about their negative and meaningless criticism of Fr. Jim and myself. She became open to new ideas and to our planned programs. Unfortunately, the other four remained adamant. They chose to leave us and sought another way of serving God. They preferred a community that was much more conservative and fundamental. They had my sincere blessing. In the end, we went on to accomplish our five-year goals in four years.

During the last two years of my Pastorate at St. Michael's in Pontiac, I received permission from the Silva Method Headquarters to teach Senior Citizens the entire $150 (the cost at that time) Course in Mind Development and Stress Control for only five dollars. That was the cost of the materials I passed out. My oldest student, Elsie, was 91 years old. Her mind was still clear and focused. About 300 seniors took the Course. It was hard to imagine how beautiful, how attentive and how active these elderly citizens were. They were a shining example to the young ones. And to me!

33. Recapturing The Vision...On Canvas

In 1975, my sister Rose was visiting us here in Michigan. We were all at St. Michael's Parish in Pontiac where I was pastor. With four of us together - Rose, Elizabeth, Tony and myself - we began to reflect on the vision we shared years ago - in 1937, to be exact.

We spent a great deal of time considering the vision. We knew that it belonged to the world beyond. Why did it happen to us? Four kids who could not possibly understand the enormous impact of such a sight? Why did it last almost a full hour, giving us time to seal the vision forever in our memory? Did our future need this experience? We had a lot more questions than answers. What *were* those forms emanating light? Were they souls? Why were some of them ascending and other descending? They were all beautiful. Was there a distinction in color or value? Was that kind of thing going on every day or was it done just for our benefit? Was it a display of Mary's role in the birth and death of the thousands who die and the thousands who are born every day? What was the purpose of it all?

We became excited with the same fervor as when the vision actually took place. After becoming sufficiently motivated by our discussion of that unforgettable experience, we decided to go back to Mt. Elliott Cemetery and re-visit the place where we witnessed the miraculous sight.

When we entered the cemetery, we went immediately to the area near the very same window frame through which we saw that awesome display of heavenly objects ascending and descending. The house we once lived in was apparently abandoned, with the windows gone and the house ready to fall;

it only looked like a skeleton of a home. (As a matter of fact, one month after our visit there the house was completely torn down. It was replaced by grass in a field.)

Standing together on cemetery soil we said a prayer of thanksgiving. Then we prayed for a response. We thought maybe we would experience another vision or perhaps a continuation of the previous one. Nothing happened! We took our time and prayed some more. Nothing! Instead of leaving and calling it a day, one of my sisters suggested that I paint what we saw. I did not think I could do justice to such an awesome task, but I agreed. I went to the car and got a sheet of paper; then we began to remember, each of us, in the most graphic way possible what we recalled. Although this was forty years later, our memories served us well. We were in agreement on almost every item. There was never a disagreement, but some minor details were overlooked by one or the other of us. We left encouraged by the fact that we went back to the spot where it all happened.

I bought a canvas 30 x 40 inches, a good size because there was a lot to put in it. I slowly began to put it together; I did not work on it steadily. I normally paint fast, but I decided every so often to add a few brush strokes. After several months, it was nearly finished. The one thing lacking was the painting of the eyes of the Blessed Lady. How could I do the eyes of such a stunning and overpowering presence? I was up till 2 am one evening. I did the eyes then scratched them out, did them again, and took them out. I just couldn't do it. Finally I left them blank and went to bed somewhat frustrated.

The next evening, I dared to face the challenge once again. When I walked into the room where the painting was, I couldn't believe my eyes. The painting was finished and the eyes of the beautiful lady were done! They were closed and she gave the appearance of looking downward in complete humility. I smiled and said, "Thanks for rescuing me again!"

There's more! Several weeks after the painting was completed and framed, I happened to be reading the story of Our Lady of Fatima. The apparitions of the Mother of Jesus at Fatima are considered authentic by the church. Believe me, it is not easy to get church approval. The investigations to prove authenticity are extremely rigorous and complete to the last detail. The three children, Lucia, Jacinta and Francisco, were playing in the area of the Cova Da Iria when they were suddenly greeted by a Heavenly Lady who was "surrounded by light" and clearly not of this world. She told them to see her on the 13th of each month and on October 13th, there would be a great miracle for all to see. It would also serve as proof of her visitations.

The children faithfully kept their appointments with the Lady at the Cova da Iria. Meantime, the story spread throughout their town and the surrounding villages that the Mother of Jesus was speaking to the three children. Their story was consistent and believable.

Some men in authority, however, did not like the popularity and the attention these visits were receiving. It was ruining their small town, people tramping through their village by the thousands, all the buying and selling and all the rest of it. They decided to detain the children on August 13th. Six days later on August 19th, the Lady appeared to them and inquired why (as if she didn't know) they did not keep their word. The children told her that the authorities held them back on that day. The Lady replied that since they held them back, she will also hold back some of the great miracle on October 13th.

When that day arrived, over 70,000 people showed up - in bad weather, no less! Although it was raining and the ground was wet and slushy, they were told to kneel. The people, expecting a miracle of some sort, were obedient. They knelt in the mud. All of them. The clouds suddenly parted, the rain stopped, the clouds very quickly parted, and the sun left its position and began to move unpredictably, like dancing in the sky. The observers were nearly frightened to death. Then the sun returned to its original position. When the people got up they noticed their clothing was not wet. It was truly a miraculous experience for the villagers and their guests.

While all the people were gazing at the phenomenon in the sky, the children saw what none of the others were aware of. There was a huge image of the Beautiful Lady of Light that took up one third of the sky; on her left was St. Joseph, holding the Child Jesus on one hand; on her right was a cross without a body on it. The three images took up the entire sky.

I was absolutely stunned. I ran into the other room and saw my painting. It was exactly the same thing. It was hard to believe: In 1917, on the Sunday before Ascension Thursday, the three children were visited for the first time by the Mother of Jesus at Fatima. In October of the same year, they, alone, saw the miraculous images in the heavens, and in 1937 - exactly 20 years later - on Ascension Thursday, we four children witnessed the very same thing. It was a thrilling moment...to think that we as children were privileged to see that which was, perhaps, reserved only for the innocent.

A fabulous result did take place after the painting of the vision was completed. Several months afterwards I asked for the *sixth time* what was the meaning of the vision we four children had. Finally, I was given the full meaning with every detail explained. I was totally overwhelmed! It took time to sink into my little mind. I was strictly cautioned about sharing that information publicly; so - what I waited for many years to discover - will have to remain in my heart until I am advised otherwise.

34. Following a Legend - My Response: "Go Pick Somebody Else!"

In the middle seventies, I was elected to be on the Assignment Board for the Archdiocese. While serving on that Committee, Our Lady of Sorrows Parish in Farmington, MI opened up since the Pastor was being named Bishop of another Diocese near Chicago. Both he and the Assignment Board, with the approval of the Cardinal, asked me to accept the position of Pastor at Our Lady of Sorrows Parish. It was one of the wealthiest and largest of all the parishes in the Archdiocese, and it was considered a great honor to be offered such a prestigious assignment. And I was guaranteed ample help.

Somehow, instinctively, I knew that such a role was not in line with my destiny. I only hesitated for a few seconds, and then replied: "Thank you all for the offer, but I'm afraid I will have to decline. As attractive as it is, I don't feel called to move in that direction." There was disappointment expressed since they expected me to jump at the opportunity. But I had to follow the intuitive dictates of my heart. I was simple and direct.

Not long after that incident, in the Spring of 1977, it was announced that the famous Fr. Kern, longtime Pastor of Most Holy Trinity Church, was retiring on July 1 of the same year. He had become a legend. He was stationed at this core inner city parish for 34 years with a reputation of defending people's rights and being a champion of the poor. Whenever there was a demonstration against companies who treated workers badly, for example, the farm workers, or if one of the unions had a confrontation with management or if there was a showdown with the City Council over neighborhood projects, he was there...and outspoken with choice words. Yet he was respected by both management and the work force. He was also well known for having an Open Door Policy at Most Holy Trinity Church. People without an appointment would come to the door asking for help, whether it was for lodging, food, money to turn the gas or electricity back on, or simply hoping for a kind word and a bit of counsel. Fr. Kern let it be known that he wanted the people that no one else wanted. He got them, lots of them.

A poll was taken throughout the State of Michigan around 1975. A cross-section of people from every walk of life were invited to select in their opinion the person who exerted the most influence for good and had the greatest impact on progress in the State. Fr. Kern was number one. Before the Governor, the Mayor of Detroit and even before the Cardinal who was enjoying at that time his greatest popularity. I remember making a statement to Fr. Jim concerning the future of Holy Trinity Church: "I feel sorry for the poor fool who follows Fr. Kern as Pastor of Holy Trinity!" Little did I know who that "poor fool" was going to be.

About a week later, I got a phone call from Bishop Gumbleton, an Auxiliary Bishop of the Archdiocese of Detroit. He stated that I was selected by the Assignment Board to follow Fr. Kern as Pastor of Holy Trinity. I told him I was flattered but I was happy right where I was. He said that I was also the choice of Cardinal Dearden and Fr. Kern himself. Priests usually apply for a parish that is open. The Assignment board then calls in each applicant for an interview in order to decide who would be the best choice for that particular parish. There sometimes could be a half dozen hopeful priests desiring the same position. In the case of Holy Trinity, however, they wanted to hand-pick the new Pastor because of the extraordinary popularity of Fr. Kern. The Archdiocese was uncertain what would happen under such circumstances.

Bishop Gumbleton emphasized the fact that everyone was in agreement that I was the right person for the job. He himself felt God was calling me to follow Fr. Kern.

Allow me to draw a picture of what he was asking of me. In Pontiac, about 25 miles north of downtown Detroit, I had just completed the goals which the staff and I had put together. The parish was in excellent condition whether seen from a financial, social, or spiritual point of view. It was a peaceful little town. There was some crime but nothing compared to Detroit which carried a local and national bad image. And Holy Trinity was located in the heart of the city...six blocks from downtown Detroit. The parish was one big Christian Service Program. The Open Door Policy kept a priest busy all day with people walking in for help. We are talking about hundreds of people each week, many thousands each year. It was unlike any other parish in the Archdiocese of Detroit. Besides, I was well aware that I would be surrendering the image of being a successful Pastor in Pontiac, to become a nobody in the inner city. Not that reputation was so important, but to follow a legend did nothing for one's self-image.

"Anyway," I was saying to the Bishop, "I never make an important decision without making a spiritual retreat."

"Then, make one," he quickly replied.

My favorite setting for a retreat was, and still is, Colombiere, which is not far from Pontiac. It was a former Jesuit Seminary, which closed because of a drastic drop in the number of vocations, but it remained open for retreats and workshops. One wing of the huge building was also reserved as a Rehabilitation Center for employees of large companies who had substance abuse problems. I did make a week's retreat there in order to sort things out and see if I would receive some kind of sign from God as to my direction. I have to say I had always received a message directly from Divine Guidance or by way of my guides. I was never left on my own except one time: to make the final decision to become ordained to the priesthood.

At Colombiere, I meditated every day, prayed, and read portions of Sacred Scripture. Each day I also took time to walk through the fields or follow a path deep into the woods. Everyday I waited for a sign. Nothing happened. I felt absolutely nothing for a whole week! When I returned to the Rectory I called the Bishop. He thought I called to tell him what he expected to hear. It was the opposite. I told him I received no sign whatsoever to go to Most Holy Trinity. So, that was my answer: "I'll stay where I am!" I presumed he would look for another priest to go there, but he completely caught me off guard.

"Make another retreat!" He said with authority.

"Now, wait a minute," I exclaimed. "I am not going to keep making retreats until I finally break down and give in!"

He assured me "You won't have to. Just make one more retreat. If, after that retreat, you still feel that you are not called to go to Holy Trinity, I will never bother you again to go there." I reluctantly agreed to make a second retreat.

While on retreat nothing happened on Monday or Tuesday. The very next day, however, I was walking through the fields behind the Colombiere Retreat House, and then it came. It was an all-encompassing feeling of Divine Presence. I was surrounded by a Power with which I had become familiar. The communication was beyond words, but I knew exactly what was being said to me: that it was in my destiny to become Pastor of Most Holy Trinity. I did not take kindly to that message. In fact, I fought it. "Go, pick somebody else!" I cried. "Why are you choosing me? You're asking an awful lot from me!"

I tried to back out of this appointment. I yelled back, wept, gave every reason not to go there, and talked to God as if we were having a typical argument between a father and a son. I was so upset I even used a small cuss-word at one point. On the part of my Divine Visitor, however, the message remained the same. After a long period of struggle and expending a lot of energy, I finally gave in. I fell to my knees out in the field. My head was bent low, and I whispered the words I said at my ordination to the priesthood: "Adsum." Literally, it meant "I am here!" To me out in a field enveloped by Mother Nature and surrounded by the Lord who gave me life, it meant "I am here to do your Will, O Lord!" I finished my retreat. Each day it became noticeably clearer to me that God would never let me down. I was protected by God's Love and God's Will.

I called the Bishop and told him that I received the message loud and clear. I was now willing to accept the appointment as Pastor of Holy Trinity. He was very happy to hear that but he did not seemed surprised. I told him "I am more surprised than you are! You must have an inside line." He said that he felt all along that it was my calling to go there.

Life at Holy Trinity can best be described as taking one day at a time, changing to "Survival Mode" and living in the continual expectation of the unexpected! "Anything goes," was an appropriate comment. It may sound impossible, but you had to give more than 100 percent, or you would be swept away by the abundance of activity and the unrelenting demands on your time and energy. And much more! As the saying goes, "It will make you or break you!"

I worked very hard at Holy Trinity and had little time for myself. I had the ordinary responsibilities of a Pastor of a parish which was a full time job in itself. Added to that we were in continual financial trouble. The parish itself only produced enough income to stay open for about three weeks. That is a fact! The families did the best they could and I was very proud of them, but it was not enough to support the church for any length of time. This was a far cry from what I had been accustomed to in my other assignments. Trinity School stayed open only because it was subsidized by the CSA (Catholic Services Appeal) an Archdiocesan Fund established to assist schools and other institutions needing help.

Besides facing the ordinary duties of a Pastor, I fully realized that Trinity Parish (the full title is Most Holy Trinity or often it is called Holy Trinity or just plain Trinity) was noted for it's outreach programs to the poor. When I arrived there in 1977, we had about 16,000 persons each year coming for help. That comes to over one thousand per month. When I left there eleven years later, we averaged 30,000-35,000 persons knocking at our door every year.

The social dimension of the Services rendered at Trinity was not possible without a parish setting. It was absolutely necessary to keep the parish open. Fund-raising was essential. Benefactors generously supported the programs, and many volunteers supplied the assistance needed. Every single day of the year there were donations in the mail. There were also several fund-raisers scheduled throughout the year. We tried not to have the same volunteers working on more than one fund-raiser in the same year since we had so many people ready to participate in any way possible. People truly love helping other people when they see results. We were grateful to the Television and Newspaper reporters who did a wonderful job of presenting articles to the public describing our work. The media should be congratulated many times over. What was most impressive to the public was the knowledge that a very small percentage of their donations was needed for administrative costs, and without question the majority of their contributions went directly into the hands of the poor.

One of the most popular and exciting fund-raisers was St. Patrick's Day. The attendance was overwhelming. Regardless of the weather, the Irish and the non-Irish came out. The Cardinal, the Governor, the Mayor, members of the Judiciary, the Attorneys, the Medical Doctors, the television and newspaper personalities, the politicians, the business people, the bag pipers, many priests to concelebrate and families from every walk of life crammed into Holy Trinity Church. Extra chairs filled every space, and the last ones in were standing by the hundreds. It was a sight to see. Those in attendance were in great spirits. They came to have a good time while worshiping the Lord. They also proved to be very generous. Trinity began as an Irish parish in 1834, three years before Michigan became a State. It was the first English-speaking Catholic church in Detroit, had the first electric lighting on Christmas of 1875 and became a temporary hospital when an epidemic broke out in 1834. From the very beginning, Trinity began outreach programs to the less fortunate since the Pastor at that time was also the City's Administrator to the Poor, a forerunner of the Welfare Programs.

Neal Shine, a very popular and well-known newspaper man and as Irish as they come, composed the letter we sent out to benefactors each year announcing St. Patrick's Day. He was also known for his wit. Having a Lebanese Pastor (yours truly) in charge of an Irish parish, he came up with a catchy title for me. I was the "Lebanese Leprechaun!" I liked it and so did the people.

Each week the doctors from Ford Hospital conducted the Medical Clinic located in the school building of Holy Trinity. They followed a schedule along with a few doctors in private practice to offer free medical service to the underprivileged. Those who came for medical assistance could not afford to go to a doctor. The Mother Cabrini Clinic, as it was called, made it possible for the doctors to come to them. After a full day's work at the hospital these dedicated physicians demonstrated a true love and service to others, and their interest and caring for the health of the poor was nothing short of remarkable.

Also, each week, the Attorneys ran the Legal Clinic in the Rectory for those who could not afford legal help. They were champions of justice protecting the rights of their clients and educating them in the various alternatives available to them.

When it comes to legal and medical problems we all depend on the expertise of professional providers. Imagine the profound feeling of helplessness that plagued the poor who could not afford any professional help. Many of them had no income whatsoever, not even from the Welfare Programs. They were the ones often spoken of that "fall through the cracks of Society."

35. Continuing The Miracle...

While still at Holy Trinity, I received a letter from Prince George King. He was the founder of the Aetherius Society and also the Grand Knight of the Mystical Order St. Peter, a world-wide Organization, equivalent to the Knights of England and the Knights of Malta. Prince George has about five or six titles and seven Doctorates he actually earned. The Headquarters of the Society was located in Los Angeles, California. He had heard of my work at Holy Trinity and sent me a personal invitation to be knighted in the Mystical Order of St. Peter at the next Knighting Ceremony. The timing was excellent. The Ceremony was scheduled to take place in the month of October, at the very same time that we have our annual family reunion at the home of my sister Rose who lives in a suburb of Los Angeles. My three sisters, Lillian, Elizabeth, and Jackie, Jackie's husband Craig, my brother Tony and myself all go there each year in October to visit. The whole family attended the Ceremony with me. Jackque Day, a friend from Scottsdale, Arizona, also joined us. The Hall was full.

Prince George was in rare form that afternoon, waxing eloquent with his enlightening message, and relaxing us with a bit of humor. Moments later, he named each person to be knighted to step forward. Then, one by one, he placed the sword over one shoulder then the other as the "knight-to-be" knelt down. Each one would then stand fully knighted. Their name was announced followed by an applause. When it was my turn to come before him, I knelt down just as the other did. He paused, then said, "Stand, Father. As a man of God, you kneel to no one!" Then he put away the sword, and said, "As one of God's chosen, you have no need of a sword." At that point, he placed his hand over one shoulder and then the other. He welcomed me as "Sir Father Jay, Knight of Grace"It was an exciting moment! There were people from Europe as well as some from Australia and other countries which I do not recall. Some already carried a high rank in their respective countries, such as the title of Duke or Prince. One was addressed as "Your Royal Highness." At the same time a few were known for their outstanding service to others. There were Dames and more than one Princess also present.

I am not into titles, but I found it amusing to witness such a gathering. When it was over, my family did not know what to call me. They were jokingly throwing words around such as "Sir Father Doctor Jay," or Doctor and Sir Reverend Father Jay." We all had a good laugh! Even Prince George chuckled when he joined us.

I would not be exaggerating if I said that a book could easily be written about my eleven years at Trinity. Case after case went through our files, and each one would be deserving of attention. Of course, our records were confidential and I would not be able to use names. When I first began my ministry at Trinity, I thought immediately of Damon Runyon and his stories about legendary people living in the questionable area of the city. "Guys and Dolls" is a good example. Not only the poor unfortunate folks from the street were interesting characters, but the staff members, business men and benefactors were equally unforgettable. Fr. Kern is one! He could be seen at any given day at Maxie's Deli, or at Leo Derderian's Anchor Bar or having a chat with Billie Joe Smith an arbitrator for the union. All of these above-mentioned persons were characters in their own right. There have indeed been books written about Fr. Kern, Maxie and Leo. It was interesting that among the four of them was a Catholic, a Jew, an Orthodox Christian and a Baptist. They got along perfectly well and enjoyed continual success with programs for the poor. That was the key that brought them together: caring for the poor and for people with problems. They raised funds by establishing the "Shakedown Society" initiated by Hank Schirmer, another Jewish friend. How did the Shakedown Society work? Simple! Any customer coming into Leo's Anchor Bar was pressed into making a donation to help the less fortunate. In time, they would solicit funds at every opportunity no matter where they were.

Joe Weaver of Channel 2 was interested in Holy Trinity and the many fund raisers arising from a wide variety of sources. He was mostly interested in Fr. Kern and what appeared to be his miraculous projects for the poor. Mr. Weaver researched Fr. Kern's work quite closely. He then put together a truly inspiring documentary made for video about Holy Trinity called "The Miracle of Porter Street." Miracles happened all the time. I can testify to that! It did not take me long to witness enough extraordinary incidents that forced me to say, "Yes, there are miracles. I don't understand them but they happen all the time."

I recall when I faced the problem of our copier breaking down. It wasn't the first time and we were told that it could not be fixed anymore. We had it for a few years and we used it beyond its normal capacity. There were many organizations connected with our work and the poor machine was in use constantly. At the staff meeting it was made clear that I would have to order another copier. I told the staff that I called the same company concerning prices for a new copier. I shared with them that we could get a very reliable one for $2,500. (Back in the early eighties that was a good price.) I added we did not have the money; if we were going to get another one God would have to act very quickly. We prayed on it. The next morning before we actually opened up our offices, the door bell rang. A man shoved a check in my hand and took off. I yelled at him to come back for a moment. I wanted to know his name and what the check was for. He told me names were not important. He said that he was the executor for his grandfather's will and he had $3,000 that was supposed to be given to a good cause. "Holy Trinity popped in my head! I don't even come here; I only heard about this place." He said he was simply following through on the suggestion made to him. Then he was gone. I never saw him again. I immediately thanked the Lord for such a quick response and with interest, no less!

A few days before Thanksgiving in 1986, we ran into another crisis. We were about $2,000 short of what we needed to take care of the Thanksgiving Dinner we put on every year for hundreds of individuals without families and also to deliver some turkeys to families who were in desperate need of one. The people in charge of that project came to me and asked what we were supposed to do about getting the turkeys, vegetables, dessert, etc. I told them confidently that we will have the money by the next morning.

"Do you *have* the money?"

"Not right now, but it will be taken care of," I said, calming their fears. Late that afternoon, three men dressed in fine suits asked to see the Pastor. I had them sit down in my office.

They came right to the point: "Father, we are three businessmen interested in helping some people out for Thanksgiving. Do you need any help at this time?" I sat again in amazement. "Yes," I said slowly so as not to sound too excited. "We need about $2,000."

"It looks like we came just in time!" Within a few minutes they signed a check for the exact amount and were on their way. Thanksgiving was saved.

Just before Christmas, we were again short. We needed two hundred more hams to fill nearly six hundred baskets of food going out to needy families. I asked Sr. Ann Currier, the

Pastoral Minister to go out and get the hams. She said "Where?" I said, "You will know!" She saw that look in my eye..meaning to *go out in faith and the Lord will provide!* She knew exactly what to do. She went out with Clayton Brundage, the Funeral Director and a benefactor of Trinity. They drove down Michigan Avenue, a main street near the Rectory. He had no idea where they were going either. After about ten minutes, she said "Let's go in there!" It was a trucking firm. She wanted to see the man in charge. She was taken into his office by his secretary.

"What can I do for you?"

"I'm Sister Ann and I need 200 hams for Christmas baskets."

This is a trucking firm, Sister, and we don't have anything like that here. Then, as if struck by lightning, he said, "Wait a minute! I know somebody who's in the ham business." He made one phone call, then hung up.

"You will have hundred hams in the morning, Sister." We did!

I know God had a lot of things to take care of, but He always took time to help us out.

One day after a Sunday Mass, I had just finished greeting everyone as they were leaving church. There was one person still standing there. He was waiting for me. He said he needed five dollars. Could I help him out. I reached under my vestments searching for my pocket. I pulled out five singles and gave them to him. He was delighted! He said he really needed the money badly. I started to take my vestments off and I noticed for the first time a business man standing off to the side. He came up to me and said "I saw what you just did."

I replied innocently, "What did you see?"

"You didn't even have time to take off your vestments and you were already helping some one out. I was deeply impressed!" He said with a smile. I didn't know what to say. He reached into his suit coat pocket and pulled out a check book. He wrote out a check right then and there. I started to say thank you as I looked at the check. It was made out for $10,000. The only thing I could say was: "Wow!!"

Sometimes God used the men from the street to help me out. On one particular morning, I was walking through the hallway of the Rectory where the people sit while waiting their turn. We had two rows of old church pews - one on either side of the hallway. That particular morning there were about twenty five men sitting quietly. Then all of a sudden one of the men began swearing at me, at God, at the Church and anything else he could think of. Then he pointed a finger at me and continued using very abusive language. I did not know exactly what to do. In my mind I said a quick prayer for help to make the right decision. I did not want the men to see me back down like a weakling...they would lose confidence in me. I was not sure about throwing him out since it could end up in a fight...which I did not want. I didn't think I should enter a verbal battle with him; he used a lot stronger language than I did. Thanks again for the help that came. One of the men sitting across from the man who was mouthing off, got up and went over to him, took him by the collar, and lifted this 200 pounder with one hand. As he raised him slowly off the bench, he said forcefully: "You don't talk to the Father like that. Now you 'pologize!!!" The tough guy with the abusive words shouted "I apologize! I apologize!" The strong arm of my "champion" let him down slowly as I marveled at his strength. He went back to his place on the bench and there was complete silence...and respect.

I also learned a lot from the clients. One day a lady came in with twelve little children. It looked like she had twins or triplets with every pregnancy. I said "Are all these children yours?"

"No, Father. These six are mine. The others belong to our

neighbors. You see, the mother and father of those children had a big fight. We could hear them clear over to our place. Then they both left in separate cars and were gone. They never came back. I went over to see how the children were doing. They needed to be fed since they were so young. So, I cooked for twelve children instead of six. I don't mind, but after a few days now, I am out of food. Can you help me?"

"Of course," I assured her. Here is a voucher that should cover a good supply of food." The voucher was for perishables, such as milk, cereal, eggs, bread, etc. Besides that, we gave her a couple of boxes of canned goods from our basement supply. I wondered how many families would take in six extra mouths to feed if they were on ADC at the time. She was alone. Even if a husband and wife had sufficient money, I still wondered how many would take in six more children not their own. Obviously, it was impressive to witness her generosity and sense of responsibility. I learned a lot that day. This story had a happy ending when the parents of the children next door returned.

I also gained an important insight about the people who wandered through the streets. Some of them preferred to remain homeless and live on the street. They liked the openness, the lack of responsibilities, the drinking and a feeling of freedom it gave them. One of these persons was - let me call him Patrick Aloysius, rather than his real name - a fine Irishman with a delightful Irish accent. His family was very concerned about him. They called one day from Bloomfield Hills, an exclusive part of town. They wanted to see him and have him come and live with them. We asked him to come to the Rectory on a certain day and time. He did, and so did his family. He went with them a little reluctantly and after a little persuasion.

One month later, in walks Patrick Aloysius! He wanted some money for a drink. I wondered what he was doing back in the inner city. He had left a beautiful place, clean, nicely decorated, three healthy meals daily, a warm bed and a loving family. It was not enough. He said he couldn't stand being walled in. The walls were definitely closing in on him, and he felt like suffocating. He needed the open air to feel like himself again. So he came back with empty pockets, walking the streets for hours, and sleeping on an uncomfortable cot at a mission down the street. We helped him as much as we could. When we accepted him back, he looked at me and thanked me by saying in a beautiful Irish brogue: "Father, ye warm the cockles of me heart!"

There is no doubt that I could fill many more pages with real stories about real people. I believe the ones mentioned should help in understanding a small part of the enormous task that faced us daily at Holy Trinity Church, but also the blessings attached to that kind of service.

36. Finding The Right Doctor

While at Holy Trinity the classes I taught in Mind Development and Stress Control expanded. I taught in the cafeteria and gave the profits to the Open Door Policy of Holy Trinity. Then came a wonderful blessing. It was around the time of Pope John Paul II's Coronation as Pope. The top half of the Michigan Catholic Newspaper had a large picture of the new Pope. The bottom half of the front page was all about the priest who taught a Course in self-improvement, stress control, improved memory, deep meditative experiences, programs for success, sleeping with out pills, and many other benefits. It showed a picture of me teaching a class in the Silva Method. Apparently, many people were impressed with the article. We received more than 600 calls. The man hired to answer the phone and the door at Holy Trinity wanted to quit. He said he had enough with all that nonsense about "that weird course I was teaching." The calls tapered off and he stayed on.

I taught the Silva Method at St. Paul of the Cross Retreat House. They were equipped to handle about eighty people at a time for retreats. They could stretch the number to 100 if it were necessary. I had no idea how many people would be showing up for the Course. That was before Tom Ewald wrote that powerful article in the Michigan Catholic. Half of those who called for information attended the full forty-hour Course at St. Paul's. Three hundred people was way beyond their capacity. But the kind and generous Passionist Fathers were extremely cooperative and patient. The people parked on the grass, all over the road on both sides and crowded in the auditorium which was also the dining room. The Passionist Fathers and their Staff were invited to take the Course without any cost. I certainly owed them that much. Everyone was delighted with the Course. They were mostly Catholic folks responding to a Catholic Newspaper. But a good percentage were not. It didn't matter one iota what one's religion was since it was not a religious course. And everyone wanted to improve their life.

I was asked by the authorities in the Silva Method, including Dr. Jose Silva himself, to become the Director of the Silva Method for the State of Michigan. Ken McCaulley had quit and started a Course of his own. I debated a long time over that decision. With the overwhelming schedule I had at Holy Trinity and using most of my energy just keeping up, I turned it down. I told them I could teach a Course three or four times a year, but not every single month. Also, I was not able to set up a program to train new Lecturers, establish a Book Store, send out Bulletins regularly, etc. and running the Center for the whole State of Michigan, while continuing a very, very full schedule at Holy Trinity. I was afraid of burn out. Nevertheless, to this day I am not sure I made the right decision. I settled for being a Lecturer teaching when I could with no additional responsibilities in the Silva Method.

Occasionally, I had speakers come in and give a talk to the graduates of the Basic Course. They would talk about various subjects, in which they were well versed. One day Frank Johnson called me and said he knew of a doctor - his name was Dr. R. E. Tent, a man I came to respect very highly - who gave exciting lectures on health from a doctor's point of view. So I called him. Dr. Tent said that he would be very happy to address the graduates. We had a most interesting conversation on the phone. He said he could *fix* a few of the people present who needed an adjustment as a demonstration of his work. I was impressed. Then he said, "Don't you want to know me a little better before I give a talk to your people? Do you yourself need anything to be fixed?"

I said "No." Then it occurred to me that I had a sore arm. It was so bad that I could not play racquetball for almost eight months. I jumped in right away: "Yes, I do have something that needs fixing." I related to him how I went over to our Medical Clinic one evening to have the doctor on duty look at it. I was told - and you can guess - to take two aspirins and call him in the morning. There was no improvement. I called and he referred me to a neurologist at Henry Ford Hospital, who took x-rays and treated me for about two weeks without any noticeable improvement. The neurologist referred me to a bone specialist who also checked it out. More x-rays and no success. Both doctors thought I had bursitis. Regardless, nothing positive happened.

Someone told me about Dr. Goodheart who had international fame because he gave credibility to the Science of Kinesiology. I went to his office and he was unable to take me personally because of his overcrowded schedule. One of his Associates treated me. After several treatments, I concluded that he was not helping me at all. Meantime, a friend told me about a Chiropractor on Michigan Avenue. I spent almost three months with that doctor. Nothing happened. Summing it all up, I had seen one General MD Practitioner, two MD Specialists and two Chiropractors to no avail. I told Dr. Tent that I would be willing to see him if he thought he could diagnose what the other doctors could not. His reply surprised me. He said "Straighten out your arm and move it upward as high as you can before it starts hurting." I let him know loud and clear when it began to hurt. "Now move your arm forward as far as it will go without discomfort," he told me. Then I was asked to move it backward. Next, to make a circular motion in both directions with a straight arm. When I was finished, he said he knew exactly was wrong with my arm. He also knew how to remedy it. I couldn't believe what I was hearing!

I replied, "Doctor, you are either the most arrogant man I have ever met, or you are the best doctor I have ever been fortunate enough to meet.

"Come and see." He said, challenging me with confidence.

I kept my appointment. I was placed in one of his rooms waiting to see this bold and unflinching man who would diagnose over the phone without instruments, without having seen me, without x-rays and yet with total self-assurance after five other doctors had previously failed to help me. *This guy's got guts*, I thought. He called for the nurse to bring out my file. On it he had written the two places he was going to adjust. One was on the spine and the other on the joint of the arm itself. After both adjustments, he asked me to move my arm around in different directions. My arm was fine! I could move it freely without discomfort. I stood there in absolute amazement. I mumbled to myself something to the effect that this man was no ordinary doctor.

He then said to me: "Is there anything else that needs attention." After thinking for a moment, I answered, "Well, I have had a thyroid problem for the last twenty five years but I doubt if you could do anything with that." I went on to tell him that on more than one occasion, doctors had given me blood tests and a BMR (Basal Metabolism Rate), verifying their diagnosis. He was undaunted. "Let me check and see." A few moments later he said: "Your thyroids are perfect. You don't have a thyroid problem; you have a iodine problem." The effect was the same but the source of the problem was different. I inquired what that meant. He said they were distracted by the symptoms rather than the cause. It would be necessary to get the body to start doing its own work again. He then asked me to take certain supplements for two weeks and to throw away my thyroid pills. I had to think about it for a moment. That was not easy for me to do, but I ended up trusting him. After all, he had just fixed my arm by diagnosing it from a distance.

Before taking the thyroid pills 25 years ago, I used to go to bed early every evening. The Pastor was getting disgusted as he had to take all evening meetings. I was fast asleep by nine. He said he would personally pay for the doctor's appointment if I went to have my thyroids and energy level checked. Which I did.

After two weeks without my thyroid pills, my energy level became normal. I was suddenly able to go to sleep at any hour and wake up any time I chose to. I still can. Whether it was ten o'clock, midnight or three in the morning it didn't matter. And I could get up at any hour refreshed. And that is still true!

37. Meeting And Hosting a Healing Priest

I have always been interested in the gift of healing. There were several occasions in which God's loving hand brought miraculous healings to someone I was praying for, besides the ones I have included in the autobiography. But I had never met a true healer whose principal work was the healing profession. While at Holy Trinity one of the graduates of the classes I was teaching told me about Fr. Ralph DiOrio, a healing priest from Worcester, Massachusetts. He traveled around the United States and abroad giving Healing Services. Not just spiritual healing but actual physical healings gave strong affirmation to his ministry.

There were three people I knew that needed a healing. One was a deacon, another a priest, and the third, a nun. That pretty well covered the bases! The deacon hurt his back and damaged some vertebrae; he could not straighten his back out in order to stand erect. Doctors examined it with the diagnosis that they would have to do some serious surgery and fuse the vertebrae, in which case his spine would always remain in the same position: stiff and straight. That was not desirable, of course. The priest was very disillusioned by his Community which reprimanded him unjustly. He was also betrayed by the therapist to whom he confided as part of his therapy. The therapist related some serious confidential information to his superiors and caused a great deal of trouble, besides breaking the oath of confidence. The priest became quite distraught and understandably despondent. (I called the therapist and told him I would never send anyone ever to him again. That he was a disgrace to his profession. I had previously sent quite a few clients to him. I kept my word.)

The nun had lost the vision in one eye and the other was beginning to fail. She was advised to begin studying braille; it seemed to be inevitable that she would completely lose her sight in the near future. The three of them had reason to seek a healing. I took it upon myself to drive them to Fr. DiOrio's Healing Service for the weekend. The only problem was that the location was Utica, New York, a good twelve hours away by car. I had a car and I took the time. So I drove them there hoping for a healing. We left early in the morning and arrived just in time for the opening service on a Friday evening. The church was already crowded. The ushers squeezed the nun in on the end of a pew near the front. The three of us were standing in the back.

As the Healing Services progressed, Fr. DiOrio stepped down near the pews and began to touch certain people "as the Holy Spirit directed him" declaring them healed through the power of God. He touched the Sister who came with us; she said nothing to us about whether she was healed or not. I was a little reluctant to ask for fear she would say no. The next morning at breakfast we were all looking at a menu, and she kept staring at it with one eye then the other. We were certainly curious as to what she was doing. Then she said in a grateful and loud voice, "I can see with both eyes!" We realized she did experience a healing that first night. She wasn't sure and did not want to be deceived by her first impression. We continued eating breakfast with happy faces, thanking the Lord and the instrument of his work: Fr. DiOrio. We all got excited that a healing already took place and we only just got there.

We attended Saturday's Service and all went smoothly. It was spiritually gratifying to hear him preach with real gusto and humor and then open up into healing. We were happy we came. And yet the priest and the deacon openly admitted that they

213

felt nothing happened to them. They appeared to be in the same condition as when we arrived.

The Sunday afternoon service was in an auditorium that held about 4,000 people. Fr. DiOrio liked having priests on stage with him. He welcomed the solidarity and brotherhood of priests when he conducted Services. I was therefore one of several priests on stage. After his usual talk about God, healing and prayer, he started to bless the people on stage by lightly touching them on the forehead. When he came to me, I said to myself: "I hope I don't end up on the floor like the others." Many of those touched by Fr. DiOrio fell back, or to use the healing term, "were slain in the Spirit."

"Not me, Lord!" Not in front of 4,000 people staring at us! No sooner had I made my request when I felt a blessing on my forehead and I went down! I couldn't believe it! How could I have fallen back when I did not ask for anything. I was not looking for a healing, nor did I have a special prayer that needed to be answered. I only wanted to remain in control to which I was accustomed. I was caught by someone and gently lowered to the floor of the stage. I decided to get right up like nothing happened. But I couldn't! I could not move a muscle! I thought: "What's going on here? Is this stuff for real?" I thought being slain in the Spirit was only an expression. I wondered if I was becoming paralyzed. Does this condition wear off? I prayed to be able to get up. After a short period of time (which seemed like hours) I regained control and got up. I was grateful! However, just as I was beginning to be in charge again, Fr. DiOrio had just blessed each person on stage and was starting to go down the steps into the auditorium. He stopped as if unexpectedly and walked over toward me. I thought he wanted to tell me something. Instead he touched my forehead again, and down I went for the second time within minutes.

"Now I am really confused" I was mumbling to myself. "I

thought we just went through this! Why on earth did he come and bless me again?" "Some blessing," I smiled. This was a genuine replay. I could not move and I am wondering once again what was happening to me? Then I heard a voice, a distinct voice saying to me, and I'm quoting: "You will be responsible for bringing Fr. DiOrio to Detroit for a Healing Service, my son." I thought to myself: "Good grief! Now I'm in this thing over my head! And getting worse! Moments later, I was in full command again and got up with more questions than answers going around in my head. Everything was moving so quickly afterwards that I did not have time to reflect on the "stage experience" again.

After Services the four of us went directly to the hotel packed, and were on our way home. We all felt good. We had one healing out of three. Not a bad average. But surprises never end. About half way home, the deacon asked me if we could stop for a moment. I looked around then said, "There is no rest area in sight." He replied, "I know, but I have something else in mind." We stopped by the side of the road. He got out, moved his back in each direction, and shouted excitedly out there in the middle of nowhere: "It's true! My back if fine. No pain, and I feel great!" He was almost doing a new dance step. He said he was feeling something going on in the spinal area, energy bouncing back and forth. He could move his spine in a limited way without pain inside the car, but he had to know if a real physical healing took place. We were all happy for him. He even requested to drive which he could not possibly have done before. I was delighted. I was getting very tired. Not more than a half an hour went by; to everyone's surprise, the priest friend took out a harmonica from his pocket and started playing songs we all knew. I had no idea he played the harmonica. We sang for hours. He said that he never felt better in years.

We finally understood what Fr. DiOrio meant when he said

that sometimes the healing begins at the Services but does not actually take visible or physical effect until later...even after we have completely returned home. I thanked the Lord many times for taking care of these wonderful friends who had embraced the religious life of service to others. They, in turn, continued their ministries that brought God's love and peace to the people they served.

Two months later, on the Sunday closest to December 12th, we celebrated the Feast of Our Lady of Guadalupe. On the southwest side of Detroit the pastors took turns having the celebration in their respective churches. Hispanics from all over the Archdiocese usually filled the church. The lot fell to me that year as the homilist for the Spanish Mass. It was Archbishop Szoka's first attendance at the annual Guadalupe Celebration. After Mass we were in the cafeteria of Holy Trinity. I was sitting next to the Archbishop. In the middle of our conversation, he suddenly changed the subject. "What do you know about Fr. Ralph DiOrio?" He questioned me.

"It's interesting that you should ask," I replied. "I met him personally in October and witnessed some physical healings of people I knew well. I believe he is authentic." Continuing my line of thought, I asked why he was interested.

"There is a group who wishes to bring him here for a Healing Service and I am looking for a priest to be in charge of this project. Will you do it?"

My first mental response was to say "No. I have enough to do. Find somebody else!" Just then, I remembered the words spoken to me while I was lying flat on my back in Utica, New York - that I would be responsible for bringing Fr. DiOrio to Detroit. "Yes, I will do it, Archbishop! Thanks for asking me." This came after a long pause. I had no idea just how popular Fr. DiOrio was. There were many volunteers who came out of nowhere to help. I called Worcester, MA and spoke personally with him. He was delighted to add Michigan to his long list of States in which he was invited to present his Healing Services.

I was trying to be honest about this whole matter. I had never met an authentic healer. True, I was present when miraculous cures and events took place. But a true healer. I didn't think there were any. The Television healers never impressed me as authentic and I had never witnessed a *real physical healing* at a service conducted by one. That is, until I met Fr. DiOrio. I placed a lot of trust in him. There were about twelve thousand people waiting for him at Joe Louis Arena. If he turned out to be a phony, my own name would be associated with him and I would carry the image of being "very gullible, naive, and easily deceived." Not to mention being the laughing stock of my priestly colleagues. Nevertheless, I had seen him in action. He was the real thing!

Being prayerful was one of his greatest qualities. It was my first clue to a clearer understanding of the make-up of a genuine healer. He prayed for hours. Nor would he eat anything all day in preparation for a Healing Service. I was deeply impressed that he was far in advance of myself in the area of discipline. His Healing Services flowed naturally from his way of life, his deep spirituality. His life work of healing was founded on a theology that placed the entire responsibility and source of his success on his relationship to the Holy Spirit: if he was true to his convictions and lived accordingly, the Spirit was active and effective. This I witnessed many times. More prayer and greater preparation resulted in a more striking demonstration of God's power at work.

I was at his side throughout his stay in Detroit. Together we had arranged his busy schedule. Besides the big arena downtown, there was the Mother House of several Religious Communities, and Sacred Heart Seminary in which fellow priests were invited. To that one even the Cardinal attended. I

217

admired this man who could stand up in front of about one hundred priests and preach a theology of healing, and then expect miracles to happen. It was not a great accomplishment to convince his audiences that they were all spiritually healed if that was their desire. But to witness a physical healing was truly astonishing.

While at Seminary, he said, without actually looking up, that one of the priests on his left was about to be healed of a leg and foot problem.

"Would you please stand up"? He asked. No one stood up.

"You are a little on the heavy side, wearing glasses and over in this section" he said while pointing in a specific direction.

No one stood up.

"You wear an insert in one of your shoes. You are about to be healed. Please stand!" Only after priests near the man he was describing pointed to him and said he was the one, did one of the Detroit priests stand up.

"Why didn't you get up earlier?"

"I didn't think you meant me" he said humbly.

"I am really stepping out in faith here considering I am in the presence of so many brother priests." Then he asked the priest in question, Fr. Don Devine, if he would please come forward where everyone could see him. He did. Then the healing priest asked him to take off his shoes and socks. He had him sit on one chair with his feet over another chair. The feet were now side by side and there was no doubt that the one foot was about two inches shorter than the other.

"Is the insert removable?"

"Yes" he replied and took it out showing everyone how big it was.

Fr. DiOrio then asked all the priests to gather around the two of them so they could get a better view.

He asked him again just to be sure. "How long did you have

this problem of one leg being shorter than the other?"

"All my life. I was born with it. I have been to many doctors, chiropractors, specialists and nothing came of it." He went on explaining that there was no adjustment or surgery that could make both legs the same length. Only a miracle could do that!

Fr. DiOrio prayed over him then slowly took both hands and gently pulled on the shorter of the two legs. Our eyes opened wide as we actually saw that leg grow another two inches. They were now both even. The Cardinal stood the closest to them with the best view. There was a hush that pervaded the chapel. We as priests were witnessing the unique ministry of a fellow priest healing another priest. Fr. DiOrio, as always, never took credit for the healings. It was the Spirit that worked through him, directed him, and gave him the courage *to do the impossible.* I felt a tear rolling down my cheek. He *was* real! The priests who came were not disappointed. There were other healings but the above was the most memorable.

At the Joe Louis Arena when Fr. DiOrio asked - rather, he shouted - how many had hearing problems, it looked like about two hundred hands went up. Then he prayed for them all that their ears would be open to the gift of hearing. When he later asked how many felt they were healed, about half of them raised their hands, smiling and nodding briskly.

I saw several people walk out of wheel chairs and others throw away their braces around their neck. A friend of mine from Livonia threw away his cane - which he always used and needed for walking - and never needed one again.

A young boy named Joey was about five years old; he could not stand on his own since both his legs were impaired. His mother explained the disease he had, but I don't recall the name of it at this moment. The healing priest asked Joey if he would like to be healed. Of course he answered in the affirmative. Father then prayed over him. He said to Joey: "You can walk if you wish!" Which he did. Then he told Joey that he could run, too! Joey ran back and forth down the hall way at Holy Trinity with a lively step.

Fr. DiOrio asked Joey who healed him. "You did!" he answered quickly.

"Who did?" You did!

"Come on, Joey. Who did?"

"God did!" This young lad was learning the Theology of Healing at a very early age.

There have been books written about the healing priest, Fr. Ralph DiOrio. He has been on national television several times on different stations. He made three separate visits to the Detroit area. The Archbishop put me in charge and I was pleased that the Lord allowed me to be a part of such a rewarding ministry. It all began when I took the three friends to Utica for them to experience a possible healing. In the end, I too experienced the miraculous power of the Almighty, actively present in the world. My faith was strengthened many times over and my mind was healed of doubt. My previous mystical experiences were re-affirmed; the Divine Presence became more of a reality than ever before.

Meeting Fr. Ralph was an unforgettable blessing that brought much light to me along the path of life.

38. Restoring Holy Trinity

Quite by accident, the responsibility of repairing and restoring the Holy Trinity church building fell on my shoulders. Certain situations forced my hand. One day, just before the organist went up into the choir loft to play, a huge chunk of plaster fell right on the bench. It would have killed him instantly. Naturally, he was reluctant to play the organ until the ceiling was repaired. We understood without question. That part of the ceiling was taken care of right away. The repaired area held up well but other pieces began to fall. Four more pieces of plaster fell on four separate occasions.

Even before pieces of plaster fell from the ceiling, another serious incident was caused by fumes that came right through the floor under the altar. I usually had people come up and stand around the altar during the daily Mass. On that particular day, a young boy about six years old passed out. He was struggling to breathe. Right away, a couple of men attending Mass wasted no time in carrying him out outside. While they were gone, others felt woozy and complained of feeling nauseous. Then I, too, was at a point of staggering. I held onto the altar just to remain on my feet. Then I edged my way to the nearest chair. It finally occurred to us that fumes coming through the floor was the culprit. It was checked out! The cause: The fumes had leaked from one of the pipes just below the altar.

It gets worse! I'll never forget what happened shortly after a Holy Day Mass when the church was filled with all the students from school: A large piece of plaster, weighing about twenty pounds fell on one of the pews in church. It was close to being a terrible near-tragedy since the plaster fell just minutes after three little children left that exact spot. It would have killed at least one of them if it fell a little sooner. It was a frightening experience. We naturally cordoned off that area and also the other areas where pieces had fallen from the ceiling.

Then came the fire. Sr. Ann Currier, the Pastoral Minister, woke me up one morning long before Mass time. It was obvious that a crisis had come up. There was panic in her voice. "The church is on fire! You better come down right away!" I was dressed and in church as quickly as possible! The entire church proper was filled with smoke. It was also apparent that the source of the smoke was the church basement. Everything was affected by the fumes and smoke: the vestments in the sacristy, the walls, the ceiling, the altar and the paintings throughout the church. An original and very dry wooden beam in the basement became overheated and combustion caused it to burn producing an unbelievable amount of smoke. There was no structural damage. Remembering the fire at St. Boniface and the Diocesan Policy concerning fires, I immediately notified the Archdiocese about the damage and the possibility of insurance coverage.

The Insurance Company responded promptly dry-cleaning all vestments, and gave sufficient money to have the walls discolored by smoke painted over. The Insurance Company also did an impressive job of cleaning up the entire church and repairing any damage in the church basement. While they were making a thorough investigation of the safety conditions in the basement, they also discovered that the balcony was supported by three small two by four wooden beams. That was all!!! They informed me that the entire balcony could collapse at any time.

Presuming that the beams would hold as they had for over a hundred years, and since we could not get those small two by fours replaced with strong metal beams until after March 17th, St. Patrick's Day, we went ahead with the annual celebration.

Every space in church was jammed with people on that day. While the festive mood continued throughout that morning until the Mass in honor of St. Patrick was over, I prayed very hard that the balcony would sustain the tremendous weight of an exceptionally large crowd. When the Mass was over without incident and everyone had left the church, I gave special thanks to the Lord. The replacement of the original tiny beams were taken care of as soon as possible.

With a bad record of disastrous events taking place in the church and in the church basement, we were told to have Masses in the cafeteria until the repair work was completed. The church building became officially closed indefinitely. We began a bold fund-raising program that would exceed one million dollars. Coming from a small inner city Parish in the heart of Detroit, that was an aggressive move. Half the money came from Governor Jim Blanchard and from Mayor Coleman Young. They used State and City funds to handle the expenses in front of the church, since Holy Trinity was a historically-designated church and desperately needed some beautification.

Another portion of the income came from the fire. That became the seed money for the painting of the church interior. Then we appealed to every benefactor of Holy Trinity. We were doing quite well. However, the expenses kept increasing and we fell short about $300,000. We received a loan from Archbishop Szoka on behalf of the Archdiocese and agreed to pay it back in six years with interest. I had the backing of some wealthy friends and thousands of supporters from every class of Society. We were confident of achieving our goal of paying it off on schedule.

We had the momentum that turns projects into success. The pieces were all in place. We were in the middle of renovation of the church and beginning to put into action the huge project of reconstructing the entire frontage of the church. However, a serious interruption took place. While all this was going on, conditions in my life had changed.

39. More Health Problems -
A New Assignment

Nothing lasts in this world, especially good health. After about eight or nine years I began to have health problems. It all started when I went to our Mother Cabrini Medical Clinic to be checked by one of the doctors. On duty that evening was Dr. Bruce Steinhauer, chief of Staff at Henry Ford Hospital. I felt a cold coming on and I wanted to get some antibiotics or whatever so it would not get worse. The doctor kept checking my chest and my back over and over. Then he looked at me very seriously and said, "I want you to go right now to Henry Ford Hospital. I want someone else to drive you and there will be a wheelchair waiting for you!" That certainly took me by surprise. I asked what was wrong. "Your heart is fibrillating and I want to take an EKG and we don't have the equipment here, of course." At the hospital, everything happened as he said. He took the EKG which verified his diagnosis.

I then confessed to him that not long before that I passed out twice in the middle of the night. I went to the bathroom and I suddenly went unconscious. I am not sure how much time elapsed. I got up and passed out again. My face was battered from each fall. My lip was swollen, my cheek stuck out and I had a black eye. When I said Mass the next morning I could not convince the congregation that I fell unconscious without a fight. They all felt sorry for me; how could anyone beat up their loving Pastor? I was unable to change their mind.

Dr. Steinhauer then set up an appointment to have me come to his office the following Monday for a complete check-up. He had a private practice in Grosse Point. He saw me more than once that week, giving me another EKG. As part of his observations, he had me wear a monitor for twenty-four hours. By the end of the week, after many tests and observations, he concluded that, apart from the atrial fibrillation of the heart, I was in fairly good health. However, he was not sure why I passed out. He recommended that I see a cardiologist. He gave me the name of a good cardiologist at Ford Hospital. I was not sure of my next move.

Meanwhile, I was praying for direction. I kept getting the same answer: "Go see Dr. Tent!" Since he was not a specialist in that field, I was doubtful that I was receiving the right suggestion. But I called him anyway. I had nothing to lose. After being examined by Dr. Tent in one session, he concluded that he knew exactly what was wrong with me and that he could correct both problems completely within three months.

"Both?" I said. He diagnosed the atrial fibrillation and also a failure of my adrenalin glands to "kick in", causing me to pass out a couple of times. I trusted Dr. Tent, since he had already helped me with other health problems. He gave me certain supplements again.

I asked him how these supplements know where to go in the body and perform a particular task.

I did not expect the answer he gave me. "The supplements were all natural and organic."

"Meaning what?" I inquired.

"That they are alive and know precisely where to go." That shook me up a little when he said they were "alive"! Then I remembered that tomatoes and cucumbers, grapes and other vegetables and fruits are also alive when we eat them. And are highly recommended compared to certain synthetic and artificial medications produced entirely in a laboratory - with their horrible side effects to the body.

Every three weeks I went back to his office to check on my progress. I was right on schedule in the process of recovering.

By the end of the three months, the last check-up indicated that I was in excellent health, with both conditions corrected. I was now ready to stay at Holy Trinity for many more years. The Bishop of the region knew of my prior health problems and so did the Archbishop recently elevated to the title: *Cardinal*. In spite of my recovery in health, the Cardinal Archbishop of Detroit made a decision that was carved in stone. He said I would be leaving Holy Trinity on July 1. It was 1988. In his estimation, it was time to put another man in there. He assured me that I had done my share and did it well; it was time to let some other young men pursue the challenges and unending responsibilities of Holy Trinity. I could not change his mind. Even the piles of petitions on his desk to keep me there and the many letters and phone calls from persons in high places did not dissuade him.

I had previously learned to put a lot of trust in dreams. When a person prays before going to bed and sincerely asking for Divine Guidance it is given, as the Master stated: "Ask and you shall receive." With that in mind, I asked for a dream to give me a sense of direction in this matter. That night I had a very vivid dream. I was singing with Neil Diamond. We were singing buddies; I had an arm over his shoulder and he had an arm over mine. We were singing words to the melody of one of his songs. The words were slightly changed to: "Goodbye my friend..." We were standing in front of Holy trinity Church and looking at it while we sang those words over and over. I slowly became aware of the fact that I was now awake and still singing "Goodbye my friend". It was so real. I looked around me. I then realized that the dream was answering my question - the time had come to leave Holy Trinity and to say goodbye. I had a second dream when I went back to sleep that same night. I was at Holy Trinity and suddenly the church changed into another building, as if I did not belong there. The second dream

227

confirmed the first one. At that point it became clear to me that it would be useless fighting to stay at Holy Trinity. I asked for Divine Guidance and I got it.

It was heart-rending to leave the place I had embraced so totally and to be separate from the work and the people with whom I had become so familiar. I had a multitude of friends: the people who came for help, a very dedicated staff, the generous and friendly benefactors, the Hispanic community: an important part of my priestly ministry, the brother priests in the vicariate, the many friends in the news media, the legendary Max Silk and Leo Derderian, the faithful Doctors and Lawyers who operated the Medical and Legal Clinics week after week, the countless volunteers for the annual fund-raisers, the Guadalupe Society, and about 30 different organizations in the downtown area. It is difficult to name them all.

But the time had come to say "Goodbye my friend..."

40. My Last Pastorate -
Artistic Skills Re-Surface

I dreaded starting all over. I was fifty eight years old when the call came to provide Pastoral leadership to another community. Life at St. Michael's in Monroe began with a culture shock. The very first Sunday Mass I said shocked me when I looked over the congregation and saw only white people. At Holy Trinity, I was used to a variety of color and culture with a congregation made up of Maltese, Puerto Rican, Native American, Mexican and African...all Americans living on the same soil, and together, forming a beautiful flower of gorgeous colors. I was proud to add an olive skin color to that flower through my Lebanese heritage. The initial shock of being in an all-white community wore off rather quickly and I was pleased to serve them as members of the parish family placed under my spiritual care.

I was totally amazed to discover that there were seventy-five churches in that little town of 25,000 people, about 15,000 of them belonging to the five Catholic churches and the other 10,000 being divided among the other seventy churches. The remark I often made about having so many churches in the same town was that "There were no atheists in Monroe." St. Michael's Church was by far the most beautiful church in Monroe. I don't think anyone who has visited the interior of St. Michael's would disagree with that statement. We even had Protestant couples come to the Rectory in the hopes that they could marry in St. Michael's.

At least on two occasions, I saw the Pastor of a neighboring Catholic church, which had just been recently renovated at a very high cost, entering St. Michael's church. He had gotten the key from the secretary. I was curious about it; so I decided to go over to church and welcome him. I had to ask what was a Pastor of a wealthier and bigger congregation doing at St. Michael's. He replied, "I wanted to show these friends the most beautiful church in Monroe." Coming from him, that was quite a compliment, especially since we had not yet begun the re-painting of the interior of the church.

Behind the church, was the famous River Raisin often mentioned in the history books when speaking of General Custer's temporary residence in Monroe. A fence blocked a full view of the river. The fence was mainly built to protect the children playing in the parking lot area at lunch hour. St. Michael's School had all eight grades plus kindergarten.

The fence also attracted my sisters to Monroe. Whenever they came down to Monroe to visit or attend Mass, they were always accompanied by plastic bags. There were many grape vines winding around the fence. My sisters would pick as many grape leaves as possible. With them they cooked one of the most popular dishes in the Middle East. The grape leaves are stuffed with ground lamb and rice. They are about the size of a cigar, and very tasty. The leaves have a distinct, exciting taste since they grow on a vine that is *sterile*. The grapes are very tiny and not edible. The energy and nutrition, therefore, go into the leaf instead of the grape. I always joined my sisters in the great art of grape leaf picking and for a very practical reason: The more we picked, the more we ate!

After picking grape leaves in the proper season for several years, the fun of grape-leaf picking came to an abrupt stop. I had to inform my sisters, my brother and brother-in law that the young folks had volunteered to clean up the fence area and several of them caught poison ivy. The ivy intermingled with the grape vines and contact with one easily included contact with the other. Their parents were a little upset, but we had no idea that the growth along the fence contained poison ivy. The kids touching them with their bare hands broke out. The persons in charge of that project realized only too late that it was a mistake to have anyone working around shrubs and vines without wearing proper gloves for protection.

While I was adjusting myself to a new life style in Monroe, I realized that I had more time. The days were about the same - quite busy - but the nights seemed longer. Many evenings after about 9:00 pm I was absolutely free to relax.

I could watch television, read, talk to parishioners, play the piano or go to bed early. I tried every one of those in the beginning. I even started working jigsaw puzzles. Compared to the hectic race that was continuous at Holy Trinity, this was actually pleasant. To my total surprise, occasionally there were some afternoons with no appointments at all. Previously, only my day off was free of schedules.

Having a little more time and being away from the city in the midst of Mother Nature, I started feeling something artistic re-awaken within me. I used to do oil painting about eleven or twelve years prior to this time. While at Holy Trinity I simply did not have that much spare energy to include painting. I loved what I was doing but the work was debilitating. At St. Michael's, the desire to get back to painting was enhanced greatly when one day, by chance, I happened to see Bob Ross producing a beautiful painting on TV. It only took him half an hour. This was impressive.

I began to follow this creative line of thought until one day I simply "broke out" and bought some art equipment. (I had given all my art supplies away when I went to Holy Trinity.) All I needed now was an art studio. I wanted a place where I could leave my easel up and my paints right where I left them. At St. Michael's I found such a room. No one had any use for that room but myself. It was perfect.

231

At St. Michael's, Monroe, there was plenty of room. The Parish House consisted of three floors, besides the basement, and I lived alone in this huge mansion. When I got there, I saw a great opportunity to finally have a place for my hundreds of books...the third floor. Some of my friends came down to help me paint the walls that were blackened with time and disuse. The result was a practical use of the four rooms on the third floor - untouched by anyone and never visited because it lacked beauty, electricity and heat. The rooms soon received names: one was my library, of course; another was the chapel; the third was the storage room. The fourth room remained open for some future purpose. When I started painting again, there was no doubt about the future of that room: I actually had my own art studio once again. And the room was perfect as a studio. The sun seemed to rise on one side of the room and set on the other. That gave me ample natural light. At night there was still poor lighting. My maintenance man, Jim, who could fix or build almost anything put in florescent lighting and added heat to the third floor. I was on my way...

I liked what I was doing. It felt good to have a brush in my hand again. Pretty soon I was on a roll. I was painting regularly - almost every evening. Sometimes I would be at it during the wee hours of the night - nonstop! Some evenings, only when my eyes got so heavy that I could no longer distinguish colors and lost all focus, did I give up. I did not like to leave a painting unfinished. I enjoyed the completion of a picture; it was a real accomplishment to me. I also had to see what it looked like in a frame already. I had empty frames nearby, just in case. Sometimes, I even painted a picture with pre-conceived dimensions, so that it would fit into a frame I happened to have ready. Normally, one would not start with a *frame*. Beginning with the *subject* or *content* would seem more appropriate. I am aware that my procedure was sometimes awkward or even backwards - but what could you expect from a person who never took lessons?

Two years after arriving in Monroe, Michigan, I experienced an example of serendipity (in which something desirable or fortunate happens *by accident*.) That is the only way to express this phenomenon. I attended the customary brunch with the eighth grade graduates of St. Michael's near the end of the school year. The students were bold and optimistic inviting the Mayor of Monroe, Sam Mignano, and the Most Rev. W. Joseph Schoenherr, Bishop of the Region that included Monroe County. I was shocked when they both showed up! As a matter of fact, I sat between the both of them. During the meal, the mayor turned to me and inquired what my lapel pin meant. It was the picture of an artist's palette. Before I was able to answer, Bishop Schoenherr chimed in "Fr. Jay is quite an artist. You should see some of his work while you're here." I did not expect the bishop to remember such details. But it started the ball rolling...the mayor became anxious to see my paintings.

After a healthy brunch with the graduates we made our way over to the rectory. When we got to the third floor the mayor's eyes were wide open. He said he could not believe what he saw. From that perspective, I couldn't either. The walls of the studio were covered with paintings. I mean everywhere. You had to take it on faith that there was a wall behind all those paintings. The chapel was also covered with paintings. Above the books in the library, paintings were in abundance. Even the storage room - a most unlikely place - had its share of paintings.

The mayor expressed amazement at the wide variety of subjects, the varied styles, technique and medium used. There were paintings of flowers, mountains, trees and rivers, paintings of people, paintings that were impressionistic, others with a flavor of modern art and still others with a metaphysical or religious message. Some were done in oil or acrylic others in watercolor, airbrush or pastel.

"Did you do all these?" he asked sincerely.

I knew by the tone of his voice he was not kidding. "Yes, everyone of them." I said simply.

"Are you aware that we have an Art Exhibit at the City Hall every year? Artists come from all over to display their magnificent work. I would like to have your art works on exhibit at the City Hall," he said excitedly.

I thanked him, but I timidly questioned having my work on display and being compared to all those established artists.

"I am not talking about you being *part* of an exhibit. I mean a one-man Art Exhibit!"

I didn't know what to say. I looked around the room and for the first time I realized just how prolific I had become. I had no idea how many paintings I had done in such a short time. When I arrived in Monroe, I had brought a few with me that I had kept through the years. The rest I had given away as gifts. Up until that time I believe I gave away at least fifty paintings. I never sold them. Was the mayor talking about an exhibit in which people would come with the intention of purchasing a painting? I didn't think so; feeling sure about that, I did not ask him.

A few days later I received a phone call from Dan Rowe, an Art Critic for the Monroe Guardian, a local newspaper. He wanted to set up an appointment for an interview concerning my art work. The mayor obviously followed through on his word even to the point of arranging the interview. Mr. Rowe, too, was amazed at the volume of paintings. He looked carefully at each one then made a comment about my style of painting. I often wondered if I had one!

"What kind of style do I have?" I was interested to know. He said he would classify me as a neo-impressionist.

"That's nice to know." I said as I smiled. "What does *that* mean?" I was sincere in asking that question. I really did not know! He asked me if I were painting buttons on a shirt, would I just dab a spot every few inches on the shirt and call them buttons? Or would I carefully make a circle and paint the holes for the thread? I quickly responded by saying that I would go "boom, boom and boom." Each boom meaning a dab and let the viewer's eye finish off the button. He said firmly "That's what a neo-impressionist is!" What an interesting surprise! After all these years of producing pictures on canvas, I finally found out that I had a specific style of painting in the world of art. I presumed he was correct.

Because of the newspaper article, word got around rather quickly that there was a priest who also paints. The interest was a lot greater than I thought it would be. Whatever were their reasons, being a priest and being an artist at the same time was apparently a rare concept in the minds of many people. They learned something about priestly life: that priests conduct worship services, preach, teach, pray and are popular community leaders, but they also have hobbies. Check the golf courses on Wednesdays and you see a lot of golfers who laid aside their Roman collars for a few hours. Priests have hobbies of every sort: skiing, racquetball, hockey, swimming, traveling, etc. They also have skills. One priest in the Detroit area is also a sculptor, and a good one! Some are accomplished musicians and attorneys.

My poor secretary was glued to her desk. The phone was ringing almost continuously. "Where exactly are you located?

"Is Father going to sell his paintings at the exhibit?"

"What is the price range of the paintings?"

"How many days will you keep the paintings in the City Hall?"

"Does Father Jay do portraits?" The questions varied with every person. I had never seriously thought about having my paintings up for sale while I was in the process of painting. I simply wished to express my feelings on canvas. It was a good feeling. Each painting was like a *child of the mind* or like a *meditation* in solid form. I was not sure I wanted to have them sold, or you might say, "adopted" by others, never to see them again. But after considering the fortuitous opportunity being presented to me, I decided to put a price on the paintings.

I had no idea where to begin. What was a painting by an unknown priest worth on the open market? Getting help was the answer. I consulted some friends who had previous experience in putting a price on paintings as well as on other goods. Two of these ladies were also artists. I thought the price range they were suggesting was too high. None of them agreed with me, and so, majority ruled. After all, it was offered as a fund-raising project for the Church. I was willing to give up any personal profit. I informed the parish that I would merely hold back sufficient funds to cover the expenses of my materials. Still, a painting has to have practical value to sell at the prices posted.

The Art Exhibit began with a dramatic flourish. The City Hall rarely had so many people attending an exhibit - and rarer still, to have so many of them from out of town. I had a few helpers sitting at a desk ready to handle the money. There were *two important things* we did not plan on. *First,* if people purchased paintings the first hour, the first day, then there would no longer be any paintings left for the Art Exhibit itself. Conclusion: they could not take the painting the day they bought it. Not everyone was happy with that arrangement but we insisted on keeping the painting for the entire week. Upon completion of the exhibit, they could be picked up at the rectory. The *second* problem became known to us only when the mayor himself whispered to me that buying or selling the paintings was forbidden in the City Hall.

"Whoops! No one told me about that!" I said surprised. "Can we put - let's say - a red tag with a number on a painting just to have someone claim it and pay for it later? Also, to let others know that it is no longer for sale?" He thought it was all right, as long as there was no indication of price or sale, and no money was handled in the building itself. I learned another lesson!

By the end of the first day, about eighty percent of the paintings were tagged as sold. By noon the second day they were all tagged. From the moment we were enlightened concerning actual purchases in the City Hall, there were no signs of sales whatsoever. However, by the end of the week, it was quite a project hauling the paintings (all framed and heavy) over to the rectory. The first floor was lined with paintings leaning against every wall of every room; then, came the job of finding the right one when a buyer came to collect. There was only one mix up in which two people received each other's painting. It was eventually straightened out. Not a bad average!

I was happy to see the children from St. Michael's School come to the exhibit. They were able to see their pastor in a new light and also have a taste of something cultural. There were over one hundred paintings on display. A few of them were not for sale - the ones that were personal to me either as a mandala (which is a painting expressing one's personal belief) or as a religious painting born out of meditation. The exhibit was far more successful than I could ever have imagined.

After the exhibit, I did not stop painting. After a few years, it was shocking to see the walls all covered again. Paintings were everywhere! Not just on the third floor, but also on all the floors and in every room. In 1995, I said to myself: "I believe it's time for another Art Exhibit," This time I had the exhibit in St. Michael's Parish Hall. It was larger and more convenient. The paintings could be carried over to the hall by hand, instead of by car. And some of them were big. Help came from everywhere. The owners of the Craft 2000 Art Store let me borrow their unused stands to hold up the paintings. Some artist friends loaned me their easels and display stands. Another volunteer was in charge of live flowers to be placed in strategic places throughout the hall. I decided not to extend the exhibit for five days, as before. Just four hours should do it. From noon to 4 pm on a Sunday afternoon, just one week before I retired. For one thing, I was packing all week and I would be much too busy to handle both projects.

A very nice article was again placed in the local newspaper after another personal interview. Many people told me they were waiting a long time for this one. The article sparked an even wider interest. The Detroit News must have read the article and wanted to have an interview with me. The interest was growing. Then Channel 2, seeing the article in the Detroit News, called about offering a "special interest story" on television about "the priest who paints." By noon on Sunday, the day of the exhibit, the entire parking lot was filled and all the streets surrounding the parish were lined with cars. We had several volunteers controlling the inflow of people at the door, so as to avoid a stampede. I had one hundred and fifteen original paintings - all framed, as before - and about three hundred prints made. The prints were included so that everyone in attendance could at least afford to make a small purchase - easily within their budget. Almost every painting and print were sold. Some folks were quite disappointed that they did not come early enough that day to get an original painting. They asked if I would do a commissioned painting for them. I hadn't thought of that! Once I agreed, others made requests as well. The orders started to come in! I ended up with thirty five commissions for additional paintings. I was astounded! I never dreamed I would have that kind of success as an artist (and with no lessons.)

By accepting the commissions for more paintings, I set myself up unwittingly for a busy first year of retirement. Especially since I promised to complete them before the end of the year, that is, within a six month period! True to form, I waited until the middle of October before I began the commissioned works. They were all done by Christmas of 1995. Paintings are sometimes called *works* of art. Well, to do thirty five original paintings in less than eight weeks *is* work! I should be more careful in the future.

At this second Art Exhibit, one of the ladies brought a friend with her. The friend wore a beautiful hat and a business suit. She was studying the paintings closely. No wonder! She worked at one of Art Galleries in a wealthy northern suburb of Detroit and was also an art critic, as she later shared with me. I thought: "Well, now I'm in trouble. An art critic. That's all I need! I kept moving away from her, but as luck would have it, she and I were suddenly facing one another. I blurted out: "Okay, give it to me straight! How do you rate my paintings? I'm a big boy! I can handle it!"

"What art school did you attend?" She inquired.

"I never took lessons anywhere." I said softly with a sense of defeat in my voice. I believed in that very moment I was ruined. She would recognize me as a phony, an imposter!

She then replied with a statement that put my fears to rest. "Don't ever take lessons!"

"I hope you mean what I think you mean..."

"Absolutely! You have a freshness and an originality that stands on its own. Your works unveil without reserve a free and creative spirit; lessons could limit that sense of freedom and creativity." She continued explaining that the purpose of art lessons is to teach techniques which, at that point in my life, could be confining.

I felt a sense of honor by *not* taking lessons. (Please don't misunderstand! I would still recommend lessons for anyone learning to paint.)

41. From Commissioner To Cardiologist

While still in Monroe, some forty miles from Detroit, I received a phone call from Governor Jim Blanchard's office. I was being offered a position on the Judicial Tenure Commission for the State of Michigan. Talk about an honor...I was overwhelmed! Imagine a Catholic priest being a member of a Commission that sits in judgement of judges, with respect to their behavior and conduct while serving on the bench. My principal comment to that appointment before accepting, was that I did not know the Laws of the State. In fact I knew very little about the whole court system, the Judiciary Department, and the complicated world of legal matters. I would hardly add any expertise to a Commission of judges and lawyers. How could my opinion be of any use in the world of Law?

It was precisely because of my unfamiliarity with the Law that I was selected. Also, my knowledge of moral law would be very helpful. The Judicial Tenure Commission did not handle lawsuits, civil suits or criminal offense. What came under our jurisdiction was the conduct of a judge, the abuse of power on the bench, the crude treatment of a litigant, partiality, favoritism, bigotry, a possible drinking problem, an unreasonable backup in the resolution of cases or using language unbecoming of a judge...to name a few. We did not have the authority to reprimand, remove from the bench, demand a rehabilitation program, etc. We sent recommendations to the Supreme Court of Michigan which made such decisions. Because of that important point, Cardinal Szoka not only permitted me to sit on that Commission but was in favor of it. Priests, having a strong background in philosophy, theology and morality, could throw much light on a situation regarding behavior and proper conduct. However, if I were involved in the actual *decision*, instead of recommending an opinion to the Supreme Court, I would have been denied permission as a priest to serve in that role.

The reason was clear! I was not the official theologian of the Archdiocese of Detroit or the Vatican, for that matter. I could not therefore speak on behalf of the church in decisions concerning, birth control, abortion, euthanasia, capital punishment and other delicate moral issues.

I filled the vacancy left by Rabbi Groner who was promoted by his authorities to a higher position, demanding more out-of-State work. I had to take an oath of office as any civil servant and completed the last year of his three year term. Compared to the other Commissioners, I was considered a "layman" on the Judicial Tenure Commission. I hadn't thought of myself as a layman for many years, going back to 1955 when I became a clergyman. Dr. Marjorie Peebles-Meyers, M.D. was also on the Commission and referred to a "lay person". We were both directly appointed by the Governor. There were two attorneys elected by their colleagues throughout the State of Michigan: John Abbott, Dean Emeritus of the Detroit College of Law, and F. Philip Colista, Esq. They were really sharp and kept us all alert with their outstanding knowledge of the Law.

The other five were judges, elected also by their respective peer groups: The Honorable Thomas J. Foley and the Honorable Hilda R. Gage, both representing the Circuit court, the Honorable Harold Hood of the Court of Appeals, the Honorable Barry M. Grant, Probate Judge, and the Honorable James R. McCann, a District Court Judge. These were some of the finest persons I had ever met in my life. They were, of course, well-versed in the Law and also the fine points of the Law. If we were only discussing the Law in each case, Dr. Peebles-Myers and I would have no chance by a longshot to add anything to the conversation. However, since doctors and clergy are as well-informed as anyone concerning ethics, proper behavior and conduct, we had some equally practical comments to offer.

There were about five to six hundred complaints against Michigan Judges each year. That sounds like a lot, but when you consider the thousands of cases brought before the bench each year, the percentage is low. And it is even much lower when you realize that the Judicial Tenure Commission dismissed about ninety percent as having no substance. I do not wish to discuss in detail any specifics since our work was confidential except what is written in the Public Record. As expected, poor losers, angry losers often complain that the hearing was unfair, that the judge was prejudiced, wasn't listening to their side, was "paid off", has a personal interest, or likes a pretty face, etc. with no evidence whatsoever coming from any other person present who also witnessed the whole thing. Even their own attorneys would disagree with them, admitting there was no basis for misconduct.

On the other hand, about ten percent or less of the cases did catch our attention. We would look at the complaint from every angle. We always did our homework before dismissing a case, giving the complainant, whose rights may have been violated, the benefit of the doubt. Which also means that judges have rights, too. We gave the judges in question as fair an evaluation as possible so that we could make an honest and proper recommendation. Since litigants and judges both have rights, we sometimes got into a hot discussion over whose rights were violated in a particular case. Every so often, unfortunately, we had to recommend that a particular judge who had been reprimanded previously on several occasions for the same legitimate complaints, step down. If he or she cooperated with the Commission and received approval by proper authority that the basis of the misconduct was completely corrected, we would recommend reinstating the judge on the bench. If correction was not assured, then the Supreme Court would remove the judge permanently.

I learned a lot about the proceedings that take place in a courtroom. It was an education but I also helped by making a contribution toward the achievement of justice and a fairer outcome for all concerned. I therefore decided to remain on the Judicial Tenure Commission for another three years when I got the call to stay on. After about a year I was nominated by the other members as Secretary of the Commission.

After serving on the Commission for about four years, I was again approached by the Governor's Office to renew my position for another three years. That was a difficult decision to make. I started having some of the same health problems once again. I was getting sick regularly, feeling exhausted most of the time, and still driving back and forth from Monroe to Detroit more and more frequently for meetings. On top of that, I had to read through ten or more cases a week on legal size paper in order to submit my pre-vote concerning the latest complaints against the judges. Some cases were more than twenty pages. At the same time, I was carrying on with a daily crowded schedule of activities in the administration of both the Parish Community and the school. Being the only priest in charge of over one thousand families and responsible for a school with grades K through eight, I, like many other priests, was beginning to experience the first stages of "burn out". It was very uncomfortable to ask *not* to renew my appointment on the Judicial Tenure Commission. I was never a quitter, and I tended to be a work-a-holic. But my health was becoming less capable of keeping up with the workload.

My personal evaluation of the health condition was soon verified. I was accustomed to giving blood every six months.

The Red Cross usually chose a different location each time, and, on this particular occasion, St. Michael's School was the place. That was certainly convenient. All I had to do was walk from the rectory to the school. I knew many people in line waiting to give blood. They were proud to see their pastor get in line too. However, the "Master Plan" had changed! The nurse gave me the required examination of my blood pressure and pulse, then made a shocking statement. "Father, we can't take your blood today."

I quickly countered with "Why not? I've been giving blood for years without a problem."

"Your blood pressure, your heartbeat and your pulse are all irregular."

"I demand a second opinion!" I said defiantly.

"Fine!" She said. "Go see the other nurse."

I did. She said the same thing, adding, "Father, you had better go see a doctor right away!"

I called Dr. Songco, a parishioner of St. Michael's. I asked if he could give me an EKG as soon as possible. "Come on over," he replied. He set me up immediately and took the EKG.

"The nurses were right" he concluded. "Your heart is fibrillating badly. I strongly recommend that you see a cardiologist. I can arrange for you to see one in Toledo."

It was strange that I felt nothing, no discomfort in the heart area and not aware of any fibrillation. From my point of view, my heart beat felt normal. So, I had to ask: "Just how serious was it? What if I refused to see a cardiologist? Was this a serious matter?"

"It depends on what you consider serious. You could easily have a blood clot while it's fibrillating, or you could..."

"Okay, you made your point!" I thanked him for suggesting a particular cardiologist in Toledo, but that I preferred to go to Henry Ford Hospital in Detroit. I knew a lot of doctors who volunteered their services at the Cabrini Medical Clinic of Holy Trinity while I was pastor. I would chat with them every week. I called one of the doctors I knew well and asked if he could put me in contact with one of the top men in the Cardiology Department.

Dr. Michael Lesch was the chosen one. He was very kind and encouraging. My blood pressure was exceptionally high which he believed caused the atrial fibrillation of the heart. The pressure placed on a pastor was multiplied enormously with the shortage of priests in our time. Almost all priests are in agreement about the pressures and stressful situations they experience compared to the past. When Dr. Lesch considered my age, my extremely high blood pressure, the twenty-five years I spent in the inner city of Detroit, and twice having trouble with the heart valve, he recommended the possibility of retirement. I was stunned! "Me retire?!! No way! The normal age to begin retirement in the priesthood in this Archdiocese is seventy." I was only sixty-three at the time!

He asked me to think about it. Then he revealed that he was the personal physician of Cardinal Bernardin in Chicago before he came to Henry Ford Hospital in Detroit. He had a lot of experience taking care of priests with heart problems. Along with many other people, professional and otherwise, he thought priests worked too long. Judging by the fact that - as of this writing - ten classmates have already gone to their reward, and a surprising number of priest friends also died well before the age of seventy, I thought very seriously about my future: "With my poor health, will I ever *see* seventy years of age?"

The cardiologist thought my condition was *hereditary* since I did not appear to be hyper or overly nervous. In fact, when I followed Fr. Kern - a legend in his own time - at Holy Trinity, everyone was eyeing me closely to see how I would hold up under such a challenge. The famous Episcopal Bishop McGee

246

when asked about such a difficult appointment, said, "Fr. Jay is *grace under pressure*." I took that as a great compliment, coming from such a notable person. It was true I rarely panicked unless the situation was totally unbearable with no alternatives.

When I shared the information with my brother and sisters about taking the medication the cardiologist prescribed, their response literally shocked me. My oldest sister Lillian said "I've been taking medication like that for years." My sister Billie added: "I'm taking the same thing!" Tony said pretty much the same. Then I remembered that both of my parents died with heart conditions. My sister Jenny died right on the operating table while they were performing open heart surgery; my sister Marie expired in the middle of a sentence. An aneurism took her that quickly. Cancer was not in our bloodline; heart conditions seemed to dominate. Not that it mattered a lot. Both were equal as *tickets to eternity*.

A retreat was almost necessary. I had to get away and think about that whole situation. I had come to another *turning point* in my life. I had done nothing deliberately to create the conditions in which I found myself. Prayer and reflection would bring me to the truth of what was happening to me. Back to Colombiere, northeast of Detroit. Walking outdoors in those fields alone under an open sky was for me the perfect place to meet God. And I am not drawing comparisons with other places to pray, such as in church or even at home in my private, sacred place. In that instance, I needed *space*. I prayed for several days, asking for the kind of Guidance that pertained to my destiny. I returned with a decision.

During my next appointment with the cardiologist, I related to him what I concluded at the end of my retreat. "I wish to wait two more years. At that time I will be ready. I am definitely not ready right now. I have too many things in the fire, too many loose ends."

He said "It was important to retire when you are ready; otherwise it was, replying with an Italian phrase, 'il bacio di morte'!" I happened to be familiar enough with Italian to know that it meant "the kiss of death," which referred to the contract of death, sealed with a kiss just as Judas did centuries ago. The doctor went on to explain how many workers who retire before their time - either by being bought off, bumped by another, or talked into it - die rather soon after retirement...that is, if they don't have any hobbies or a *life* outside of work! I assured him that I have a lot of hobbies to keep me busy.

I went through the whole process of preparing for retirement: writing a series of letters back and forth with the Archdiocese about the possibility of retiring - I needed permission and approval - and meeting with my superior, Cardinal Maida, in person, with two letters in my hand from the cardiologists. He was very gracious and understanding. Then I had to inform the Parish Family of St. Michael's in Monroe where I had served for seven years and had come to love as my own family. After that came the slow and quite painful meeting with groups and individuals I had worked closely with about my leaving in the near future. First and foremost was my secretary, Rita Marino, who was all that any pastor could ask for regarding efficiency, competence, cooperation and an abundance of patience. There was the rest of the staff, the parish council, the commissions, the committees and so many individual parishioners who were deeply involved in parish activities - both as co-workers and friends - with a firm resolve to accomplish our parish goals and dedicated to preserve the Parish community.

It was a bit heartrending to say goodbye to my friends and to retire from my principal work which was the focus of my life for the last forty years. There was help from everywhere. I needed it. My last Mass at St. Michael's as pastor saw a very crowded church with parishioners and with friends from the past, many of whom I had not seen for years. Naturally, there were mixed feelings of great joy and sorrow. Priests are human beings who come from human families. They have the same emotions and feelings as anyone. They hurt when they must leave a congregation which they had endeared to themselves in ministry. I was assigned to nine different parishes in my active ministry of the priesthood. And I am one who dislikes "Goodbyes." Believe me, it never gets easier. The older we get, the more we appreciate family ties and friendships. With age comes a natural change in values, and the values, more often than not, include others. We become more interested in the person rather than appearances.

My heart, even till this day - two years after I retired - is filled with love and gratitude for all those wonderful people with whom I had the privilege to cross paths. Since I do not believe in "accidents," I am sure the many thousands whom I addressed from the pulpit throughout the years were meant to hear me speak about spiritual laws, spiritual values and our spiritual destiny. I hope I have given them the right message. I spoke only from my convictions, right or wrong. It's dangerous in a way; we become responsible for persons, animals or anything, for that matter, which we have touched, loved or influenced. The thought occurred to me: those are the very words the fox said to the prince in Exupery's classical story of The Little Prince. The fox said: "You are responsible for that which you have loved." He was referring to the rose which the little prince was watering and protecting from the elements.

Except for Divine Providence once again, I would not have lived to retire at all. About six months before I officially retired, I drove to St. Vincent's Hospital down in Toledo, Ohio, to visit a parishioner. After conferring the Last Rites, I was on my way back to Monroe. I took the road called "125" and was just south of Alexis road. When I arrived at the crossing, there were a few cars lined up waiting for a train to go by. I followed suit and drove up behind the last car. I was not even there for ten or fifteen seconds when suddenly I distinctly heard a loud voice yell, "Get out of that lane immediately!!!" I swerved over into the lane nearest the sidewalk (which I did not see previously.) As soon as I made it to the other lane, I heard the most horrible noise. I thought it was an explosion. A van smashed directly into the last car where I was parked just moments ago, hitting it with the full force of its velocity and weight. The van was obviously speeding, and turned the small mid-size car into an accordion. I was frozen for a moment! That was exactly where I was. I could have been killed instantly, or permanently injured, paralyzed or what have you. Many thoughts raced through my mind. When I recovered and focused on the situation, I called the police with my car phone.

As I was getting out of my car, I heard someone yelling that the driver of the van got out and was running away - across an empty field. Two other men started chasing him. I ran, too, but by the time I caught up with them, they had grabbed him by the arms and were bringing him back to the scene of the accident. Just then the police arrived and took over. There must have been a police car in the vicinity...they were there so fast. I told one of the officers that I would serve as a witness if necessary. I still did not have a chance to see just how much damage and injury took place. I started to look inside the squashed car that was hit with the full impact when the police told me to move my car immediately. I was blocking a long line of traffic and the train was gone. As I was walking to my car, I could easily see that all four cars in the other lane were damaged. The one in front was pushed forward to within inches of the oncoming train. They must have been frightened to death. I still do not know if the two people in the last car died or miraculously survived.

On my way home, I had thoughts racing through my mind how I was incredibly spared a very possible instant death or serious disabling injury. Someone was watching over me...and got my attention. I had just come from giving the Last Rites to someone else. I almost needed the Last Rites myself, except for a heavenly warning. If someone was in charge of keeping me alive to fulfill my destiny, I certainly have kept that guardian very busy. Death was knocking at my door several times that I know of, but it wasn't time. I continue to thank God every morning upon awakening.

The message is that I still have some work to do. The future will always be mysterious. I have the strangest feeling that this book is one of the reasons I have been spared so many times. I am not even sure what that means. I don't know why my story would be better than anyone else's. There are billions of people on the earth today, approaching the twenty first century...and they are *all* exciting! Perhaps there are people who wonder what goes on in the mind of a Roman Catholic priest; he lives in this world but he is spiritually motivated and driven by his conviction that the world of spirit is a very real world. So much so that his priestly life of sacrifice and service would have no meaning and would even appear insane if indeed there were no afterlife awaiting us.

42. The Testimony of Personal Experience

LIFE'S greatest teacher is personal experience. What we experience, is *real* to us! Whether we interpret the experience correctly or not, it is real. It really happened! If I broke my arm and it is in a cast for six months, I would affirm without the slightest doubt that it happened to me. If I did not pay my taxes one particular year and the IRS got on my case and added a penalty to my payment, I would not forget it because it was real. The same is true with a mystical experience. If I am awakened during the night and I am greeted with an extraordinary experience of lights or a voice or a being of light or even a nightmare or a thunderstorm - regardless of the nature, I would remember it as a reality, that is recorded by my senses, whether it is a good or a bad memory.

I am not referring to a situation in which a person has a documented history of hallucinating either because of taking drugs or is out of touch with reality. Or someone victimized by mental illness. In such cases, what is experienced as *real* to the person, exists only in one's mind.

On the other hand, people from every walk of life - professional or uneducated, male or female, young or old, people from every race, creed or culture - claim to have extraordinary experiences, such as a *near-death experience*. They appear on the monitor as brain-dead and then come back into their body after being told it was not their time to leave the earth. I read in two different articles that literally millions worldwide are having such an experience.

Speaking of credibility, one's background and lifestyle have a lot to do with it. Lourdes in France is visited by more than five million people each year, the result of a heavenly visit to Bernadette Soubirous, a rather uneducated young lady who was as innocent as a young child. She was told that the visitor was the Immaculate Conception. Bernadette did not know what either word meant. Only after water gushed out of an area where there was no water, and only after proven and authentic healings took place as a result of being washed in the "miraculous" waters of Lourdes, was she believed. The life she led afterwards until her death was perfectly consistent with the life of a saint. And after years of investigation concerning every aspect of her life she was indeed canonized a Saint in the Catholic Church.

Mother Teresa is well known throughout the world as an example of a saintly life. I heard her give a talk in person on two different occasions and I was deeply impressed with her unwavering faith and also with her *continuous communication* with God. She attributes *nothing* to herself. It is *God* who has empowered her to accomplish such marvelous and extraordinary deeds. On both occasions I spoke with Mother Teresa afterwards. Those moments represent a couple of highlights in my life.

Neither one of these saintly women were prone to "hear voices" that led them down an unreal path. Rather, the life they led and their accomplishments gave authenticity to their mystical experiences.

We can add many names to that list. Dr. Martin Luther King was a powerful religious leader who raised his followers to a level of equality, freedom and pride...far beyond their previous self-image as a race. He is revered also as a saintly person who was martyred for the cause of righteousness and truth. He spoke of being up "on the mountain" where God dwells. His belief of being led by Divine Guidance is universally acceptable because of his sincerity, his accomplishments and his lifestyle.

I pray that my lifestyle has been consistent with the mystical experiences, the miraculous healings and the most unexpected gift of Divine Guidance I have received or witnessed since my childhood. Was I just *lucky* to be in the right place at the right time? I doubt it. The *extraordinary* happened too often. And I attribute none of them to myself. My whole life has gone in a direction I never planned. I simply wanted to do God's will and to fulfill my purpose for being here, with the help of the Holy Spirit.

If I followed my own instincts and went through life without ever having the benefit of the spiritual Guidance I have presented here, I would have probably led an ordinary life, had an ordinary job, married a wonderful girl, had children and be a retired grandpa today. That, of course, was not my destiny in this life. The path I chose - and was encouraged to follow - began when I changed from the school of my choice, which was St. Joseph High School in downtown Detroit, to Sacred Heart Seminary.

I had said that *personal experience* is the greatest teacher. In my seminary and post-seminary academic career, we learned a great deal about other people's experience. We did not own it, we did not claim it, we did not live it. It was part of the curriculum. We did make a deep study of the philosophy and theology of St. Thomas Aquinas. He was an original thinker. His works are prolific and awesome. In fact, he held the enviable position as the official theologian of the church from the thirteenth century up to and including most of the twentieth century. He was good, very good! His theology was literally the foundation of our belief system. For over seven hundred years we relied on the same material. There was only one problem; there were no alternatives! Aquinas and a few other theologians compatible to him were presented to us.

As a matter of interest, Aquinas, at one point, wanted to burn all his works. He considered them as "straw" compared to the mystical experiences he had later in life. The truth of his personal encounter with the Lord of Truth made his works appear totally unsatisfactory to him. He was, however, prevented from destroying his many volumes. What he thought was *straw* was still enlightenment to the rest of the world.

My quest was to become a priest. I wanted to serve God in priestly Ministry. My goal kept me on course. But I had many doubts along the way. After all, I had twelve years to make up my mind. Part of our training was not to rock the boat. It would be dangerous and rebellious! Discipline was absolutely necessary to run a Major and Minor Seminary with about five hundred students at that time. Being a seminary, there was also the additional importance of insisting on conformity to Catholic Teaching. Naturally! We were eventually going to be the ones to teach and preach the Catholic System to others.

I kept the rules and kept my mouth shut. My doubts would surface in almost every aspect of seminary education, from an abundance of traditional and/or *obsolete* regulations in Canon Law, to the incredible *power* and *grace* of the Sacraments, or from the fixed Dogma of belief to an enormously complicated pattern of behavior expressed in Moral Theology, or even to the very understanding of God. (Did St. Thomas Aquinas become aware of a totally different view of who God is after having his mystical experiences? I think *yes*!) Did I object to anything taught us? Of course not! Ask questions for the sake of clarity? Yes, very carefully and with reservation. Did I share my concerns with my classmates? Rarely! And very much in private. I did not know if they had similar doubts. We inherited a concrete, systematic thought system of a church that had withstood opposition and argumentation, schism and religious division for two thousand years. It had gone through many periods of self-examination through its General Councils.

Two Councils stand out in modern times. In 1545, the Council of Trent was convened, following the founding of the

Lutheran Church by Martin Luther, a Catholic priest, and the separation from Rome by Henry VIII, enforcing the practice of the Anglican Faith throughout England.

Then came the Vatican Council II which began in 1963, seven years after I was ordained. It was refreshing and exciting. It was also necessary! As Pope John XXIII stated, "Let's open the window and let some fresh air in!" It was time for another self-examination of Catholic belief, practices and policies. This time it was done in the presence of religious leaders of many denominations. It was bold. No other religion has ever done this before or after! The Catholic Church came out of the Middle Ages! And just in time! The *window* was open and massive changes began. Deep feelings and silent convictions emerged all over the entire Catholic world. Questions locked for many years within the heart were being addressed and some issues were resolved...but raised other *larger* questions. A case in point: as a by-product of the Council, the centuries-old policy of a celibate priesthood suddenly became ajar! Thousands of clergy and religious left the active ministry...and with the blessing of the church! Some did not wait nor even cared for such a blessing. At the time we called it a *brain drain*. Some of the finest minds in the church chose another profession and the married state. I, for one, thought seriously of leaving the active ministry in the early sixties. However, many of my doubts were resolved with the Vatican Council Documents, and I was given spiritual encouragement by my guides. However, I cannot deny that *there are still some serious questions that are untouched.* But I still believe my choice to remain in the active ministry of the priesthood is the right one!

Nevertheless, the Vatican Council was a noble effort, the phenomenal attempt to update a church with about one billion members world-wide! The updating, unfortunately, is still being trickled down to the total membership. Some areas in the world are still in the pre-Vatican mind set. In some cases, only the changes that are convenient have been implemented. We see the same principle in the minds of some of our older generation who prefer the *good old days*, but they would never give up their *television sets* or *car* or *air conditioning*! Being selective has always been an open option.

43. The Path Is Lined With Surprises

In 1970, I was amazed at the prophetic aspect of my dream life. One of my most vivid dreams concerned eight of my classmates, who were also my closest friends. We spent our days-off together each week, either skiing or golfing or playing racquetball, depending on the season. Our annual vacations were usually spent together as well. In the dream, we were walking on a long dock at the end of which there was a huge ship about to launch out to sea. I kept urging my buddies to hurry along or we would miss the ship.

They shrugged their shoulders as if to say "Stop worrying, Jay; we'll get there when we get there."

I tripped over a can. I said "Come on, hurry!" I then fell over a barrel; then there were pieces of glass to walk around; next, there were a few banana peelings to get by. There was a continuous array of obstacles to discourage me or at least to slow me down. But I didn't! Finally I got to the dock and the ship began to pull out. I leaped and barely reached a stairway a few feet from the dock. There were many steps that led right to the main deck of the ship. By the time the ship was about one hundred feet from the dock, my buddies showed up. I said, "I *told* you guys to hurry!" They simply shrugged their shoulders again and showed no real concern about not being on the ship. I woke up.

At that period of my life, I was recording my dreams faithfully. I remembered them almost every night. Sometimes I had two or three dreams in a single night. I was becoming quite competent in the interpretation of my dreams - with the help of my guides, of course. I learned to interpret dreams sufficiently on my own after a while. I would then check with my guides to see if I was drawing the right conclusion. In almost every case I was correct - or at least partially correct. In the beginning, I had no idea how to interpret dreams. I did not realize that there were often several levels of interpretation.

With regard to the above dream, as soon as I recorded it in my Dream Journal, I immediately wrote down what I thought was the meaning of the dream. To me, the meaning was simple and clear: I got on a ship which went off into the sunset. Therefore, I was the one leaving the priesthood. I was struggling to get on that ship, boarded it and went away...into another life, another career. Not a bad interpretation, but it didn't happen that way. All eight of my classmates standing on the dock left the active ministry of the priesthood within two years of the dream. This came as a complete shock to me since none of them spoke of leaving at that time. At least not to me. I remained in the active ministry, totally surprised. My guides cautioned me about making a hasty interpretation of my dreams. So I continued to check with them, but *only after* I first tried to interpret the dreams myself. I wanted to become totally independent of my guides, which I believe I eventually did achieve. That was their goal as well! Sometime afterwards, I was giving entire weekend workshops on the interpretation of dreams. I spoke from years of experience.

I do not wish to give the impression that by staying in the active priesthood I find myself in a superior position than my classmates. There is no better or worse. We are *not competing* in the unfolding of life. In my opinion, the major premise of serving God and fulfilling our purpose on earth remains the same for myself as well as for my colleagues. There are many channels of service to others: through the priesthood and religious life or through marriage, widowhood or the single life. *All are equally valid.* What is essential is the dedication and commitment in the application of service.

Though I remained in the active ministry, there were certain unexpected events that helped to change my values and my spiritual direction. My mother played an important role in opening my eyes to see things differently. At the end of college we received our B.A. Degree; we majored in philosophy and minored in English. As "philosophers", at least in our own minds, we were being given profound and important knowledge passed on through the ages. Also, we were being prepared to answer even the most difficult questions people in the world might have.

Besides our academic background part of our religious training was to make a directed retreat every year. During the retreat, the priest was giving us an example of the length of time spent in hell. This was not considered doctrine, but merely an example of the everlasting fires and eternal suffering for the poor souls sent there. The retreat-master said that if a bird were to take a bite out of a large mountain every hundred years and place that morsel in another area and keep taking a bite from that mountain every hundred years until after millions and millions of years the entire mountain was moved to another place...you might call that *the beginning of hell*. He literally scared the hell out of us! One mortal sin, one action against what the church calls a serious sin would separate us from God for all eternity. Eat meat on Friday, miss a day reading the Breviary (official prayers of the church), miss Mass on a Sunday, break the fasting laws during Lent, and you are doomed to an eternity of hellfire and damnation, never to see God or enjoy heaven. There was no hope!

During the next visit home, I was relating these ugly facts of hell to my mother and a couple of my sisters about what that retreat master said, not really to scare them, but to share with them some important facts every Catholic should know. My mother didn't buy it! She disagreed completely. I said, "How can you disagree?" We learned this in the seminary, and the church teaches the eternity of hell.

My mother replied with perfect logic: "God is our Divine Parent. I'm a parent, too! I would never be happy without my children with me. Since God's love is greater and more perfect than ours, I don't believe for a minute that God would be happy either. If there is some suffering after death, it can't possibly be forever. No parent would allow that to happen...especially not God!"

She shook my belief system to its very foundations. I neither denied or affirmed what she said. But her response raised a lot of questions in my mind. And the more I thought about it, the more I sided with her argument. My mother often spoke with great wisdom. I marveled at her perception of reality which, of course, was born out of the experience of life. After all, she only completed the third grade in school. (Her parents moved a lot between Lebanon, Canada and the United States when she was a child. Going to school was almost impossible.) My mother demonstrated an unshakeable faith and a common sense attitude. I am happy to say that much of it rubbed off on me. Her opinion about hell and other issues helped me to think more freely, regardless of what we were being taught in the seminary.

Another incident that helped me to seriously question our seminary training occurred several years after I was ordained. I was on retreat at St. Paul of the Cross Retreat House with several classmates and many other fellow priests. The retreat master, Fr. Eugene VanAntwerp, happened to be the Rector (or President) of St. John's Major Seminary in Plymouth, Michigan, where I spent my last four years of study before ordination. He spoke about some of the more recent changes in seminary life: radical changes in curriculum, more freedom in the seminary and more free time away from the seminary. All of that was new to us. Except for vacations at Christmas and Easter, we were more or less confined to the boundaries of the seminary.

At one point, Fr. VanAntwerp paused and opened the floor for questions. I could not hold back. I had to raise my hand and ask if St. Thomas Aquinas was still taught as the principal source of theology in the Major Seminary. I expected a "yes" answer.

"St. Who?" he shouted emphatically! I was sitting with several classmates. We all looked at each other, puzzled and confused, mumbling to each other:

"Does that mean that what we learned is now obsolete?"

"Are Hegel, Kirkegaarde, and Descarte, to name a few, now the good guys?"

"Where do you draw the line?"

What else did they throw out?"

"Sounds like we need an update!"

The foundation of my convictions received another wave of tremors. *"Perhaps there is no absolute truth, after all!"* I thought to myself. It was about this time that I began to meditate every night for many years seeking some answers about the nature of God, the essence of truth, my future path and the fulfilment of my purpose.

I shall continue to pray, meditate, say Mass daily and serve others in priestly ministry in my retirement - for as long as I am able.

Even so, I continue also to have deja vu experiences or visions of a past life, especially when traveling to other parts of the world. Something seems to open up to what I can only call *a warp in time* in which the past or future is going on right now. Suddenly what is happening is *timeless*.

For example, when traveling in Germany, I was conducting a tour of Europe with 26 other people. I went as a Spiritual Director. While going down the Rhine River on a boat, I decided to go outside and take pictures of some truly gorgeous scenes. When I finished with my camera, I sat down and was taking it all in, so to speak. It was breathtaking!

All of a sudden I began to see what looked like fireflies, little sparks of light jumping around. I thought *How can I see fireflies on a bright sunny day?* Then the *lights* started to form a circle in the sky, a large circle. A very clear picture appeared in the circle, very much like a television screen. It was a farm scene in which a mother and father and their two children - a boy and a girl about twelve or thirteen years old - were binding up wheat, beautiful golden wheat, and stacking them on a flat-top wagon drawn by horses. The man, *with whom I identified* - did the heavy lifting of the bales of wheat while the children pushed them close together in an orderly fashion. The mother was sitting down holding the reins of the horses.

They were speaking German and I understood every word (Although at that time I did not know a word of German except perhaps *auf wiedersehen.*) Soon the wheat was ready to take to the river to be sold to a man waiting on a barge. The area was near the place called Lorelei. When they came to the river, I could see that it was exactly the same place in the vision as on the ground. The two images were the same. Money was exchanged for the wheat. The family returned home to share a nice warm meal. A large kettle was over the fireplace...and the stew was ready. I could even *smell* it as the stew was placed in bowls. The children were chatting in German about the work they just finished and about school.

I was taken by surprise when Al Schlicht (of happy memory), one of the passengers on the tour, came up to me and shouted "What are you doing out here?" I said, "Al, what do you see in the sky?" as I pointed to the middle of the picture.

He replied, "Clouds and blue sky."

"I am seeing something else. I wish I could share it with

you." The scenario lasted about a half a hour.

Shortly after that experience, we docked. I then surprised everyone, including myself. I knelt down and kissed the ground, then went to the nearest tree and hugged it. They thought I was happy to be on land again. That I was afraid of the boat ride. Not quite! What really happened was that I felt a tremendous sense of freedom. I am sorry to admit this, but as a kid during the World War II, I hated the Nazis, Germans included and the German language. They killed so many Americans that I thought they were all evil. I never wanted to learn German, although I had a choice to learn it in the seminary. As I was hugging the tree something inside of me was saying "You will be back to Germany and you will be learning German." *No way!* I thought.

Our next stop was Rome. We happened to be there for the Canonization of the first American born Saint: Elizabeth Ann Seton. As Americans, we had seats right up front. The day before, some of our group invited three German ladies on a holiday, to join us. They were from Munich, and only one of them spoke English. I managed to get them tickets to sit with us. They were so delighted that they took me out to dinner after the Canonization, and invited me to come to Munich.

After returning home, I received a couple of letters again asking me to visit them in Munich. I finally said I would. I took a ten-lesson course in German with Berlitz, and made the trip. In the two weeks, I picked up a lot of German words. Then, after my third trip to Germany, I was speaking German almost fluently. I had to! The one elderly lady who spoke English had moved to New York. The other two did not know any English.

One of the husbands spoke Spanish. (He sold plane parts in El Salvador.) Whenever I got stuck, especially on the first trip, he helped me out. Thank goodness for Fritz. The whole family seemed embarrassed when I first arrived; they would not walk with me in public. They would stay behind or in front of me but not with me. Fritz explained that night. "You look like a Turk!" I said "So What!" He explained that after the war in which Germany had lost about five million men, German authorities were desperately looking for men from other countries. Many Turks came, and they multiplied and multiplied. Soon they were all over the place and a bitter resentment grew among the German people. I happened to have a moustache at that time and with my dark skin and black hair, I looked just like one of them.

For the sake of getting along, I shaved the moustache off that night and all was well.

I had other scenarios take place in my travels besides the one in Germany: one in Israel, one in France, two in Spain, one in Italy, three in Mexico, and most recently, one in Egypt.

I have never looked for something to happen. I never desired something to happen. They always happen unexpectedly. I am surprised every single time, without exception. Why they keep happening to me, I have no idea. With my academic background I should be the last person in the world to experience such things. And I am not trying to prove anything.

44. It Won't Be Long Now -
Our Home Is Just Beyond The Horizon

I am sure every person on earth has a story to tell - an interesting one at that. I am simply one of those who became strongly motivated to do it. It is perhaps a form of therapy to reflect on and revisit one's past life from childhood and become astonishingly aware of all the different paths one has walked in one lifetime. It is surprising to note how often the Lord has stepped in and changed the course of events. At the time, every experience seems to be simply an unfolding of life...normal and ordinary. But upon reflection, at least for me, I can name a dozen times and more in which the Divine Helper was at my side, protecting, guiding, teaching - ever the constant Companion.

I hope that someone reading this simple autobiography of a simple priest who served his church in sincerity and to the best of his ability, will receive even a morsel of encouragement or motivation to see life differently. There is always a better view; there is always another way of looking at the world, at God or at oneself.

One of the greatest lessons I learned centered on the importance of being determined, consistent and serious. Krishnamurti, a great teacher in our time, stressed not only the *importance* of being serious but also the *necessity* of seriously seeking one's path. He also stated that "Truth is a pathless land." I thoroughly agree with him. My path and your path may differ but our purpose is the same...to seek Truth. Our starting point will naturally differ, depending on our background. One could hardly expect a Chinese person, steeped in thousands of years of an Oriental culture, to approach Truth in the same manner as a kid from the Bronx. Yet, each of us is bonded in an everlasting relationship with the very same Creator Who may be known by many different names and in many different languages.

Before our Creator, we are all *created* equal, though we may not be *born* equal. We are God's creation, His sons and daughters, His co-creators. All together we form a oneness in the Mystical Body of Christ, regardless of sex, creed, culture, color of skin, intelligence, ignorance, etc. The images I received during my forty nights in a row demonstrated clearly to me that we are all part of God's life. Unfortunately, *Religions separate* while a *Way of Life unites*. As an example, there is only one Christianity, but there are over three hundred different Christian Religions. That's just *Christian* Religions. The same applies to all the ways of life in all cultures of the world.

Is one better than the other? If I were God looking down upon the earth filled with my children who were, without exception, all created in my own image and likeness, and I sustained their life and sent my Spirit to guide each one *without exception*, I would see no religion, no path, no way of life better than another. They all have the same purpose: to discover Me and to discover who they are; namely, to seek the Truth. I would love all my children, one hundred percent, regardless of their differences. Maybe, it's their very differences that pleases Me. Just as the variety of flowers do! After all, each one is unique, and their *uniqueness* is beautiful to Me. Yes, I would say these things if I were God. However, I don't have to be the Almighty One to know that from the Holy Scriptures, God's attributes are Infinite Love, Truth, Wisdom, Knowledge and a host of other Divine Qualities.

It is my opinion that all of us seeking Truth will eventually find the object of our search: The Divine Lover, The Ultimate Source, Who gives meaning to our life. Or as Paul Tillich would say: we would find God, the Ground of our being. I happen to have a strong Roman Catholic background and my path is through the church in which I was raised and still embrace as an adult. That is my path. Your path is where you are. It is not the path itself that is important. As we discussed before, Truth is a pathless land.

"Seek and you shall find," said the Master. Seriously ask for Divine Guidance *which is always available*. Open your heart whoever you are, wherever you are, whatever your religious convictions. You have a *life*, you have a *future*. Let God's Spirit touch your spirit, and your eyes will be open perhaps for the first time...and you shall embrace the Truth as never before. You shall soar above your highest ideals. Beyond your dreams! We have been given a *promise* by the Lord: "Blessed are the pure of heart, for they shall *see* God." That is quite a promise!

The next step is yours. Give thanks for your life, for the Hand of the Lord that has carried you this far will never let you down. Get ready for the *quantum leap* that comes with perseverance and trust. You and I - members of God's Family - are all on the same incredible, spiritual, cosmic journey, following many different paths, but we all have the same destination in mind: *we are all on our way Home.*

To order additional copies of "On My Way Home",
complete the information below.

Mail to: (please print)

Name_____

Address_____

City, State, Zip_____

Day phone_(_____)_____

___copies of "On My Way Home" @ $14.95

Total amount enclosed $_____

Make checks payable to Rev. Jay Samonie

Send to:

Rev. Jay J. Samonie
34664 Spring Valley Dr.
Westland, MI 48185